OXFORD BOOKS OF REFERENCE

THE value of the great works of reference published by the Oxford University Press is everywhere recognized—the *Oxford English Dictionary* (which began to be published in 1884, and of which nine volumes are now complete, the tenth and concluding volume being in course of publication); the Dictionaries of Hebrew and Syriac, Sanscrit, Greek and Latin, Icelandic, Anglo-Saxon (the *Anglo-Saxon Dictionary* by BOSWORTH and TOLLER is now complete), and Middle English, and the great Etymological Dictionary of SKEAT; the *Dictionary of National Biography*, 30,000 Lives in 30,000 pages, now published by the Press; the *Oxford Survey of the British Empire* in six volumes; Mr. POOLE'S *Historical Atlas*.

But these monuments of industry and learning, though all may use them in public libraries, only the fortunate few can buy and house. To the larger and non-specialist public the Press offers a series of more compendious works, which, it is believed, combine with the Oxford standard of accuracy that brevity and simplicity which are essential for popular use.

The Concise Oxford Dictionary of Current English, adapted from the great Oxford Dictionary by H. W. and F. G. FOWLER, containing 1,072 pages (including *Addenda*), is the only dictionary which is in all its elements (save the concluding letters, for which the Great Dictionary was not available) based directly and *cum privilegio* upon the unique authority of the parent work. The price of ordinary copies in stout cloth is 7s. 6d. net. There are also editions in leather bindings, on thin paper, from 12s. 6d. net, and on India paper, from 14s. net. Over 150,000 copies have been sold.

'If there is a better or handier friend of the literary man than this I should like to hear of it.'—Mr. E. V. LUCAS in *Punch*.

The King's English, by the same authors, first published in 1907 and frequently reprinted, has been recognized as a classic. The price is 6s. net. There is an abridged edition for schools, 3s. net.

'I am afraid to set pen to paper.'—ANDREW LANG.

In preparation, by the same authors :—

The *Pocket Oxford Dictionary ;* a still 'conciser' work, which has the advantages of relying upon the Great Dictionary for all but a fraction of the vocabulary, and of including all noteworthy war-words and other recent neologisms.

A Dictionary of English Idiom (by H. W. FOWLER).

The *Oxford Shakespeare Glossary*, by C. T. ONIONS, one of the editors of the Great Dictionary. Second edition, revised, 1919; contains in 272 pages all that the general reader, or any but the most advanced student, is likely to require, and makes it possible to read Shakespeare intelligently in any edition and without any need of notes or special vocabularies to individual plays. Now that Prof. Max Förster has once more informed us that Shakespeare is more German than English, and that the English do not read and cannot understand him, it is worth while to mention that the Oxford Glossary has relieved English scholars from their former dependence upon the Lexicon of Schmidt. (Prof. Förster himself describes it as 'das beste der *englischen* Shakespeare-Wörterbücher'.) The price is 5*s.* net; on India paper, 6*s.* net.

The *Concise Dictionary of National Biography* consists of the *Epitomes* of the main work and of the 1901–1911 Supplement; it thus covers the whole ground down to 1911, and in 1,580 pages affords succinct biographies of 32,000 national Worthies. The *C.D.N.B.* should be in universal use by all who cannot peruse or use the main work in 23 volumes. There is a handy edition on India paper, the price of which is two guineas net; the ordinary edition in half morocco is three guineas net, in cloth 32*s.* net.

Other smaller Dictionaries issued by the Oxford University Press :

The *Student's Dictionary of Anglo-Saxon*, by HENRY SWEET. 10*s.* 6*d.* net.

A Concise Dictionary of Middle English, 1150–1580, by A. L. MAYHEW and W. W. SKEAT. 6*s.* net.

A Glossary of Tudor and Stuart Words collected by W. W. SKEAT, edited by A. L. MAYHEW. 5*s.* net.

A Concise Etymological Dictionary of the English Language, by W. W. SKEAT. Cloth, 6*s.* net; on thin paper, 7*s.* 6*d.* net.

A Latin Dictionary for Schools, by C. T. LEWIS. Constructed from Lewis and Short's Latin Dictionary. 16*s.* net.

Elementary Latin Dictionary with brief Helps for Latin Readers, by C. T. LEWIS. 10*s.* net.

An Intermediate Greek Lexicon founded upon Liddell and Scott's Greek-English Lexicon 'from Homer to the close of Classical Attic Greek'. 16*s.* net.

An Abridged Greek Lexicon, chiefly for Schools. 8*s.* 6*d.* net.

[*October 1922.*

THE
CENTURY OF HOPE

A Sketch of Western Progress

from 1815 *to the Great War*

BY

F. S. MARVIN

AUTHOR OF 'THE LIVING PAST'

Truth justifies herself, and as she dwells
With Hope, who would not follow where she leads?
The Recluse

SECOND EDITION

OXFORD
AT THE CLARENDON PRESS
1921

OXFORD UNIVERSITY PRESS

LONDON   EDINBURGH   GLASGOW   NEW YORK

TORONTO MELBOURNE CAPE TOWN BOMBAY

HUMPHREY   MILFORD

PUBLISHER TO THE UNIVERSITY

PRINTED IN ENGLAND.

PREFACE

THIS little book attempts to look at Western history in the last hundred years from the same point of view from which *The Living Past* treated Western progress as a whole. It concentrates mainly on the chief centres of civilization in the West, and from them endeavours to exhibit the growth of humanity in the world, taking as a leading—though not exclusive—thought, the development of science and its reactions on other sides of national and international life.

The war, which has filled all the period of its composition and came to a close just before it appears, has no doubt left a large impression on the work, though I have striven not to allow it to become the dominant feature. In one respect the war made clear what many have always held to be a cardinal truth in European politics, that good relations between France and England are a most valuable asset to Western progress—perhaps the most valuable of all—and that a study of the parallel development of the two countries is the most enlightening approach to an understanding of modern history. This, therefore, I have borne in mind throughout, though the contributions of other nations, and, especially towards the end, of the United States, find, I hope, due treatment so far as my narrow limits permit.

So much for the purpose. A few words may be useful as to the general plan. There is an attempt throughout to combine a roughly chronological treatment with the form of short essays on successive great topics as they become prominent in the hundred years from 1815 to 1914. The chapters are therefore planned to take up as far as possible the most salient feature in the successive decades.

Chapter I is introductory.

Chapter II treats of the revival of liberalism—the principles of freedom in both domestic and foreign affairs—which is the most striking feature of 1815–30.

Chapter III, on Literature, has perforce to traverse much the same period from another point of view, going both backwards and forwards rather farther than Chapter II.

Chapter IV, on the Birth of Socialism, follows this, because the socialistic agitation which set in after the Revolution of July, and is represented in England by the Chartists, becomes the prominent public feature until the Revolution of 1848.

Chapter V, on Mechanical Science and Invention, turns on the railway and telegraph, which were introduced in the 'forties and 'fifties, and of which the triumph was symbolized in the First International Exhibition of 1851.

Chapter VI, on Biology and Evolution, centres, of course, on the *Origin of Species*, which appeared in 1859.

Chapter VII, on Nationality and Imperialism, deals mainly with the unification of Italy and of Germany, and the Civil War in the United States. These events are the most striking political facts in the decade 1860–70.

Chapter VIII, on Schools for All, selects the Education Acts and the development of public and of higher education as the most salient events in the 'seventies.

Chapter IX, on Religious Growth, has necessarily a wide outlook, both before and after, but the death of T. H. Green and of several other religious leaders in the 'eighties seems to fix its place there.

Chapter X, on the New Knowledge, is compelled to go back to Dalton and the Atomic Theory and forward to the discoveries in radio-activity. But the central portion, on astrophysics, relates to discoveries which were being made about three-quarters of the way through the nineteenth century.

Chapter XI, on the Expansion of the West, falls naturally to the last decade of the nineteenth century, when friction was most acute between ourselves and France, and when, in Africa and in the Far East, the Western Powers seemed to be completing their partition of the world.

Chapter XII, on Social Progress, may be attached to the first decade of the twentieth century, for it was then that a policy of Social Reform was first adopted as its primary object by an English government supported by a large majority of votes, and began to be realized in measures like the Old Age Pensions and National Insurance Acts.

Chapter XIII, on International Progress, is connected, paradoxically it may seem, with the second decade of the present century, which will always be remembered as the decade of the greatest of wars. Yet if the war was the greatest, so also was the world-alliance for humanity and international law which brought it to a victorious conclusion. So also, we believe, will the world-union be the greatest, and most permanent, which will arise from the devastated earth and the saddened but determined spirits who are now facing the future with a new sense of hope, which enshrines our sorrows and has overcome our most oppressive fears. Is not the new and abundant harvest of poetry one of the best signs of life and hope?

Of the many friends who have assisted me with good counsel and encouragement, I owe a special debt of gratitude to Miss Melian Stawell, who has helped me most generously throughout, and notably in the revision of the proofs.

To Mr. T. H. Riches I am indebted for reading Chapters V, VI, and X. and for his invariably sound and careful advice upon them; and to Miss G. N. Dewar for kind co-operation on the Index.

F. S. M.

Berkhamsted,
17 *Dec.* 1918.

PREFACE TO SECOND EDITION

A TIME Chart has been added to this issue, based on the general plan of the book, but rather more comprehensive in the facts which it records. A few explanatory notes are given in their place.

The other improvements are due mainly to kindly criticisms which the author has received from various sources, among which he is bound to mention with special thanks the letters of Professor Hearnshaw, of King's College, London, and Professor Desch, of Glasgow. To the former some corrections in the political chapters are due, to the latter some additions to the chapters, especially X, on science.

Of the more general criticisms the burden has been, 'Why not more about so-and-so'—Tennyson or Browning in poetry, Mendel on evolution, &c. ? And the answer is the same in each case. The plan of the book—taking the salient feature in each decade and making the chapter turn on that—precludes any full treatment of the earlier and later development. Only allusion is possible. It is no doubt a defect, but it seemed better to give in its due place a rather more adequate account of Darwin, than to attempt a complete summary of the development of biological theories.

On the general thesis the author stands to his guns. He does not believe that the hopefulness of the last century has been exhausted, but that the sources of hope are unimpaired, though our conclusions from them must be tempered by our wider experience. A more complete answer will be found in the introduction to the volume on *Recent Developments in European Thought*, shortly to be published by the Oxford Press.

F. S. M.

BERKHAMSTED,
10 *Oct.* 1919.

CONTENTS

I

THE LEGACY OF THE REVOLUTION

THE eighteenth century—in this respect like the Middle Ages—has borne some shrewd blows from moralists and historians. To be called an 'Age of Prose' is perhaps a bearable reproach, for it was very good prose. But it has also appeared to many of them as mainly a time of relaxation, of moral and political depravity, after the strenuous efforts and glorious achievements of the seventeenth century. Walpole after Cromwell, Louis XV after Richelieu, even Voltaire after Descartes—the change seems a measure of decadence. But if we approach the matter from another angle and ask for ourselves and the other nations of the West one simple but far-reaching question, the answer will lead to a different and rather remarkable conclusion.

At what period in history did modern life begin, life really like our own ?

If it is an Englishman who answers first, he would probably reply that it is in Dr. Johnson's time that he first begins to feel at home. He would find sympathy there, in the club with Goldsmith and Burke, which would be wanting even in the Mermaid Tavern or the parlour of Queen Anne. The Elizabethans and Milton and Cromwell are heroic figures, belonging rather to another world. But we might have talked to Dr. Johnson had we dared, and we should have loved to discuss the war with Fox, and compare Napoleon with the Kaiser.

It is not of course merely a question of language, though that counts for much. Many new things had lately entered into the national life, and still more were surging outside for entrance, of which the Elizabethans and even William of Orange had no inkling.   There was the free speech of parliamentary leaders beginning to speak for a nation that was to govern itself.   There was a new industry arising, which was to build the cities of the nineteenth century.   There was a Britain overseas, asserting an independent life and pegging out estates for the free allied nations of the twentieth.

If this was so for England, it was even more clearly a new epoch for the United States, for Germany, and for France.

To the United States the latter part of the eighteenth century was the actual beginning of their existence as a nation.   The wave that carried the rest of us to new moorings raised them for the first time above the gulf of time.   And they in their turn accelerated that movement of change which was beginning to run at full flood throughout the world.

The Germans—and we must think of them primarily as under the leadership of Prussia—go back also to the latter part of the eighteenth century for the foundation of the national existence which they now enjoy.   Territory enlarged, internal organization strengthened, national pride created and national speech approved, a new spirit in Lessing and Goethe which was beginning to clear away the shallow formalities imported from France and to found the great era of German thought : all this comes between the accession and the death of Frederick and is again something to the credit of the eighteenth century.

Frederick the Great died just three years before the French Revolution began.   The Revolution, which was to put the stamp of novelty on so many things which had been growing quietly beneath the surface, makes the end of the century a new starting-point for France, in some ways more complete than even the War of Independence for America.   There can be no doubt for any Frenchman that his modern world begins with the men who destroyed the *ancien régime*, who organized the nation, codified the law, and made his country for the time the dominating force in Europe. What the Revolution meant beyond that and beyond France, we shall consider in a moment. But it meant at least that for France, and France therefore, even more than any other country, looks to the end of the eighteenth century for the beginnings of modern life.

The coincidence of so much national interest on the same period in history must give pause to the detractors of the century, and provides all of us with a problem.

The question which must occur is this, Was there not a common cause, or set of causes, operating at least throughout the Western World to produce results which have obviously much in common ; and if so, what were they?

The only answer we can attempt here must be a brief one and must take a good deal for granted. For any true answer in history leads the mind farther and farther back, never stopping at any one point as a real beginning but finding everywhere threads that connect the sequel with something earlier, and so on into the infinite past. But of this change into a modern world we may discern some outlines. There was a time when the Romans, having welded together the lands adjacent to the Mediterranean Sea, governed them as a unit, on principles partly derived from their own experience, partly from the practice and philosophy of the kindred Greeks. Then came another time, when this rule and unity had disappeared, and there was a welter of conflicting principalities, held together loosely by the surviving traditions of Rome and more strongly by a new power, centred also in Rome, but exercising control over men's minds and conduct on different principles and with a different object in view. Such was the mediaeval system, which lasted for some thousand years after the Roman Empire broke up in the fifth century A. D. This fresh attempt at unity broke down in its turn, and we may fix for convenience the fifteenth century as the date for the opening of another act in the *Divina Commedia* of Man. But now it becomes more difficult to be sure of the characters and to hear all they say, for the stage is much vaster and we are soon taking part in the play ourselves. But we know that the action ever since has become more and more rapid than it was, and that we are now assisting at one of its most tremendous scenes.

It may be thought that we have reached a contradiction to that conclusion as to the eighteenth century with which we started. But the explanation is easy. We asked at what time in modern history can the nations recognize themselves : and this, as we saw, would be towards the end of the eighteenth century. But the pioneers and premonitions of modernity appear some centuries before. Columbus, Luther, Galileo— to take the first great names that occur—were all pioneers of the modern world in which we live. Their influence began at once to spread in widening circles, but we may speak of 'modern history' in the fullest sense when it has taken shape in social forms. Thus, the new lands discovered by Columbus in the West are now the thriving settlements of millions, and a powerful factor in the order and progress of the world. This was first appreciable at the end of the eighteenth century. The new ideal, too, of personal and public morals apart from the Church, first becomes prominent in the same century, when rulers like Frederick the Great and Joseph II avowed themselves the ministers of their people, and the people themselves first realized, as in France, that their interests were the true end of government. And it is the same century which saw the final alliance first cemented between science and industry which, in spite of war, in spite of the blindness of many who are actually carrying out the work, has continued ever since to transform the social and economic condition of the West. Here is the work of Columbus, Luther, Galileo, and their compeers of the Renaissance in its social form.

Let us then see in a little more detail how these changes had taken effect in the four countries we selected. New lands, new knowledge, new religious, moral, and political energy, this was the fresh matter thrown into the melting-pot of Europe.

America is the simplest case, for she was born on one of the new lands which the Renaissance had added to Western civilization, and she was reborn in the eighteenth century by an act of severance, political and religious, from the Old World out of which she sprang. Not till our own day did she return to that community of older nations who have the world's fortunes in their keeping, and she returned with a rich experience of knowledge organizing industry, liberty shaping government, and religion released from tradition.

Germany was the other extreme of the four, for in the eighteenth century she had the maximum of antiquated political machinery and the minimum of outlook for industry or expansion. The fratricidal slaughter and destruction of the Thirty Years' War had postponed her development for a hundred years, but in the eighteenth century she resumed her place in the general movement. Frederick, so far as superficial culture went, borrowed from France and wrote French from preference till his dying day. Meanwhile he developed in Prussia the type of strong government and thorough organization from which the whole world has learnt—and suffered—since, and which lends itself so well to the requirements of a society based on science allied with industry. It is on this side of the modern movement that Germany, under Prussian guidance, has become a type. But at the end of the eighteenth century there was also in Germany an array of great writers and thinkers who handled all the new knowledge of the age and prompted its spirit in the same direction as those of Britain or France.

It was, however, in France and England that the tendencies of the age were most clearly marked, though they had contributed comparatively few to the pioneer figures of the fifteenth century. These came mostly from Italy, with stray names of fellow-workers from other lands ; for Italy was the original home of the New Birth of thought, as Greece was of the old. France and England took up the lead a little later, and they were better able to maintain it, for they had already achieved their social unity in national form. The nation is the typical group for modern history, and England and France were the two first countries to attain their nationhood.

Both countries are geographically compact ; both stand in the European system, and both lean to the West. France is more central in Europe, Britain more oceanic. Near enough for constant intercourse, separate enough for national independence, they have developed on parallel but often contrasted lines, with frequent though diminishing hostility, always in modern times the leaders of European progress, now, as we believe, united in a permanent bond of friendship for freedom and mankind.

When the new life of the fifteenth and sixteenth centuries had begun to flow in the veins of Europe, France and England responded first to the stimulus as nations, and in the seventeenth century it would be difficult to draw the balance between them. In splendour of form, in wealth and population, in general respect for the things of the mind, France was then our superior; but we could show a national spirit of freedom and activity which ultimately placed our political order above the danger of violent revolution and gave us in the eighteenth century a definite preponderance of power. We owe this partly to that Puritan strain which made itself dominant for a time in the seventeenth century and has been a source of strength as well as narrowness to us ever since. In gifts to science, philosophy, and art we were perhaps at least as rich as they. For their Descartes or Pascal or Molière, we had our Newton, our Milton, and our Locke. But in the eighteenth century the differences which were to be ultimately resolved in the revolutionary war became more accentuated. In that age the intellect of France outdistanced ours, while we were accumulating a superiority in national resources which in the conflict with Napoleon proved decisive. Above all we had two advantages. Politically the nation was united, and by the Revolution of 1689 it had acquired the means of making its will prevail in constitutional forms. Practically, both in government and in industry, we had a greater power of adapting means to ends. While the French were classifying the elements of chemistry and compiling an encyclopaedia of all the sciences, we had found out the way to govern India with a handful of settlers and to make a steam-engine which would really work.

The crisis came when at the end of the century France, intellectually the most advanced of European countries, gave a violent impulse to the forward movement which was going on throughout the West. As with the Greeks, as with Galileo on his tower, as with Columbus poring over Tuscanelli's map, it was then, as always, the critical mind which moved.

For if we accept the truth that not economic conditions nor geography nor the ambition of governments is the *primum mobile* in human affairs but the Spirit of Man itself seeking greater freedom and expansion, then we are bound to turn to the movement of thought which preceded the Revolution as the chief explanation of its occurrence and its results. The men of the seventeenth century, looking back to the Greeks for inspiration and forward to the interpretation of Nature and the triumph of Man, had started a new impulse of human activity which came at the Revolution into violent contact with the old order in Church, Society, and State. England surmounted the crisis without a breach, but in France the conditions were sharply distinguished from our own. In religion the old Catholic régime, after a period of doubt in the time of Henri IV, had finally survived in nominal supremacy, while men's minds had drifted farther and farther away from her official doctrines. In England the multiplicity of ' Protestant variations ' had prevented the sharp conflict of orthodoxy and unbelief. The Crown in France had surrounded itself with a court of satellite nobles divorced from the land, and the burden of taxation fell upon a mass of peasantry, despised and neglected by those who lived on them and should have made their welfare the first object of concern. In England there was poverty enough and a drift of countrymen into the towns, but on the whole the landlords recognized a duty to their neighbours and lived among them, while the government of the State was in the hands of the same landlords, known to the people whom they had to govern.

In the middle of the century there was a general movement, felt more on the Continent than in England, towards a reform in administration, towards making the welfare of the people, as understood by their rulers, the main object of government. There was also a growing belief, born of the scientific movement of the previous age and especially of Newton's triumphant generalizations, that the actions of men could, like the phenomena of nature, be reduced to simple principles and counted upon by philosophers and statesmen. The success of Frederick in Prussia was the best example of many similar attempts to govern on this plan. But France was in another case. Her Government was less capable and her people more enlightened than those of any other great State just before the Revolution began. Her Government was atrophied by selfishness and want of contact with the national life, and the nation was readier than any other to take its salvation into its own hands.

The dominating mind in France, that general will which

carried the nation through the crises of six years and finally left it an instrument in the hands of Napoleon, was inspired by several of the general or philosophic ideas of the time, which, crude and misleading as they sometimes appear in revolutionary mouths, will be found among the foundations of the nineteenth century. There was the notion of the infinite perfectibility of human nature which finds so noble an expression in Condorcet. There was the passion for freedom and nature in Rousseau. There was the belief in the unlimited power and right of the sovereign people. Now all this, and the subsequent work of the Revolution, showed itself to a conservative mind like Burke's only on its destructive side. ' Man is born free,' ran Rousseau's famous motto, ' and everywhere he is in chains.' If this be so, the breaking of chains must be the preliminary of any free movement ; but the chains of Rousseau are to Burke the sacred and indispensable traditions which hold society together.

On this plane of thought the conflict is eternal. Every age, every man will look on the past primarily either as a thing to flee from or a thing to follow, will either prefer to build a house for himself or to live in his ancestors'. What we need is a temper or a principle which will take us above this unceasing clash, some ideal for the sake of which we shall be content to abandon our father's house even if we love it, some plan to guide us in building the new one for ourselves if we are compelled to do so. Can we out of the so-called ' principles of the Revolution ' extract any constructive principles of this order ?

Clearly we can, and they will become more and more apparent as we proceed. Take the republican watchwords of Liberty, Equality, and Fraternity. Each had its purely revolutionary or destructive side, often salutary enough. But each contains also an element of reconstruction and growth. To the man of 1789 Liberty implied in the first instance the

destruction of feudal obligations and, as the Revolution proceeded, the destructive impulse spread to the abolition of all
kinds of traditional authority. But it also carries with it the
implication of freedom to develop the full capacity of the
individual, and this capacity, as we are taught by the doctrine
of perfectibility, is infinitely great. Equality meant in the
height of the Revolution the striking down of any superiority :
even the eminence of Condorcet or the science of Lavoisier
weighed for nothing in their favour. But the idea of equality
also contains the constructive notion that every human being
should have an equal opportunity—so far as society can make
it equal—of realizing his powers, and that every man should be
equal before the law. Fraternity, though misused by republican
armies when aggressive, was the most positive of all the watchwords, and, allied with freedom in the true sense, will be found
a continuous force in society, growing in intensity down to our
own time. Tolstoi, the figure of purest humanity in post-
Revolutionary days, recreates the passion for us with no touch
of violence, in the form of an ideal Christianity—a religion
based on brotherhood and self-suppression.

We know that all these good things were implicit in the
'principles of the Revolution', and were sincerely and pas-
sionately held by many of the actors in it ; but when we turn
to their issue in the wars and reaction under Napoleon, still
more when we compare the French ideals with the actualities
of England, we are brought to an abrupt and bewildering pause.
The world was not ripe ; the principles were inadequately
thought out ; the means adopted were inconsistent with the
ends proposed. Such are the various explanations that force
themselves on the mind.

Let us then retrace the main stages of the Revolution, having
England mainly in our eye, and afterwards restate the under-
lying principles with such corrections and enlargements as later

experience has impressed upon mankind. It is only in this broader sense that the Revolution can be regarded as the seed-plot of the modern age.

England, when confronted by the daring innovators of France, gave various response. There was the enthusiastic sympathy expressed by Wordsworth, but by no means confined to him. For the ideals of freedom and human progress, like all the greatest things in history, were current with us, and in Germany as well as in France. The spectacle of a great nation—the most famous in Europe—throwing off the fetters of an autocratic government, determined to control and to improve its fate, struck most intelligent observers with as much admiration as the Russian revolution aroused among us in 1917. They knew the lot of the French peasants to be a poor one—worse, travellers said, than anything in England. Men rejoiced to see them entering into a new state of being, where the prospect of individual power and happiness was open to them, and the face of every man would brighten with the joy of others. But there were other thoughts. It has never been the English way to obtain an object, however desirable, by a violent breach with the past. We love, like the ancient Romans, to find some way of attaining our end which seems naturally to follow on what has gone before. Cromwell, our greatest revolutionist, strove to the last to preserve the ancient forms, and lost his power when it was seen that between the old and new order there was no common link. The final settlement of 1689 succeeded by keeping as close as possible to the ancient dynasty and constitutional law.

This tendency of Britain's had been strengthened in the century which succeeded our own revolution. The Georges by their habits and language had thrown us back on ourselves. Scotland was at last assimilated, and the triumphs of Chatham East and West raised the national fervour again, in a larger

theatre, to something like Elizabethan heat. Such was the
background of Burke's immortal panegyric on constitutional
order and social growth. The French portent and challenge
came to men who had lived through and learnt all this. Across
the channel, within sight of our coast, our rivals of the century
were hewing down their own institutions right and left without
restraint and without reverence. For this, though all were
amazed, the wiser among us saw some reason, though a doubtful
prospect. Then came the moral revulsion, abhorrence of the
suffering inflicted on innocent people for reasons of State.
Lastly, in the aggressive stage, the Revolution began to over-
flow France and sweep away the rights and possessions of other
people wherever they conflicted with its own interests : at this
point the patriotism of 1793 was merged in the imperialism of
Napoleon, and the whole world was driven to arms.

We were so clearly right to resist Napoleon that it is the more
necessary to insist on the value of the ideal elements in the
earlier French movement. It was a light to the world, the
flaming-up of subterranean fires which had been kindling the
mind of Europe: and for France herself it burnt the dross
and forged new tools.

If we compare the state of England and France in 1815 when
the fires had at last died down, there can be no doubt that, in
spite of revolutionary exhaustion and her final defeat under
Napoleon, the civilization of France had been in many points
advanced beyond our own. Her population as a whole was
awakened, as ours was to be in a milder form by the Chartist
agitation. The French were from that time forward ready,
under repression, for the rebound. Her soil, by the sale of
Church land and the increase in peasant proprietors, became
able to support a far larger number of thrifty and contented
people than our own. The Convention, on the eve of the
Terror, had planned a general system of primary education which

was a model for later years, and had actually established several higher schools in Paris of which we had no conception until well on into the following century. It had compiled a code of law which Napoleon completed and issued in his own name. He himself, while doing little to supply the educational needs, reformed the financial, judicial, and administrative system and set a permanent stamp on the abolition of feudal privilege. Merit, if it could be recognized, was henceforth to be the rule of promotion and the guidance of France, a wholesome advance on the chance and scramble of a pure democracy, and a rule for which we have struggled with imperfect success ever since.

Now Britain during her conflict had done none of these things, but she was passing through the acutest stage of a parallel revolution in industry. She had grown strong at sea and rich as a nation of shop-keepers. Her constitution, by weathering the storm, had gained fresh lustre and added strength. Factories at home, fresh possessions and expanding trade abroad, confirmed the nation in its policy of isolation and internal strength. But this strength itself was subject to serious abatement when one looked beneath the surface. The public debt had risen mountains high, a greater weight in proportion to our wealth than the Great War had imposed upon us after three years. But actually more injurious were the poverty and degradation of the manual workers. They had crowded into the towns, their wages were at the lowest point, and the remedial legislation of the nineteenth century had not yet begun; it was not in fact contemplated by the accepted philosophy of the day. For the movement towards freedom, which in France had swept away thrones and privilege, had taken in England the form of removing the ancient restrictions on industry. The rules of apprenticeship, the limitations of the poor to their own parish for relief, all regulations which might hamper the extension of that commerce by which we had defeated France, were relaxed in the name of liberty : but it was liberty without the content of a human life. The first small effort to ameliorate the lives of young workers—the climbing boys—was not made till after the turn of the century in 1802. Politically the stream of reform which had begun to flow in the early days of Pitt was completely stayed. The removal of the least abuse in the political machinery seemed like a step towards the abyss, and every one who asked for free speech or a free vote was a Robespierre in the making.

Such was, for the time, the contrast established between the two leading nations of the West. Yet beneath the surface the same streams of thought were surging on.

In England, when the war was over and the reaction dying down, Adam Smith and Bentham became the guiding stars in the first period of reform. Both of them were international in the fullest sense and strongly influenced by the group of men who gathered round Diderot's *Encyclopédie*. The whole group in their turn, and all the philosophy of the day, drew largely from Hume, the most penetrating critical intellect of the age. There are continuous links on both sides, for Hume's thought goes back to Hobbes and the scientific movement of the seventeenth century, while Kant in Germany begins by a reconstruction based on Hume and is stimulated also by Rousseau, and Voltaire is largely indebted to Locke. And of the lesser but still important forces Helvétius, who sought by an analysis of the mind to establish the necessary identity of the interests of the individual and the whole community, set Bentham thinking, and thus leads in the early years of the nineteenth century to the doctrine of the utilitarians ; while Italy contributed Beccaria to the movement, who strove by an analysis of penal legislation to strengthen the elements of humanity and reason.

The growth of a general or European frame of mind was never more clearly demonstrated than at the period when our sketch begins. But it is one thing to believe in and to realize this, and quite another to trace its workings in the manifold difficulties and turnings of practical life. Here is the supreme task which faces any one who attempts what may be called a philosophical view of history—to satisfy our reason which demands some justification of human doings from a rational standpoint without falsifying the facts which are so often full of perversity and unreason ; in short, to reconcile the ideal with the actual. The one plan, ordinarily followed in special histories, is simply to narrate the sequence of events in the particular department or period of study without regard to the general coherence or purpose of the whole. The other extreme, represented by such a writer as Hegel, is to consider the whole merely as the evolution in time of one or two general ideas and to evacuate these of nearly all their content, of personal passion, accident, and mistakes. Either alternative is gravely erroneous, but surely the worst of all errors is to ignore or deny the validity of the ideal aspect which is just as real a fact in the minds of men as the cannon-shot or the actions of leading individuals—things only put in motion by human thought in the mass. We shall endeavour in the twelve short chapters which follow to avoid the worst evils of either method while returning constantly to the main intellectual tendencies which seem to have marked the last hundred years of Western history. They are new in their concurrence in so many independent centres of civilized life, new entirely in many of their applications, new in the strength with which they are held by multitudes of men, not new of course in their appearance in the world. Such newness, without root or preparation in the past, would be, if conceivable at all, only an evidence of transitory illusion. But newness in the other sense, of a wide-spread application of great ideas which had before been regarded as the visions of isolated dreamers, we hold to be manifest in the period of our review. It was, and is, a moment of new life such as the world has seen more than once before even in the short span of man's recorded history. The advent of Christianity was such a time, when into a world just knit up by Greek thought and Roman action there came a new passion for moral purity and for living and loving in this world as a preparation for another. There came another moment somewhat like it when in the thirteenth century St. Francis and his fellows preached again a gospel of kindness and simplicity after the reconciliation of Catholic theology and Greek philosophy. But the new birth of humanity at the Revolution and after brought even a larger store of thought and force and idealism together. We need before entering on a more detailed review to disentangle what appear to be the leading motives in the drama.

We should put first the growth of knowledge, and of knowledge in that connected and ordered form which we call science. The dominance of this factor in modern life has not escaped, could not escape, the notice of any philosophic mind which surveyed the field. One may find it amply dealt with in such an utterance as Mr. Balfour's presidential address to the British Association in 1900. But it is a reminder which we in England have always needed more than any other great nation in the modern world, much more than our neighbours either in France or Germany. We gave the world the greatest herald of the coming change in Francis Bacon, and we have contributed at least as richly as any other people to the progress of the scientific knowledge which Bacon hailed. But we have never appreciated knowledge as a nation or made it an ideal as others have. Those Englishmen, like Bacon himself or in our own time Spencer, who spoke as prophets of the value of science, have always found a readier hearing abroad and become greater heroes than at home. The French *Encyclopédie* of Diderot, which ushered in the Revolution, is an impressive symbol of respect for modern and coherent knowledge. It rallied the leading thinkers of France and gave them a platform which they could find nowhere else. They refer constantly to Bacon as their apostle and use his language to express their purpose. Like him they set out to found an ' empire of virtue ' and to increase human happiness by the growth and spread of science. Where shall we find such a group in England ? Hardly in that Club of Johnson's which was prevailingly Tory in politics, and did not attempt any work of sustained and collective intellectual labour. Perhaps the nearest parallel would be in Scotland, among the group of men who gathered round and followed Adam Smith and Dugald Stewart ; and there we should find an instructive contrast. The outcome of their intercourse, the nearest analogue as a piece of concerted effort by a group of advanced thinkers in Great Britain, was undoubtedly the *Edinburgh Review*, proposed by Sydney Smith in 1802 at the famous supper in Buccleuch Place and carried out by Jeffrey, Brougham, Horner, and Smith. Their motto, to be set beside the Encyclopaedists' ' empire of virtue by the spread of knowledge ', was Sydney Smith's, ' I have a passionate love for common justice and common sense '. For while the best mind in France has been devoted to ideal constructions and to science, the corresponding preference has been given in England to business and practical life in politics and elsewhere. But this will not prevent us from seeing in the growth, application, and appreciation of knowledge the first of the leading traits which characterize the modern world. The difference arises from the fact that the comparative political freedom of England had given a greater scope to talent in that direction. We are now, a hundred years later, entering on a time when it will be impossible thus sharply to distinguish between the different nations in the Western family. In the interval the English political habit has overspread the world, and we, in our turn, have been learning the general value and fruitfulness of knowledge. We have still far to go on that road. But in the end we shall have learnt to prize, to teach, and to apply it as we already have taken our full share in building it up. This scientific structure, embracing more and more of our own nature and the surrounding cosmos, with its attendant developments in industry and wealth and population and its attendant organization and specialization both of thought and life, is the first and most important of all the salient features of the modern age.

The second feature is less easy to define, but no less certain, when once we apprehend it. To some men—Lord Acton was one—it seems supreme, the end of all our life and effort : and they call it freedom. It means, among a hundred other things, the opportunity for every one of exercising more power in the direction of his own life and the life of the community in which he lives. We shall see in the next chapter how a movement of this kind began again with vigour as soon as the repression of the French war was withdrawn. But personal and political freedom is allied to much else in the development of man's life, and belongs really to a larger conception which is perhaps better described in other words. There has been in this modern stage of history a progressive effort to gain for one's self and to secure for others a fuller life on all sides, the fullest life of which the individual is capable. This is the largest aspect in which we may regard the search for freedom ; and so regarded, the increase of knowledge by science, the deepening of thought in philosophy, the aspirations of the poet, the creations of beauty, are all seen to contribute their share to the ideal. But the poets have done most to build it up in men's minds. For us in Britain Burns and Wordsworth and Shelley were the most powerful voices, but a host of others join in chorus throughout the Western world. We shall see later how the literature of the age, and particularly the earlier part of it when the fervour of the revival was at its height, speak of a new ideal of life, free and full, in harmony with all sides of our own nature, in harmony too with something in surrounding nature which seems to call on us for a reply. To the reflective mind Wordsworth expresses this most fully ; to the simpler soul Burns is the trumpet-call, and the echo which his songs have roused throughout the English-speaking world, springs from the depth of passion.

> The social, friendly, honest man,
> Whate'er he be,
> 'Tis he fulfils great Nature's plan,
> And none but he.

This is the basis of what is called the ' democratic ' movement in the nineteenth century ; and to this belief is added the necessary corollary that if the simple man, merely through his humanity, is the fulfilment of Nature, so he, by that very fact, can claim from society, as his own fulfilment, a share of all the goods that society has acquired. Hence the movement for social reform and popular education which we shall trace ; and we rank it second among the outstanding features of the modern world.

If we call this, which to Lord Acton was freedom, by the wider name of the ' growth of soul ', another step will take us to the collective aspects of that growth which are no less obvious in the same age. The family, the town, the church, the State, have all such a real super-personal existence and affect us in ways distinct from the separate individuals who compose them. Of all these forms of collective being the Nation plays the largest part in modern history. Here again the nineteenth century is the period of chief expansion, not for a new or passing fashion, but for a fundamental condition of human life which had been taking shape for ages and gained a special strength at the Revolution. France gave the national principle electric force by the violence of its internal struggle. So violent was it that in effect it was a new nation which flowed over Europe, doing vital work of preservation and of propaganda. By defence at Valmy and Jemappes, by conquest with Napoleon, France consolidated herself within and inspired other nations without, some by example, others by reaction. The Congress of Vienna and the 'Holy Alliance' which followed were unable for long to repress the current. First Greece and, through an un-broken course down to the tragedies of recent years, every part of Europe has since been struggling for a strong national system.

Yet even nationality is overshadowed by the still larger growth which marks the century of our study. For by a strange, apparent contradiction the bitterest and most determined struggles of nationality have taken place in a world tending to greater unity. We might, in fact, speak with equal truth of the age of rising internationalism as of competing nations. This will become clearer as we proceed. Science and industry have knit up the world, but it has not yet fully found its soul. That soul is nascent, just as the soul of France was nascent in Jeanne Darc and born in the Revolution, and the soul of England stirred in Chaucer and was born with Shakespeare. So in the world a wider consciousness, though nascent, has still to come.

That we believe in its coming, even in the midst of the greatest war, is of all symptoms the most striking of an Age of Hope. And in this quality of Hope we have another of the profound characteristics of the age. Since the reforming pio-neers of the Revolution a hundred and fifty years ago, men have been living for the future and believing in it as they had never done before. Some writers have seen in this dominion of the future the principle of a religion, the solution of all the problems of our being. We are content here to observe it, as every student must, and to connect it with other aspects of modern life. With one other aspect the connexion is intimate and full of meaning. We have been living for the future and living in hope. Whence comes this assurance, on what do we rest this hope? It is not a blind or instinctive confidence; and no undeniable, external voice has in this recent period revealed it to us. We must unquestionably find the food for the belief, the impulse to the future, in the deeper knowledge and understanding of the past that has developed with it. It is an age of history as truly as an age of hope. And history has taken shape in the same years, no longer as a statement—true and well explained as may be—of what took place at any given epoch in the past, but as the revelation of an illimitable upward process in which mankind and all creation are labouring together from moment to moment and age to age. History in this full sense is also the child of the eighteenth, the adolescent of the nineteenth century. And history has helped immeasurably to fortify the early hopes of reformers by showing that, imperfect as we are and bloodstained as our path has been, we yet have risen already from a lower state and have it in us to advance to one still nobler. A life which hope can turn to, but to be won by effort and hastened by stronger effort—this is the guarantee of history.

The historical spirit of the century is thus closely bound up with that inclination to look forward and work for a better future which is also a mark of the times. The two interests do not always dwell together in the same brain, and might seem, like those of nations and of humanity, to be antagonistic. But, as in that contradiction, so here, the opposition is ultimately to be resolved in a deeper unity, until at last we may feel that in passing from one to the other we are really studying the obverse and reverse, concave and convex, of the same object. History can describe the past and give us some guarantee for the ideal future. It is for the poets to picture it and inspire the will. In that imaginative world, to which we turn in moments of aspiration and distant visions, Shelley among English poets reigns supreme. The darkest moments of the reaction did not extinguish Hope in him and what he wrote in 1819,[1] exaggerated by passion as it is, might well be taken as the paean of modern Hope sung in the hour of despair. At that day too, Time seemed to have grown grey in waiting for a better world; and Hope alone of all Time's children was left, wandering distraught. At last, as she is lying in the street, waiting for the feet of Murder, Fraud, and Anarchy to trample her down, the lightning flashes and the clouds are seen piled up like giants in the sky; and then the stars shine out and there seems to come a new presence in the air. And when the prostrate people looked, the maid had risen and, ankle-deep in blood, was yet walking on with a quiet mien. Suddenly she breaks out with that tremendous song in which patriotism, history, and humanity all conspire to stir the soul :

> Men of England, heirs of Glory,
> Heroes of unwritten story,
> Nurslings of one mighty Mother,
> Hopes of her and one another ;
> Rise like lions after slumber !

[1] 'The Mask of Anarchy'.

II

THE POLITICAL REVIVAL

We take certain dates and striking events in history as turning-points or starting-points in new epochs; and 1815 is one of them. But it would be a gross error to overlook the continuity of movements before and after the chosen point. France in 1815 lost all her conquests and returned to the monarchy of the *ancien régime*. But she had gained in the revolutionary and Napoleonic periods a fresh national spirit, a compactness and a readiness to act, which she had not known before. Her judicial and administrative system had been recast and strengthened, and her peasant proprietorship enlarged. In these respects she was now in advance of us. But we too had been moving, even in the time of the strongest reaction against the Revolution. The reforming spirit of 1780 of which Pitt was the constitutional spokesman was never quite extinct. In the sphere of administration, for instance, inquiries and reforms were being constantly discussed and sometimes carried out. In 1809 a law was passed forbidding the sale of public offices; in 1812 a bill was introduced for the abolition of sinecures and the founding of pensions for public servants with the money saved: it was thrown out by the House of Lords but was not without certain indirect results. But the war and the king together were able to prevent any serious political changes, and the Prince of Wales, who had been the hope of Whigs and reformers when in opposition, became, when he succeeded as Regent and as George IV, a worse Tory than his father. We have to look outside government circles for the mainsprings of the reform which was to come. The growth of science and industry, and, on another line which must ultimately coalesce with them, the growth of a new spirit of sincerity and humanity in religion, these were the deepest causes, and their action is clearly traceable even in the dark days before our proper story begins. Take three or four typical lines of action on which far-reaching developments were to follow. The evangelical movement in religion, with Wesley as its leading figure, had preceded the end of the century. It was a revolt against the coldness and formality of current religion, strictly and closely analogous to the revolt against artificiality in literature for which the great Romantics stand. The ' methodist ', outside the official order, despised by the ' world', might well feel some of that quiet confidence which marked the Christian of the first and second century A. D. His time was to come, not perhaps in the distant personal visions which sometimes attracted him, but in a new earth where all slaves would be free. The campaign for the freedom of slaves, in the technical sense, had practically been fought out before the nineteenth century began. In 1807 the oversea traffic in slaves was abolished. It was another manifestation of the growing belief in the value and dignity of the individual human soul. Wilberforce and Clarkson were prophets of the Revolution as truly as Rousseau or Shelley, and they found ardent sympathizers in the French Convention. It was a proper and necessary application of their principles to go further and say, if you are so anxious by State action to prohibit certain relations between human beings abroad in the interest of the weak, why shrink from imposing, also in the interest of the weak, certain conditions on the employers of labour at home ? Not slaves in the legal sense, the miserable pauper child in the factory, the half-starved, half-naked woman in the coal-mine, were quite as unable to defend themselves as the negroes on a plantation. Are they less needy of sympathy and protection because they are white ? This fight also was really determined in principle before our period begins. The first Sir Robert Peel had passed an Act in 1802 protecting the climbing boys, and Shaftesbury is in the succession of the humanitarians of the eighteenth century.

Another humanitarian movement which arose in the eighteenth and led directly to the wider reforms of the nineteenth century was the agitation for the improvement of prisons, in which John Howard took the leading part. Howard's work was done before the Revolution broke out : he died in 1790. Mrs. Fry, who carried on the same task for women which Howard had begun for men, did most of her work in the twenties and thirties of the nineteenth century in the full swing of the political movement which we are now to consider.

There are two points about all these and similar movements. which should be laid to heart as soon as possible, and often recalled. One is their coincidence in history. We cannot avoid the conclusion that they are varied symptoms of one common and general movement in the mind of man. The other point confirms this. The same people who interest themselves in one branch of philanthropic work are nearly always led, so far as their time and powers permit, to extend their efforts to kindred subjects. Howard went on from prison-reform to the study and amelioration of sufferers from the plague. Mrs. Fry built schools for children as well as reforming prisons for women. The cause of the young, the weak, and the suffering is closely allied, and humanity is built up by manifold services.

The movement for reform which we have called the ' Political Revival ' centres in England on the passing of the Reform Bill, and in France on the Revolution of July 1830. There was, as we shall see, an actual connexion between the two events as between so many critical steps in the two countries. The French landmarks are significant of the general trend of thought and very useful for us and other countries. The Revolution of

1830 was middle-class like our Reform Bill of 1832. The Revolutions of 1848 were proletarian or working-class, and the corresponding movement in England came a little later in the Reform Bills of 1867 and 1884. Corresponding with the democratic imperialism of Napoleon III we find a general reaction on materialistic and aggressive national lines which may be brought down roughly to the end of the century. Then, at last, with the new century we reach what we trust may be the permanent approximation of the liberal and reforming forces in the world, beginning to work out their problems of social progress deliberately and in consultation.

The first phase which culminated in France in 1830 and in England two years later, while alike in its main features and issues, differed in its details just as the whole social and political systems of France and England then differed. The aim of the French Revolution of that time was to secure a system of constitutional government, ministers responsible to the elected chamber, and freedom of press and speech. The political issue for us in England appeared primarily as a clearance of abuses which had overgrown the system of freedom and justice, which is the birthright of every Englishman. So it has appeared at most of the crises in our national history, and it is well for us that we feel it so.

The main public interest therefore in the first twenty years after 1815 was political, devoted to the task of securing a more perfect expression of the public will in both England and France. The Government in both countries was to act in accordance with what was then thought to be the best opinion of the nation. The story in England is a striking example of the political instinct of our people, and their concentration on one issue, remote apparently from the most urgent needs of the moment, and not in fact of immediate benefit to the great majority of those who were agitating to promote it.

For consider what were actually the most urgent needs of the country when the war with Napoleon came at length to a close.

The first was, unquestionably, to relieve the poverty and distress of the people. Wages were extremely low and work was scarce. Some whole parishes were deserted by their inhabitants, who tramped the country in search of employment. The workhouses were teeming with inmates, and the poor law tended to increase, and not diminish, the number of paupers. The returning soldiers, for whom no foresight had been exercised by the State, swelled the stream of the workless poor. The price of corn was kept artificially high by corn-laws which were maintained by a landlord Parliament in the landlords' interest. To crown all this, came a succession of bad harvests ; that of 1816 was specially bad. This, then, was the primary and most pressing need.

Next to this the impartial well-wisher for his country's weal would have put better provision for the education of the people. Sunday schools had been started by Robert Raikes before the end of the eighteenth century, and benevolent persons such as Hannah More and Sydney Smith had been setting these up in various places for general instruction in the rudiments of reading and writing. But the supply was far too small and unorganized. The State knew nothing of it : and though George III and the Royal Dukes showed some interest in the schemes of Bell and Lancaster, just as Charles II had played with physical science, there was no attempt to support or regulate public education by State action until after the Reformed Parliament had met.

Thirdly, in the order of national evils, our reformer would probably have put the barbarity of the law and the weakness and partiality of its administration. There were still, in 1818, 223 capital offences known to the law, and in the same year 107,000 persons were counted in gaols. And just as there was barbarity and excess of legal precaution in the defence of property, especially of all property connected with land, so there was a deficiency, in many cases a complete absence, of legal protection for the weak and poor. Some slight obligations in the matter of children's health and instruction were imposed by Sir Robert Peel's first Factory Act of 1802, but the mass of the workers were entirely unprotected. The Combination Laws punished severely any attempt by the workers to enforce better wages by a strike or even by an agreement ; but no employer was ever punished for open agreements to lower wages. An unemployed workman could be sent to prison for refusing to accept work on the employer's terms.

Yet in spite of all this it was the corruption and inadequacy of the parliamentary system which finally rallied all the reforming forces in the country. It was this which brought us several times near a popular rising, and the insistence on this which made each successive step in the improvement of the representation—in 1867, in 1884, in 1918—an easier and a more generally accepted reform. Men felt, as Mr. Gladstone afterwards said, that if you wished to shave easily, you had better first sharpen your razor.

It was quite in harmony with the general political keenness of the working classes that their first demonstration after the war—at Spa Fields in 1816—displayed the tricolour and demanded reform in a revolutionary spirit. The fires of France were still alight though smothered for the moment. Starving and oppressed, the predominant idea of the active-minded poor was not to rob or to destroy the rich, but to create a better political system which would guarantee happiness and justice to all alike. Unfortunately any suggestion of political reform, above all any overt connexion with revolutionary France, threw the governing class into a panic. It was the red flag of the Terror. Things were to become still worse before they began to mend. The demonstration at Spa Fields in London was followed by another at St. Peter's Fields near Manchester in August 1819, for in those days Lancashire followed London. This was repressed with loss of life. It inspired Shelley's 'Mask of Anarchy', and was the nadir of the century. The Six Acts, passed in November of the same year, limiting the right of public meeting and penalizing political writing, were the turning-point. Public meetings were held all over the country to protest against a massacre that seemed to mock Waterloo. In the West Riding the meeting was presided over by the Lord Lieutenant, a great Whig landlord. It was the first step to the hearty union of Whigs and popular reformers which gave us the Act of 1832.

In the decade which followed 1819, before the Revolution of 1830 gave the signal for our own constitutional change, there were three noteworthy political events, the repeal of the Combination Laws engineered by the incomparable and indefatigable Place, the Catholic Emancipation won by O'Connell, and the revival of a liberal policy abroad due to Canning. The last we shall deal with in its place later on. On the two former a word should be said before we pass to the struggle for the Reform Bill and its sequel.

All the activities of Francis Place are of extreme interest, as coming between the era of revolution, war, and reaction, which culminates in 1819, and that of the new age of social and political reconstruction which begins after the great Reform Bill. Place himself was one of the most remarkable and powerful characters who have ever influenced from the background our national history. Beginning life as a journeyman tailor, he lived in his earlier years with his wife and the first one or two of his fourteen children in a single room in the heart of London on the smallest income which could have sustained life. But at that very moment he was fully resolved, first, to make a fortune; second, to educate himself to the utmost limits of his capacity; thirdly, to become a force in politics in the interests of the working class to which he belonged. This was in 1795. Within twenty years he had built up a prosperous business as a tailor at Charing Cross, had accumulated in a room behind his shop what was probably the best library in London on modern social and political subjects, and had become the recognized friend and adviser of all the leading reformers of the day. His was the strongest practical head in the Mill, Grote, and Bentham group, and he alone kept the reforming party together in Westminster at the time when Westminster was the typical free constituency in the country. He took his part in all the forward movements of the time, supported the Lancastrian schools in their early days, protested against Peterloo, gained the repeal of the Combination Laws, invented the poster which 'stopped the Duke' and secured the Reform Bill, drafted the People's Charter, and lived on to support the repeal of the Corn Laws. As a rule an enemy and merciless critic of both official parties, of Whig perhaps even more than of Tory, he was yet the strongest advocate of an alliance at any time when, as in 1831, it seemed the obvious means of reaching the goal. As a critic of the Whigs on the one side and the newborn Socialists on the other, he fits in admirably to this period of transition.

The repeal of the Combination Laws exactly suited the temper and politics of Place and his closest allies, for it was a step towards the enlargement of personal freedom and the removal of a legal restriction which had operated in practice to the detriment of the poor and the advantage of the strong. 'Let workpeople and employers be free to make their own bargains without the interference of the State'; this was the gospel, and to it Place—the father of fourteen—added as a necessary corollary, 'Let working people restrict their families, so that there may not be so many of them competing for the same jobs.'

Both these propositions remind us, in their crude form, of how much had yet to be done by inquiry, by reflection, and by organization before government could approach the scientific state which the men of the eighteenth century had thought so easy to attain.

The fight over the Combination Laws took place in 1824 and 1825. The repeal of the laws against Catholics and Non-conformists was to follow in 1828 and 1829. The stiff reaction of the first years after the peace had begun to yield.

The change in tone coincides with Canning's succession to Castlereagh in 1822, and his influence was largely responsible for it. The growth of freedom which now set in, the greater confidence in the reasonableness and right feeling of mankind, was not confined to foreign policy, where for six years Canning was supreme.

We may trace it also in home affairs, which always take on a similar hue. In this case the connexion and the explanation are clear enough. Castlereagh had been Foreign Secretary and practically Prime Minister from 1810 to his death in 1822. His character was so good, his life so strenuous, and his prestige so great, that the leadership of Lord Liverpool was not much more than nominal. Now Castlereagh had been on the diplomatic side as much responsible for England's triumph and Napoleon's defeat as Wellington was on the field. Together they stood for England in the eyes of Europe, and they rightly gained a corresponding weight in the counsels of their countrymen at home. This weight was always thrown on the side of extreme caution, of the least possible change, and, if necessary, of forcible repression.

Canning, inferior in character to either of them, was yet by mental outlook and by personal antecedents freer to take a new line. Doubtless we may trace his influence in the later diplomatic papers of Castlereagh, which Canning used without

alteration after his accession to full power in 1822. Thus the
policy of England advanced without a break from the caution
and moderation of Castlereagh's attitude at the Congress of
Vienna to the bolder line of encouraging the aspirations of
struggling nationalities which was the glory of Canning and
finally severed us from the alliance of the reactionary Powers.
After Canning's death in 1828, Wellington became Prime
Minister within a year. By that time the diė was really cast.
Reform was bound to come in England and the bourgeois
Revolution in France. But the Duke was then too old and
too blind to read the signs. He agreed to give the Catholics
their freedom, and then went out before the storm. It was
his final term of power. For two short periods he joined Peel
in later ministries and was still the staunch and patriotic
friend of colleagues and of country. But the relief of the
Catholics was his last, as it was his best, act of personal responsibility. It was the leading political question in home
affairs in the last years before Reform, and the concession by
the Duke in 1829 prepared the way for the solution of the
larger issue. When the Catholic religion, connected with
traditions of disloyalty in England and with the recent rebellion in Ireland, was at last declared no bar to office or a
seat in Parliament, it began to dawn on many a timid mind that
a larger and truer representation of the people might not be so
terrible a risk. If we are to trust the Catholics, as even the Duke
was at last prepared to do, may we not trust the whole nation ?

So far as the Catholics were concerned, Pitt, who had abandoned general reform under revolutionary stress, had remained
liberal as long as possible. It was the well understood sequel of
the Act of Union that, deprived of their independent Parliament,
the Irish—including of course a Catholic majority—were to be
free to sit at Westminster. But George III had found here an
insuperable stumbling-block. His coronation oath to maintain

the Protestant religion appeared to him to forbid his consent, and Pitt resigned in 1801. The straiter Tories (Eldon throughout, the Duke up to the last practicable moment) supported the King. Ireland herself, led by O'Connell, forced the pass. The Catholic Association, dissolved and quietly reconstituted, refusing to pay taxes and threatening an insurrection, at last broke down the resistance when George IV was king. It gave England an example which Birmingham and many other towns were ready to take up in 1832.

The Reform agitation which led to the first great Act will always remain a little epic of English political life. The absurd and wellnigh incredible anomalies which had to be removed, the pleasure mixed up with the abuses, the humours of the contest, the grim determination of the few, the skilful marshalling of all the reforming camps into one striking and ultimately irresistible force, the exaggerated hopes of the enthusiasts, the quiet acquiescence of everybody when the deed was done, all this, with its strength and its weakness, we are ready to believe is typically English. What we do not recognize so readily is the coincidence of our national timepiece with the moments of the European clock. This Reform, like the Reformation, like the Tudor monarchy, like the rise of science and the Industrial Revolution, was synchronous, though in a different tone, with events abroad and especially in France.

The confusion and corruption of the old franchises have been so oft and so fully described in the history books that we need not dwell long upon them. One or two facts will suffice. Of 658 members of Parliament 424 were nominated either by government agents or by private individuals. These, therefore, were in no sense representative of the constituencies, and in many cases the constituencies themselves had ceased to exist. They might lie under the sea, like Dunwich, where the proprietor took a boat on the polling day and conducted the election some fathoms above the ancient borough. Or they might be deserted sites on ground like Old Sarum or Bute, where one elector returned the member. Many large modern towns, even Manchester and Birmingham, had no member, while the whole of Scotland had only 45 to Cornwall's 44. In the election of 1818 there had been only 100 contests; and of these the majority, owing to the loose and open method of voting, the mustering of their tenants by the landlords, the jovial intimidation which prevailed, could not by any stretch of imagination be considered as a serious expression of opinion. The election was rather a rowdy meeting on a succession of market-days; and when the Duke declared, on the eve of the final contest, that it would have been impossible to devise a more perfect system if we were starting afresh, a shout of indignant laughter ran through the country. The Duke had no sense of humour, and though an excess of this quality has sometimes proved fatal to a statesman, its complete absence may on occasion be found almost equally inconvenient. For we had at this crisis, more perfectly combined than at any other moment in our history, all the strongest forces of the nation against the feudal inheritance of a handful of landlords and their dependents. There was the solid commercial interest of all the rising towns, centred in Birmingham. There was working-class opinion, organized by Place and his friends in London, expecting no doubt more from Reform than it was ever likely to give them, but determined that the change should be made. And clinching all these, and giving them voice, was the intellectual element which had been struggling to power for fifty years in newspapers, pamphlets, and reviews, and had found its most telling expression in the *Edinburgh*. The day of triumph had come at last, and one can still hear the echo in that immortal story of Sydney Smith's mass meeting at Taunton Castle in

October 1831. There, before a keen and crowded audience of all classes, he acted, with vigorous gestures and every appearance of anger, the great apologue of Dame Partington determined to sweep back the waves of the Atlantic. The speech was dispatched by special post to London to be read by Lord Grey and his colleagues in the Whig Cabinet, which was to carry reform in the next session. Grey had taken office in 1830 after the accession of William IV. When the new king's first Parliament met, the Duke had assured them that 'human nature is incapable of attaining at one stroke so great perfection' as the British Constitution. True in one sense as this undoubtedly was, the House of Commons had refused to accept the assurance as a reason for not attempting to make the Constitution even more perfect.

Though the new king was more favourable to reform than the old, stern measures were still needed to clear the last obstacle, the adverse majority in the House of Lords. The final stage came on a wrecking amendment of the Lords in May 1832. For some days there was no Government. Grey refused to go on without assurances from the King. The Duke was egged on by the die-hards to take office, without Peel, against the Commons and the nation, and with increasing evidence that only armed force and a doubtful issue were before him. Birmingham and other places were preparing barricades on the new French pattern. Then came the famous placard 'TO STOP THE DUKE GO FOR GOLD'. It was struck out by Place among his friends in the library at Charing Cross, and by the aid of his associates soon posted all over the country. The mere beginning of the run on gold, added to the other symptoms, completed the enlightenment of King and Duke. Wellington accepted his defeat, and Grey returned to power with the necessary pledge to create peers.

The placard deserves its place, besides Smith's apologue, in our national annals. It was the marching orders of the man of action beside the *mot* of the man of wit. Together they symbolize the union at this crisis of working-class Radicals and middle-class Whigs.

The first Reform Bill, in spite of the enthusiasm it aroused, was a very moderate measure of democracy. In this respect it was valuable rather for the removal of abuses than the wide extension of freedom granted. But it gave an impulse to other reform. Many measures were passed, and more discussed, in the ten years of Whig supremacy which followed. For as the Whigs had carried the Reform, they naturally dominated for some time the reformed Parliament which they had created.

That Parliament, true to the principles of its founders, extended the representative system to the government of municipalities, first to Scotland in 1833, then to England in 1835, and, finally, after many years of conflict with the Lords, to Ireland in 1840. It carried out the humanitarian spirit of the earlier reformers, conspicuously in the abolition of slavery in the colonies. The abolition of the venal boroughs at home at once led to the public purchase of the slaves' freedom for £20,000,000 in 1833. It carried further the amelioration of the criminal law which Peel had begun in 1821, when he removed 100 capital offences from the list. It set up a Central Criminal Court in 1834. On three other lines it commenced the work of social reform which becomes the predominant interest in the politics of later times. These three lines were education, poor law, and factory legislation. In education the first State grant was given to schools in 1833, and a Committee of Council appointed to inspect them in 1839. In poor law the great Act was passed in 1834 which formed unions from parishes, imposed a workhouse test, and endeavoured to check the growth of pauperism and of the poor-rates which in many places exceeded the annual rent of the land. In factory legislation it passed the first serious Act, on Lord Shaftesbury's initiative, in 1833, prohibiting the employment of children under nine years of age, and limiting the work of women and young persons under eighteen to twelve hours a day.

To reach the same point in French and European politics which we have now touched in home affairs we need first to retrace our steps. The Charter of 1814 under which the Bourbons returned to power was in some points, especially on paper, more democratic than the contemporary English system. The franchise, though high, was uniform, and every one was equal before the law and equally admissible to all public offices. So much of the Revolution was left unshakable. A good deal of the constitution was directly borrowed from ourselves: two chambers, one nominated by the Crown, the other the House of Representatives, elected by a small body of electors paying a considerable sum in taxes, from a still smaller body of those paying a still larger sum. There was thus legally constituted in France a 'governing class' on a purely money basis, which one might compare instructively with those 'governing classes' of England, which had grown up irregularly, as the nation grew, in the manner that Burke had taught us to prefer. The French Charter also borrowed from England the theory of 'ministerial responsibility'. The King's ministers were to answer to the chambers for the acts of government. But the Charter unfortunately also reserved to the Crown certain rights of making ' regulations for the safety of the State', and the King was stated therein to have ' granted the constitution to his people' by his own sovereign power. It was on this rock that the royal ship went down.

The reign of Louis XVIII was a period of violent struggles between the rival parties in France, the 'liberals' who aimed at widening the element of popular control, the 'ultras' or clericals who first took sanguinary vengeance on the old republicans in the 'White Terror' and then definitely entered on that course of opposition to popular sovereignty and all freedom of thought which did not end till Dreyfus was set free. But while Louis lived the throne was safe. He was personally adroit and moderate, and averse from the extreme measures taken in his name. But towards the end of his reign, after the murder of the Duke of Berry, it became clear that the State of France was unstable. Secret societies, called 'la Charbonnerie' after the kindred Carbonari of Italy, began to flourish. The Duke of Berry, heir to the throne, was murdered in 1820. The 'ultra' government replied by repression more and more severe. In 1823, just after Canning had given a more liberal turn to foreign policy in England, the 'ultra' government in France, against the wiser feelings of the King and his prime minister Villèle, but in concert with the sovereigns of the 'Holy Alliance', sent a French expedition to suppress a popular rising in Spain. The immediate effect was a temporary triumph for the reactionaries, and Charles X, who succeeded his brother in 1824, succeeded also to the most reactionary Chamber elected since the restoration, a chamber which at once voted itself seven years' power. It was like—and yet unlike—the blind confidence of the Iron Duke six years later in England. His eyes were always opened in time to save the country, though not his own system of government. Within eight years both systems, in England and in France, had crumbled never to revive.

The relations between the Duke and the King of France in these last years before the Revolution of July are a curious study. Charles X, far from wishing to develop the French Charter on English lines, set out at once on a course of whittling down the scanty liberties which it provided. He declared that he would sooner saw wood than be king on the same conditions as a king of England. Various reactionary laws were passed in the first three years of his reign, laws strengthening the rights of eldest sons, religious laws threatening savage punishments for thefts in churches, and, most serious and unpopular of all in France, laws penalizing the press by taxes and regulations—a worse edition of one of our own Six Acts. Public opinion was so much alienated that the next Chamber elected, that of 1827, had lost nearly all its reactionary majority. After a year and a half of uneasy government with a more liberal ministry, the King, on the advice of the Duke of Wellington, appointed Prince Jules de Polignac as premier, a man more reactionary and less enlightened than himself. For Polignac, besides being a son of one of the earliest *émigrés* of 1789, had actually refused to swear to the Charter by virtue of which his master was on the throne. He had, he believed, a personal mission from the Blessed Virgin to save the country by other means.

Such was the guidance which drove France in 1829 to the Revolution of 1830.

Another election in 1830 gave a chamber even more hostile than the last to the King's policy. Paris was now awake, and organized by the intellectual leaders of the country. Four royal ordinances promulgated in July set fire to the train. By a violent misuse of the dangerous clause in the Charter, the King attempted to introduce a new and more limited body of voters and annulled the recent elections. Within four days the barricades were up and the King and his Government had gone. The *Farce de Quinze Ans* was over.

The fall of Polignac in France undoubtedly hastened the defeat of his friend and patron in England. The Duke had known him when French ambassador in London, and thought him the best agent for averting a revolution and saving the Bourbon monarchy. He misjudged the situation on both sides of the Channel, and his complete and speedy discomfiture in France gave hope and courage to his opponents at home.

For the Revolution of July was a brilliant success for all the Liberals of Europe. It was prompt, moderate, and almost bloodless. Instead of their excesses of 1792 the French of 1830 were glad to accept a constitutional king, cousin of the deposed monarch. They preserved and improved their Charter of 1814; they maintained their Code Napoléon, and began to apply in a quiet and systematic way the principles of 1789 which in the hands of their first apostles had led to ruin. Englishmen might be pardoned for thinking that the common sense which they had always professed, was on its way to become the law of Europe. But they must lose no time in setting their own house in better order.

The new government in France showed its kinship with the reforming movement in England. The same ideas may constantly be traced prompting legislative action on humanitarian and moderate democratic lines. Municipalities were reformed and created. The criminal law was softened as in England. Prisons and asylums were brought under better control. In two important matters the French at one stride outdistanced us. Their fundamental law establishing primary schools coincides exactly with the beginning of State action in England. Guizot's law was passed in 1833, when the first grants were voted in England. But whereas the French law imposed the obligation of establishing schools on every commune, and is thus comparable to our School Board Act of 1870, the English Government of the same date only offered a dole of £20,000 to the existing societies. And in the matter of child labour, their first factory law of 1841 prohibited the employment of children up to twelve years of age.

But we have now to consider the parallel activity of the two Western Powers in the larger issues of nationality and international concert. The French Revolution had brought into prominence, both in France and other countries, the spirit of nationality, which is one of the two greatest factors by which the peace of the world must be ultimately settled. The revolutionary wars had been wound up at Vienna by a treaty and an alliance which were a narrow but honest effort to reconcile competing State interests in a larger and permanent system. The line taken by the two liberal Powers in response to these two impulses forms in view of the future the most important study of the historian who has an eye on the ideal. We cannot in either case make out a clear and consistent policy developed from the first. We are compelled in both instances to recognize many deviations and a large admixture of selfish motives and mistaken judgement. Yet on the whole the action of France and England tends to a common goal of general good. The hundred years which elapsed before the Great War prepared them for the crucial moment when they were to be allied in a determined struggle to assert a new order of national justice and the free union of nations.

The Congress of Vienna was sitting, amid the tense expectations of Europe, during the interval between the defeat of Napoleon in 1814 and his return for the 'Hundred Days' in 1815, and again after Waterloo ; but it failed in its greater object. It could not at that day establish a new and permanent polity for Europe on the principles of nationality and freedom which were beginning to inspire the hopes of the world. It led to the re-establishment of the *status quo* with certain changes mostly in the interests of those who had come strongest out of the fight. Holland and Belgium were united, and Sweden and Norway ; both unions were subsequently dissolved. England received the Cape of Good Hope and a few colonial islands. The great cases of nationality which called out for treatment—the Polish, the German, the Italian—were left unsettled, and the whole Eastern question was untouched. It gave a breathing space merely, but in the course of its meetings the position of England and France were defined in relation to the three military Powers of the North and East—Prussia, Austria, Russia. Two great men had charge of their countries' interests at the Congress, Talleyrand and Castlereagh, and their actions from different motives tended to converge. It was Talleyrand's part to re-assert for France her due weight in the councils of Europe. It was Castlereagh's object to check the ambition of any individual Power and establish a stable equilibrium ; and he was charged by England to gain if possible one special object—the agreement of the Congress to the abolition of the slave trade. Both statesmen succeeded in their definite and limited objects and their pursuit brought the two Powers together. A further step towards their co-operation took place at the Congress of Troppau in 1820.

The Eastern Powers, who after the Congress of Vienna had under the initiative of the Tsar Alexander drawn more closely together in the Holy Alliance, found themselves confronted by liberal risings in various parts of Europe. They went on to bind themselves to mutual help in suppressing any attempts of the peoples to alter their governments. Alexander had attempted to inspire the Alliance with Christian principles. Metternich, the Austrian minister, had supported it in the interests of autocratic power. Both were agreed that any movements of nations against their legal sovereigns must be put down by force. This at Troppau the three Eastern Powers agreed to do in common, and to exclude from the European Alliance any State which had undergone a revolution of which they disapproved, until, ' by peaceful means, or, if need be, by arms, they had brought back the guilty State into the bosom of the Grand Alliance '. This was the climax of Metternich's ascendancy and the definite breach with the Western Powers. For Castlereagh had already in 1819 protested against the policy of leaguing the Governments against the peoples, and at

Troppau the representatives of France and England were shut out.

It was a significant prelude to the series of revolutions which from 1822 to 1835 altered the Governments of Greece, Belgium, Spain, and Portugal, all in the direction of national freedom and self-government and in each case with the assistance of England and France.

But before this England and the United States had, from 1810 onwards, supported the fight of the South American colonies for freedom from Spain. Englishmen had fought as individuals for Bolivar in his heroic lifelong struggle for the independence and union of the South American states, and Castlereagh had intervened in 1817 to prevent a European Congress from supporting the claims of Spain over them. Again, after the French expedition of 1823 had revived the hopes of Spain, a movement for European intervention was frustrated by England and the United States. At last it fell to Canning in 1825 to recognize the revolted colonies as independent, and to conclude commercial treaties with them. In this early case England gave the signal to the other Powers.

The case of Greece brings France and England into joint action, and is a direct link with the politics of our own day. It is full of interest of every kind. The Turkish Empire was the part of the world where the idea of nationality was least developed and most deeply overlaid by a military depotism, alien in race and largely in religion. In the Balkans, the latent nationalities, much confused among themselves, were cherishing the memories of ancient greatness and national conflict with their present masters. When they regained their strength and full national consciousness, this alien mastership would be ended. With the decay of the Turkish power in the eighteenth century they began to stir, and north of Turkey lay the Muskovite giant ready to abet every movement of the Christian communities against their foe. Peter the Great at the beginning of the eighteenth century first avowed the Russian ambition by styling himself 'Petrus I Russo-Graecorum Monarcha'. Catherine II carried the idea farther and had her nephew baptized 'Constantine' in order to succeed to the Greek throne which was to be. The end of the century saw more than one abortive rebellion and the spread of a secret organization of Greek patriots to promote the independence of their country. In 1820 a war between Mehemet Ali, the Pasha of Egypt, and his nominal suzerain the Sultan gave the Greeks the opportunity they sought. The revolt of the Greeks in the Morea was followed by a war of extermination on both sides. The Greek patriarch Gregorius was executed by the Turks, and pyramids of Greek skulls adorned the headlands. Three things drove Canning to take action with the passionate sympathy of Western Europe behind him.

The first was the romantic ideal of the West, which, half history and half hope, was beginning to project new national forms for the future wherever common deeds and common sufferings had laid a large foundation in the past. Greece struck this cultured imagination more strongly than any other land, and men dreamt with Byron that she might still be free,

> For standing on the Persians' grave,
> I could not deem myself a slave.

Greece, the ancient mother of modern thought, thus became the leading case in the modern world of a struggling nationality brought to birth by the collective action of progressive Europe.

The second motive, which led to England's intervention in 1823, was the apprehension of a war between Turkey and Russia, as the result of which the Northern Power would, or might, have become completely dominant in the East. This larger aspect of the problem came up again for solution in the Crimean

War, when for the first time the whole Balkan question passed under the joint review of the Concert of European Powers. On the first occasion, in 1823, England and France forced their way in by the side of Russia to wrest from Turkey the independence of the most easily detached of her dominions, and the most sentimentally attractive.

The third motive, the actual occasion for our intervention, was the necessity of making some one responsible for policing the seas of the Greek archipelago. The Turkish fleet was impotent, and piracy was rife. In 1823 Canning recognized the insurgents as belligerent. On this the Sultan made up his quarrel with Mehemet Ali, and, for the price of Crete, the Morea, Syria, and Damascus, an Egyptian fleet and army were sent to finish with the Greeks. In 1825 the Morea was overrun. In April 1826 Missolonghi, where Byron two years before had been drilling troops almost to the day of his death, fell at last. But in the same month the Duke of Wellington, who had been sent to Petrograd by Canning to concert joint measures with the new Tsar Nicholas I, had drawn up the protocol by which in three years' time Greek independence was secured.

In the interval events hurried on. The Greeks made a formal application to England for help. Canning, relying on the agreement with Russia, went a step further and consented to a 'pacific blockade' of the Morea, which would have starved out the Egyptian fleet locked up in Greek harbours. France had come in, and a treaty of the three Powers was concluded on the basis of the protocol. The Turkish and Egyptian fleets, shut in by the fleets of the three protecting Powers in Navarino Bay, showed fight, and were annihilated on October 20, 1828, by the Allies under Codrington the British admiral.

The death of Canning had unfortunately preceded this famous battle by two months, and the weakened English Government proceeded to express diplomatic apologies to the Porte. But the deed was decisive. The fighting by land was carried on by the Russians, the military occupation of the Morea by the French. In 1830 the independence of Greece was agreed to by all the Powers, and, after the fall of Wellington, just before the Grey Government passed the Reform Act, the new Greek kingdom somewhat enlarged, under the Bavarian Prince Otto, was established by the Treaty of London in May 1832.

The growth of a humanitarian entente with France, the anticipation of a triple entente with Russia, the sequel of these events in the Great War of to-day, all give a singular prominence to the story of modern Greece. The concurrent case of Belgium has a more tragic issue. But an Englishman will rejoice that the two pivots of our policy in Europe, East and West, have remained true to the same direction of national liberty in face of the varying dangers of a hundred years. In 1826 we played our part in winning the independence of Greece from the Turks while keeping Russia at our side ; in 1832, when Palmerston had succeeded to the inheritance of Canning, we secured the independence of Belgium from Holland with the assistance of France.

The Revolution of Belgium was the immediate sequel to the French Revolution of July. The Belgians had chafed for fifteen years under their forced union with Holland, with a Dutch king and an administration largely Dutch. They were the more numerous portion of the combined kingdom, and mainly Catholic while the Dutch were mainly Protestant. They refused to coalesce. If we seek for causes of the failure farther back in history, we may find them in the premature death of William of Orange, which reduced the provinces of the Netherlands, which might have been united in freedom, from seventeen to seven. That greatest of modern statesmen might have achieved this union. Perhaps by doing it he would have averted the greatest of wars. But the crude handiwork of the statesmen of Vienna had no permanence. The Belgians hailed the outbreak in Paris as their signal, and rose against Holland. Palmerston, at the conference which met at London in November, persuaded the five great Powers to recognize the claim of Belgium to independence. Louis Philippe refused the crown for himself or his son, and a perfect compromise between England and France, Protestantism and Catholicism, was found in the kingship of Leopold of Saxe-Coburg. He was a Protestant, widower of the English Princess Charlotte, and uncle of the Princess Victoria who was to succeed to the English throne; and, within two years of his accession, he had married a daughter of Louis Philippe and satisfied the Belgian majority by contracting that the children of his marriage should be brought up as Catholics. The French by land and the French and English by sea had to complete the eviction of the Dutch. The famous treaty by which the neutrality of Belgium was guaranteed by the five great Powers was finally executed in April 1839.

Canning's life-work and the earlier activities of Palmerston, while he still made a good understanding with Paris ' the pivot of his policy ', complete our picture of England's attitude abroad in this first period of revival. It was a policy of making England's influence felt in the councils of Europe but strictly limiting the exercise of our powers, a policy of preserving a balance between the ambitions of competing countries and giving a chance, wherever possible, to other nations struggling for such liberties as we possessed ourselves. But the proper prudence with which we pursued these aims gave some colour to the charges of our critics that we did nothing for the good of others without an eye to our own advantage. Poland rose against Russia in the revolution year of 1830, but her struggle gained no support from us. On behalf of Spain and Portugal, however, where a British fleet could come into play, Palmerston formed an alliance with France in 1834, which secured the constitutional parties against their clerical and reactionary foes. This was his most successful effort, and he carried it out almost single-handed.

But the heavier tasks were still to be accomplished, the larger ideas to spread. Germany had yet to be made a nation, and Italy. And all the peoples of the earth had yet to come together and realize their common destiny and common duties.

In 1831 an exiled Italian landed at Marseilles, a man in whom the passion for national independence was better tempered by an enthusiasm for the kindred good of all mankind than in any other thinker before his time. Mazzini, the Carbonaro, the man of letters, the life-long martyr to the humanitarian ideal, is the best link in this age between philosophy and the politics of nations. And in the league of ' La Giovine Italia' which he founded as an exile in France, he proclaimed the gospel of the coming day—'Moral unity and Fraternity in a faith common to all Humanity.'

III

THE NEW SPIRIT IN LITERATURE

We saw that the eighteenth century was a period of prose, much of it great prose—the first modern prose in English, but predominantly prose. At the end of the century when the Revolution took place which was to transform industry, politics, and social life, a change came over literature as well. The next period was an age of poetry. Nothing to be said in this chapter can exceed the importance of this. Rightly understood, all we have to say is but a commentary on this text. One of the greatest poetic epochs in the world's history begins when Lessing and Goethe go back to Shakespeare, when Wordsworth turns to nature, when Victor Hugo tears up the conventions of the French stage and founds the Romantic movement.

This simultaneous phenomenon and its place in general history are strong presumption for us that we are in presence of one of the turning-points in man's evolution. Homer and the poets of Athens appeared when Greece was founding the world's thought in which their works were to be part of a common inheritance. Lucretius and his successors were spokesmen of a society again at the head of civilization and laying the foundations for a world-order which was to follow. Dante in like manner speaks to us all of a common ordering of thought and life which, in his time, had come to its zenith. When, with the Elizabethans and Shakespeare, we come to the next great outburst of poetic power, it is dispersed among the nations, but still produces, in varied colours, common forms. The Spanish drama of Lope de Vega and Calderon is near of kin to ours, and is followed shortly by the classical drama of France,

E

So at the Romantic revival towards the close of the eighteenth and the beginning of the nineteenth century there is again a general movement in the leading countries of the West, but its common features are more difficult to discern.

The name, or rather the want of a good name, perplexes us. ' Romantic ' is of all possible terms perhaps the least satisfactory. Literally it refers back to languages which derive from Latin, by association it suggests the creation of striking but unaccustomed visions of life. Nothing could be less like Wordsworth, or the main purpose, if not always the actual achievement, of Hugo. Let us search further and try to find the common points and connecting links without imposing any strain on our subject-matter, without ignoring the individuality of the men of genius who make up a ' movement '. Genius is complete but not isolated. This one assumption we must make at starting. The work of these poets and their successors, individual as each must be, distinguished as they also are by national divisions, has yet its common roots in the contemporary civilization of Western Europe, and has moulded the social life which followed, in some respects to common ends. To trace these is the historian's primary object. The individual colours will brighten the picture and enliven us as we proceed.

We are still perhaps too near these great men of a hundred years ago to give them their final place among the eminences. We are far enough away to discern the mountain chain, not yet far enough to place it in its due relations to those on other sides and behind them. So far mankind has not agreed that any one of the group will rank with the very highest of the past, with Homer or Dante or Shakespeare, though some might, even now, give such a place to Goethe or to Victor Hugo. But on the group as a whole it may be safe to venture one or two conclusions. Has there ever been in the world before so rich an outburst of creative power in literature within the same space of time, so varied, so well distributed among the leading nations, and, withal, so closely knit by common traits in its inspiration and its purpose?

The magnitude of the creative power is the first and most striking aspect. To most students the lifetime of Goethe seems to cover more of the best literature of Germany than all her other years; and it is also the flowering-time in Germany for music and philosophy. For France the lyric and reflective poetry of the nineteenth century, especially its earlier portion, are of incomparable value; the bulk of their fiction falls within the same period, and their drama of the nineteenth deserves comparison with that of the seventeenth century, the only other to be mentioned in their history beside it. In England our stretch of the greatest literature is longer—longer than that of any other people. Yet, putting Shakespeare out of the account, he would be a bold man who denied that the nineteenth century, especially its earlier portion, outweighed both in volume and in value any other period, some might even say the greater part of all the rest together. For in this time we have Wordsworth, Byron, Shelley, Coleridge, Browning, and Tennyson, as well as Scott and the greatest school of novelists in the world.

It is attractive to set this great creative act of European mind beside the creations of other sorts proceeding at the same moment. Are they not all parts of one creation which is fashioning science, transforming industry, and widening liberty in parallel and related movements? Man, it seems, was becoming conscious of all his powers at that revolutionary moment and found them more varied and of wider scope than even the Greeks or the men of the Renaissance, who had felt earlier stirrings of the same spirit. The infinite scope of science was now added to his aspirations and the possibility of organizing the whole world in the service of human good. We cannot doubt, though we cannot prove, that as with the Greeks of the fifth century B. C., as with the artists and men of science of the sixteenth and seventeenth centuries A. D., so at the end of the eighteenth there was a real and intimate connexion between all these creative acts in science, literature, music, and liberty.

A new spirit of freedom is, next to its creative power, the most striking general feature in the literature of the age. It is this which connects it most closely with the political movement which we have sketched. Lessing's is the clearest voice of the new freedom in Germany, Victor Hugo's in France, Wordsworth's in England. The accents must be as varied as Freedom is, as varied as the vision of the men who gave it utterance. To Germany, as to the ' Romantics ' a little later in France, the freedom meant primarily the breaking of the conventions with which the French stage had bound itself by a mistaken and narrow rendering of Aristotle. This may seem a small thing, and remote enough in origin and in distance from the main interests of human life. Yet, when the issue came to be fought out in France, all society was divided and an actual battle raged, as fierce as any contested election in politics. The ' unities ' in a play had become a symbol of a literature where everything—language, character, and action—was to follow the accepted types. Yet Shakespeare was the greatest figure in the whole world of drama, and he was unconscious of these categories of character, unities of time and place, conventions of language. As a creator he made men and women living and individual, and he used his material not as the topiary artist cutting live trees into dead birds, but as the sculptor using rough blocks for new and vivid shapes. Hence for Lessing, Goethe, Victor Hugo, new life for the drama called for the study of Shakespeare, and since the Puritan revolution the drama meant for France and for Germany incomparably more than it did for us. This was one aspect of the new freedom. Rousseau had expressed it in other forms—in a new gospel of freedom in education, and Diderot in a fresh and personal criticism of art.

In England the drama does not express the change. We look rather to work of another kind, and find the same mark in Wordsworth's meditations on man and nature, in Byron's revolt and passion for liberty in his own days, in Shelley's visions of an ideal world. In all these there may be traced the same desire to break away from hampering traditions of the past, the same confidence that human nature, relying on its own impulses, may create a better world in the future, which were felt by Rousseau, Condorcet, Godwin, Turgot. Freedom, directness, and greater simplicity in language were to them, as to the French and German 'Romantics', the badge of greater freedom of the spirit. For the new poets everywhere there was to be no court livery in the service of their mistress poetry.

It is a fact akin to this that all these men get nearer to the truth of human nature. But here we must distinguish, and the distinction will throw light before and after in the line of literary evolution. The truth that these men aimed at in their delineation of life, was not the microscopic, photographic study of human nature which passes by the name of naturalism. Such study tends, as in later writers, such as Balzac and his successors, to an exaggeration of human faults. The search for truth of the earlier writers found it rather in the appreciation of those traits in character which tend to greatness. Idealism there must be in every work of art. Are we to look for it in a brilliant picture of the weak and little in our nature, thrown by a powerful magnifying light upon the screen, or in the delineation of those characters and those features in any character, which, subject to given trials of circumstance, become heroic, sometimes in action, sometimes in suffering, but always in growth? This is also truth to nature, but truth developed to a higher power.

It will be observed, of course, that in thus proceeding from the truth of human nature and idealizing it, the men of the new age in literature were doing no new thing. The greatest makers, Homer, Dante, and Shakespeare, had done it before and thus won their immortality. The test of greatness is, in fact, precisely the same with the new school of poets. Wordsworth and Scott take men and women of their own world, the poor countryman of the dales, the Scotch peasant, the Covenanting preacher, and show them as heroic in their own sphere, acting with perfect truth to their own nature, as the chiefs of Homer or the Romans of Shakespeare. This is the glory of these new poets, and we can say it of no others before them since Shakespeare.

But we come now to another feature in which the writers of the new age surpass those of any earlier period. It is not primarily an individual quality, but it is a debt which Scott, Victor Hugo, Thackeray, and all the writers of the time owe in varied measure to the spirit of the age. This is the historical spirit which we noted before as a general characteristic. Gibbon had lived, and Montesquieu; the beginnings of history had been laid at the end of the eighteenth century. All succeeding writers appeal to history in different tones. Byron's free Greece of the future is the Greece of history. Shelley, the least attached to tradition, is constrained by the same spirit to appeal to the heroic past of England as well as the empire of Hellenic thought. Scott lived in a recreated past. Victor Hugo crowned his life's work by a *Légende des Siècles*.

In this respect their truth to nature aimed at another and deeper aspect of the truth, for the poets, often unconsciously, were compassing the same task which the historians and philosophers had just begun of set purpose, i. e. to understand the being and destiny of Man by studying his becoming. It is the supreme task of interpretation, the comprehensive truth of which but one facet here and another there will gleam through the minds of the greatest masters. Scott saw the past, but had no inkling of the forces which were transforming the present. Shelley saw a future so radiant that the present seemed but a procession of hideous crimes.

Of the characteristics of the nineteenth century which we noted as emerging from the great industrial and political revolution, two remain to be considered in their relation to the new spirit in literature ; they are, we believe, to be the most decisive in the end. One is the force of science, of organized knowledge, in framing and inspiring life. The other is the goal of human thought and activity, the community of all human beings conspiring to a common end by diverse means. This is the problem of humanity, and it covers those partial aspects which we know as nationalism and the international question. Now both of these kindred forces and ideals begin to be felt in the poetry of the early century, but do not yet transfuse it. Their presence and their growth during our period are palpable enough. Most significant of all is their mutual relation. Those thinkers who appreciate best the meaning and the value of the scientific evolution are those to whom the ideal of humanity is most apparent.

Of all the poets of the time Goethe is the most scientific, and he is also strongly international in spirit. Science is to him primarily a noble and attractive object of human interest— perhaps the most attractive of all—at times even more so than his own liege mistress poetry herself. At times he gives us also a glimpse of the organizing aspect of science as the product of joint human labour operating through the ages. But for the notion of science as the basis of social progress we have to wait. The social question, as we now understand it, did not exist till after the industrial revolution, and Goethe's mind is essentially pre-revolutionary. Wordsworth, as we shall see, takes us a step farther in his Preface to the *Lyrical Ballads,* where he describes with marvellous insight both the right relation of poetry to science and the difficulties which hinder its realization. And Shelley, through his higher imaginative power, expresses the future ideal of knowledge transfused by love and power, more perfectly than any other poet of the age. It is to him that man appeared not as men but as ' Man, a chain of linked thought, of love and might to be divided not '. In this, the sublime chorus in the *Prometheus Unbound,* he attains a fuller vision than even Victor Hugo, to whom ' science is beautiful and Aristotle great, but Socrates and Zeno greater still '.

On the whole the great writers of the Romantic school are more concerned to expound the heroic in the individual soul as supreme above any achievement of the collective mind. It is not till later in the century that writers appear, individually less magnificent, but primarily interested in the collective problem. Then the growth of science becomes the guiding thought and social progress the greatest subject. George Eliot is a type in England, Sully Prudhomme in France, and they speak with a voice of philosophic reflection, pitched in a lower and less passionate key.

From similar causes national sentiments are stronger in the earlier writers than any feeling of the unity of mankind. It was an age of rising nationalities when France was recovering her national strength and Byron was breathing new life into the crushed frame of Greece and Canning setting free young nations in the New World. Hence nearly all the great writers of the age are full of national enthusiasm, and even the rebels among them, such as Byron and Shelley, cannot escape from it. If, like Byron, they find nothing to inspire them in their own country's achievements, they find a spiritual home elsewhere. For heroism, when it once advances beyond the Cyclops' cave, must have its fellows to work with, its traditions to feed on, its common goal of victory to attain. The larger ideal of a hero of humanity is as yet but faintly traced ; it is apt to take the form merely of a Man of Sorrows. Carlyle gives us no picture of the hero as Man of Science. But we can see its need in the national self-complacency of Englishmen in those early decades, in the lyrical exaggeration of patriotism such as Victor Hugo's. But the larger ideal is in the making ; it gains a philosophic expression in many writers : one day it will find its sacred poet.

This new outburst of poetry may be dated from that famous year [1] when Wordsworth, Hegel, and Beethoven were born, 1770. Scott's birth followed in 1771. Turner, the painter of nature, was four years younger. Within those five years therefore five men were born, makers of new things of the first moment in the thought of Europe. There is something kindred in their depth of feeling, their scope of imagination, their creative force. The two great national poets, Goethe for Germany, Victor Hugo for France, are not quite in this group. Goethe was just over twenty years senior and has firm roots in the *ancien régime*. Victor Hugo is thirty years later and is a child of the nineteenth century. Goethe looks as much to the past as Hugo looks to the future. But the five men were on the watershed. From them the streams were descending, of which we will trace a few of the brightest stretches until they are lost in the great expanse of the later century.

As we are tracing these great movements only, and within those limits endeavouring especially to see the common points and the contrasts between ourselves and France, it is necessary to select a very few of the acknowledged and most typical masters, and view the rest in relation to them. Taking the period from 1770, which was remarkable for the birth of so much genius, to 1850, when a fresh revolution had taken place in Europe and

[1] See Dr. A. C. Bradley in *English Poetry and German Philosophy*.

Wordsworth and Scott were dead, there can be no doubt as to the most representative names. We must take Wordsworth and Scott in England, Victor Hugo and Balzac in France. To select these is not to give four first prizes for genius. Genius is an individual and incomparable thing, and who shall say that Shelley is not as great a genius as Wordsworth ? In some of the most brilliant poetic qualities, in imagery, in glow of language, in creative imagination, he is manifestly his superior. But Wordsworth holds so central a position in English poetry, brings together so many threads of religious and philosophic thought and has spread his influence so wide in later literature, that no one can dispute his claim to the most serious study if we would understand the part that England played in expressing the new spirit of the age. To some critics this has become so clear that one distinguished French historian of the nineteenth century tells us that ' Wordsworth is, or is to be, the true national poet of England '.[1]

If this be so, we must yield an exclusive national possession of Shakespeare, and allow him to belong, like Homer, like Dante, like Goethe, primarily to all mankind. And clearly there is a sense in which this is true. There is a class of great poets for whom the world and humanity at large eclipse their national background. For all there are local roots and national and temporal attachments, but with some the branches spread so wide that they cover the earth and we are apt to lose sight of the narrower origin. Such were Homer and Dante, and Shakespeare and Goethe. Such was not Virgil or Milton or Racine. Such were not those whom we have mentioned as the most representative writers in France and England in the early nineteenth century. Victor Hugo comes the nearest to universality but hardly reaches it, while Wordsworth, with all his kinship with German philosophy and all his early enthusiasm for the

[1] M. Élie Halévy.

French Revolution, ends as an Englishman of the English. Byron and Shelley are of course much more cosmopolitan than he, but ' cosmopolitan ' is not the proper name of this universal quality. The universal poets have all a strong and deep root in their local or national environment, but develop their nature to embrace mankind. Byron and Shelley rather turn to mankind for comfort and redress against the ills, real and imagined, that they have suffered in their natural home. This is the mark of the cosmopolitan as distinguished from the more thoroughly human and universal quality of mind.

Now of all the great writers who occupy the early part of the nineteenth century, Wordsworth most perfectly combines strong national feelings with a mind open to new thought. And all he received from without, from the impressions of nature and the converse of friends, from political revolutions and philosophic thought, he made his own and transmuted into one substance by an intensely individual and sympathetic temper. Thus, while not a great creative poet, in the Shakespearean sense, not cosmopolitan in any sense, he became the first and most powerful of the philosophic poets, who, with the novelists, are the literary distinction of the nineteenth century. We find in him all those features which we analysed as the ideal legacy of the Revolution. ' We live by admiration, hope and love', he tells us, and, in words that aim at science and might be taken as the motto of the age,

> Truth justifies herself, and as she dwells
> With Hope, who would not follow where she leads ? [1]

The Prelude gives us the ' growth of the Poet's mind '—his education and early history ; above all the interest and passion aroused in him by his visit to France in the summer of 1790, when the French were celebrating their first National Fête

---

[1] *The Recluse.*

and hailing their king as first citizen and constitutional chief
of a regenerated country. The generous enthusiasm, the love
of freedom, the hope for the future found an echo in his soul
which never died. He supported the revolutionists until
Napoleon's aggression alienated him, as it alienated the other
greatest prophet of freedom, born in 1770, Beethoven. Then
came that period of deep depression which turned him to
science and the inward vision, and in which his poetry and even
his sanity were preserved by the constant love and companion-
ship of his sister.[1]

Lyrical Ballads, one of the milestones in English poetry,
appeared in 1798. It was the result of a visit of Coleridge to
Wordsworth at the time when Wordsworth was living in
Somerset. The friendship there formed was decisive for
Wordsworth in many ways. Coleridge was able to introduce
his friend to the thought of foreign philosophers, especially
of Spinoza. He gave him confidence in his own powers, and
the stimulus of another point of view, kindred and yet different
from his own. The influence of Coleridge thus deepened
and widened his own individuality. Coleridge, a mystic,
with his mysticism strengthened by his philosophic training,
inclined to supernatural subjects for poetic treatment. He
contributed 'The Ancient Mariner' to their joint book.
Wordsworth, inclined to simple subjects of common life,
wrote 'We are Seven', 'The Idiot Boy', and many more of
his familiar short poems. But the collection also contained
the 'Lines above Tintern Abbey', and most of the poems
showed that deep insight into the natural, that power of seeing
something beyond the natural in the commonest object
which is his peculiar gift.

In 1800 a second edition was called for. A number of new
poems were added, some of Wordsworth's best, 'Ruth',

[1] *The Prelude*, Book II.

'The old Cumberland Beggar ', ' Lucy Gray ' ; and he added a Preface, defending and explaining his poetry, which is one of the most important documents in English criticism. It stands to English poetry in much the same position in which Victor Hugo's *Preface to Cromwell*, published twenty-seven years later, stands to French. The contrasts as well as the communities of thought between the two manifestoes, equally famous in their own countries, are of the highest interest and significance. We will return to them when speaking of Hugo. The main points of Wordsworth's Preface are : his account of the nature of poetry itself and of the language in which it should be expressed.

What is a poet, he asks, to whom does he address himself, and what language is to be expected of him ?

' He is a man endowed with more lively sensibility, more enthusiasm and tenderness, who has a greater knowledge of human nature and a more comprehensive soul, than are supposed to be common among mankind ; a man pleased with his own passions and volitions and passions as manifested in the goings-on of the Universe, and habitually impelled to create them where he does not find them.' Wordsworth accepts the dictum of Aristotle that poetry is the most philosophic of all writing, for its object is truth, not individual and local, but general and operative ; not standing upon external testimony, but carried alive into the heart by passion. It is the image of man and of nature. And where the historian has a thousand obstacles of detail standing between himself and the person to whom he has to convey his picture, the Poet, granted his superior endowment of feeling and imagination, has no other obstacle except the necessity of giving pleasure to any human being ' possessed of that information which may be expected of him not as a lawyer, a physician, a mariner, an astronomer, or a natural philosopher, but as a Man '.

The necessity of producing pleasure is not to be regarded as a degradation of his art, but an acknowledgement of the beauty of the Universe and a homage to the native dignity of man, who knows and feels and lives and moves by the ' grand elementary principle of pleasure '. ' Pleasure ', understood in this wide sense of ' Joy ', a sense in which Wordsworth agrees with more than one of the great contemporary schools of philosophy, is the universal ingredient and stimulus to action. The man of Science has no knowledge except so far as he has pleasure, and the Poet works by creating in the minds of his hearers or readers that degree of pleasure which is inseparable from sympathy with the complex of ideas and sensations which surrounds us all, and which the Poet idealizes and evokes. The man of Science has also to recreate and evoke the actual, but he ' seeks truth as a remote and unknown benefactor ; he cherishes and loves it in his solitude ; the Poet, singing a song in which all human beings join with him, rejoices in the presence of truth as our visible friend and hourly companion. Poetry is the breath and finer spirit of all knowledge, the impassioned expression which is in the countenance of all Science. He looks before and after ; he is the rock of defence for human nature, carrying everywhere with him relationship and love. In spite of difference of soil and climate, and language and manners, and laws and customs ; in spite of things silently gone out of mind or violently destroyed, the Poet binds together by passion and knowledge the vast empire of human society. The objects of the Poet's thoughts are everywhere ; though the eyes and senses of man are, it is true, his favourite guides, yet he will follow wheresoever he can find an atmosphere of sensation in which to move his wings. If the labours of the man of Science should ever create any material revolution, direct or indirect, in our condition or in the impressions which we habitually receive, the Poet will sleep no more than at present ; he will be ready to follow the steps of the man of Science, not only in those general indirect effects, but he will be at his side, carrying sensation into the midst of the objects of the science itself. The remotest discoveries of the Chemist, the Botanist, or Mineralogist, will be as proper objects of the poet's art as any upon which it can be employed, if ever the time should come when these things shall be familiar to us as suffering and enjoying beings. If the time should ever come when what is now called science, thus familiarized to man, shall be ready to put on, as it were, a form of flesh and blood, the Poet will lend his divine spirit to aid the transformation, and will welcome the Being thus produced, as a dear and genuine inmate of the household of Man.'

It is interesting to see this point recurring later in our century, when in 1906 we find Sully Prudhomme still lamenting the little influence exercised on the inspiration of poets by the prodigious conquests of science. But Wordsworth's immediate lesson is that the Poet is the man of greater promptness in thinking and feeling the general passions and thoughts of men, and greater power in expressing them. Science, therefore, has to pass into the common stock before it will be matter for the Poet to deal with. He must, if he is to do his own work well, express these matters of common interest in the language best fitted to put his reader into the closest communion with his own thought, and to give the appropriate pleasure in the highest degree. All rules of metre or of choice of language are dictated by these simple considerations. Metre also, he suggests, not only gives pleasure directly, but also enables us to bear a degree of pathos which is almost intolerable in prose.[1] It tempers and restrains our passion.

In the longer poems—*The Prelude* and *The Excursion* with

[1] Goethe makes a similar remark to Schiller about Faust.

the lately published fragment of *The Recluse*—Wordsworth was labouring to express that complete synthesis of his ideas and feelings upon which he fell back after his early disillusionment with the Revolution. They are often long drawn out and full of passages little distinguishable from prose. But they are invaluable as the outpouring of a profound and faithful mind struggling to set forth in simple terms the beliefs which he had arrived at in a long life of concentrated thought. These beliefs contain a glimpse of the great truth, first dawning on the men of his day, that the mind of man is a progressive thing, gaining depth and power from age to age ; but he is dominated by the idea, in which also he was a spokesman of his time, that this evolving mind of man is in communion with something behind Nature, which has a kindred existence and is qualified in some deep and half-inscrutable way, to call out a response from the human soul. Byron and many more had also given expression to this feeling ; he tells us in *Childe Harold* :

> I live not in myself but I become
> Portion of that around me ; and to me
> High mountains are a feeling.

But to Wordsworth it was a far deeper, more constant and more governing thought than to Byron or to any other man. He gave himself in all his later life to the lakes and mountains and the society of a few, simple congenial spirits in order that this frame of mind might be supreme ; and it is his reward, like that of other men—an Augustine, a Descartes, a Comte—who concentrate wholly on one line of thought, to become its immortal prophet and expositor.

We may pass on to Sir Walter Scott through the medium of a sentence in Carlyle's essay on him. He says—it is one of many suggestive partial truths in the midst of a generally inadequate and unappreciative treatment—that ' a great man is ever, as the Transcendentalists speak, possessed by an idea '.

By this test we have judged Wordsworth great, and Carlyle would have us judge Scott not great. Obviously it is only a test of one type of greatness, and inappropriate to creative genius of vast and varied scope. Shakespeare would not be great, judged by this standard, nor Homer nor Molière. Wordsworth had this mark of greatness, as we have seen, and, of the greatest poets, Dante. Each had a philosophic moral idea which possessed him and transfuses all his work. Scott was a genius of the other order, receptive, creative, abundant. He was born in the year after Wordsworth, and bears many traces of the same environment. But his mind being of a different temper, he used his material to quite another purpose.

He was from his earliest years fed on the wild legends of the Border country in which his own Scott ancestry played a large part. A born storyteller like the Homeric rhapsodes of ancient Greece, he began to think, in adult years, of how best to make use of the rich stores with which his mind was full. It was the raw material of epics such as the Norse Sagas or the books of Joshua and Judges, or the primitive lays which grew into the *Iliad*. Then some one introduced him to *Christabel* and to the German ballads of the Rhine, and he began his work in verse. He went on to translate Goethe's *Götz of the Iron Hand*. But his poetry, which was at this time reckoned second only to Byron's, seems to us now too facile, too little analytic, with too little insight into character. In this respect he is clearly not in the main line of nineteenth-century development. But in other points, perhaps, of equal moment for our present purpose, he is fully representative of the age. As heartily as Wordsworth or Hugo, he eschewed the stilted artificial images and language of the eighteenth century, and spoke in simple words which glowed as they ran and carried the eager mind along with them.

Many lines, such as the ' unwept, unhonoured, and unsung', have become a part of ourselves.

The prose romances, on which mankind has rightly decided to rest his chief fame, had been begun with *Waverley* quite early in the century at the time of the first ballads ; but they were laid aside. In 1814 *Waverley* appeared, and from 1814 to 1832 when he died, the year of Goethe's death, followed the unmatched series. The tragic side of the story—the business speculations, the heroic labours to pay off debt, the premature exhaustion of a strong physique—this does not concern us here. We take with admiration and gratitude the greatest gift of British genius to the imaginative reconstruction of the past since Shakespeare, for we know that but for Scott long stretches of our national annals would still have lain but faintly illuminated in the national consciousness. Through him the France and Flanders of *Quentin Durward*—scene of our greatest struggle in the war—the Highlands of *The Fair Maid of Perth*, the Lowlands of *Old Mortality*, the England of *Ivanhoe*, have taken on as vivid a colour in our minds as the England of Shakespeare.

Herein we touch Scott's chief link with the nineteenth century, and it leads us on to the great French master of romance, who carried the historical spirit a stage further, and combined with it a creative power in poetry of all kinds.

Hugo was born in 1802, when ' *ce siècle avait deux ans* '. He is thus more entirely the child of the nineteenth century than either of the great masters of whom we have just spoken. He shows his modernity in a fuller appreciation of the historical process than either Scott or Wordsworth. Scott was historical by virtue of living in the past, but democracy had not dawned for him. Wordsworth had an inkling of the contributions of the past and shows it in various passages of *The Prelude* and

The Excursion, but his supreme interest was the unfolding of the individual soul in communion with nature and living men. To Victor Hugo the historical pageant was the dominant thought : he sees it moving on to the future as well as issuing from the past, and the future was a vision of democratic freedom and happiness and triumph. Here especially he represents the nineteenth century, and above all France.

He was himself the son of one of Napoleon's generals, and spent a large part of his childhood in Spain, imbibing the language, the literature, and the spirit of that home of romance. That element, therefore, held through life a larger place in his mind than the philosophy of Germany or the science of the West. Devoted to his father, he was always loyal to his father's chief, and his later democracy and freedom in religion were grafted on a stem originally Catholic and authoritative, carefully nurtured by his mother, a royalist of La Vendée. With him, too, there was a ' growth of the poet's soul ' towards freedom, and he gives some account of this in various passages of his work. In the Preface to *Cromwell,* at the age of twenty-five, he threw down the gauntlet to the conventional spirit which still held the stage in France : it was taken up and the battle fought out on the production of *Hernani* three years later, in 1830. To compare and sum up the differences between this Preface and Wordsworth's is the essay in criticism which we suggested above. Brilliance and breadth in the Frenchman, thoroughness and profundity in the Englishman, would be on our balance-sheet. Hugo does not attempt to tell us what superiorities distinguish a poet's mind, nor does he touch the question of how poetry will ultimately appropriate and express the achievements of science. Here Wordsworth cuts deeper than Hugo, though his tool produces less finished, less varied, less attractive images. Hugo sets out to explain how different ages in history have been expressed by different types of poetry, and how the drama, if allowed to develop, would be the perfect and complete type of poetry. He is primarily a dramatist, as Wordsworth is a philosophic poet, and to him the drama is ' *la poésie complète* '. He decries any system of thought, but, like a true French-man, at once throws his sketch of poetic history into systematic form. When the primitive man awakes in the primitive world, poetry awakes with him. His first word is a hymn. His thought being fugitive and passionate, the earliest type of poetry is lyrical. Then as society settles round the priest and the king, another and more connected type of poetry appears. It is the epic which commemorates the migrations and conflicts of peoples. It sings of the lapse of ages, of nations, and of empires. Homer is born, who sums up and dominates all ancient society. Even the historians, with Herodotus at their head, were epic poets. The ancient drama is but another form of this all-per-vading epic. Not only are all their stories drawn from Homeric sources, but the same religious, heroic, gigantic spirit runs through them all. What the rhapsodes sang, the actors now declaim : that is all the difference. Then with Christianity a real change comes. Poetry becomes more spiritual, more true to nature, more full of melancholy and of the grotesque. Shakespeare at last appears, the summit of modern poetic art, combining by one supreme genius grotesque and sublime, comic and tragic. Shakespeare is drama itself, because he is the whole of life, seen at the angle of the stage.

Here is another law of the three stages, to be set beside the kindred thoughts of Comte and Hegel, and recalling Vico's earlier suggestion of a triple sequence—divine, heroic, human. Hegel's order, as given in his Aesthetic, is nearest to Hugo's, and must, one would think, have contributed something to the latter's. Hegel finds in art a progress from the ' Symbolic ',

typified by such monuments as the Pyramids, through the
'Classical' of the Parthenon and the Greek drama—beautiful,
complete, and limited—to the 'Romantic' of modern times,
when the infinite breaks up the perfect, finite sufficiency of the
Greek spirit. To Hugo the Bible is the model of the first stage,
the Iliad of the second, and Shakespeare of the third. '*La société,
en effet, commence par chanter ce qu'elle rêve, puis raconte ce
qu'elle fait, et enfin se met à peindre ce qu'elle pense*'; and he
illustrates this with a wealth of brilliant epigrams and figures.
The early ode is like the lake among the mountains, the epic is the
river that rises from it and rushes down, watering the land and
dividing the nations, the drama is the ocean in which all waters
are finally collected and the world of the skies is reflected for
ever.

But he is far from attempting to carry out this division in any
rigid way. Every stage has some elements of all, and every form
of literature some germs or examples of the others. The
supreme merit of the drama is that, to be complete, it must
actually contain both the others. It must have its story to be
unfolded, and this is an epic *in petto* ; and in the highest form
of drama, as in Shakespeare, it contains abundant lyrical and
emotional poetry.

Just as Wordsworth had his own public to convince, and uses
his philosophy of poetry as an introduction to arguments
about the legitimacy of his methods, so to Hugo these wide
generalizations and brilliant *aperçus* are but the substructure
for the new drama which he was about to launch in France.
He is really proving two things of which the latter is a corollary
of the former. The drama is a picture of life, and has grown
up and changed its character with the society from which it
springs. And if it is to be a picture of life, its language and
its technique must be free from the restrictions which the

eighteenth century had been imposing upon it in the name of Aristotle and decency and order. Thus the national poet of France and the future national poet of England are struggling to the same goal from different starting-points and by different methods.

Of these differences the most striking is the greater prominence given to the drama in France. Hugo uses his first play as the stalking-horse of his new and wider theory of poetic art, new to his generation, but true because it rests upon the natural and permanent relations between man's social and intellectual attainments and his means of expressing them in beautiful language, appealing to the emotions. To the Frenchman, as to the German, the drama first occurs as the obvious way of doing this. Lessing had raised the banner of the free drama sixty years before, and Goethe, who had won the same fight over *Götz* in 1771, completed it by *Faust*. Both Germans and French looked back to Shakespeare as their unsurpassable model. But England, which had given birth to Shakespeare, had since his day lost its national taste for drama. None of our great poets of the revolutionary age makes his appeal through the stage. In England the battle of *Hernani* was fought out over *Lyrical Ballads*. The ' This will never do ' of Jeffrey in the *Edinburgh Review* of 1815 was the protest of conventional England corresponding to the scene in the *Théâtre français* on October 24, 1829, when the groans of the bourgeois in the boxes were borne down by those wild youths with long hair and flaming waistcoats who had sworn allegiance to Hugo as the new master and the rising hope of revolutionary poetic France. By 1830 the battle was won for the new drama as it was for the Constitution, so that a poet and an official historian [1] of French poetry can declare that as 1789 created ' *notre patrie*

[1] Catulle Mendès.

politique, 1830 *a créé notre patrie littéraire*'. Two years later
Goethe died, the acknowledged king of German literature,
while in England Wordsworth was at last acknowledged.
In poetry the three great Western nations were keeping
pace.

But true to our insularity, our greater exclusiveness in the
early century, we never went to France for our poetic models
as the French went to us. In politics there had been Corresponding Societies but not in literature. Young France wor-
shipped Shakespeare, admired Byron, imitated Scott, but it
was a rather prevalent belief in England, not yet extinct, that
there is no real poetry in French. The forms of poetry are, in
fact, a strong national boundary. Poetry does not, in spite of
Wordsworth's glowing language, unite all nations as abstract
science does. Not only is the national language different while
an equation is the same for all, but the language of poetry being
by its very nature more carefully chosen than that of prose,
and fitted into forms that are not universal like the forms of
science, may be an additional barrier to community of thought.
And in these matters of form and the choice of language in
poetry the French have the stricter standard. Hence, while
the nineteenth-century Englishman has read his French novel
on the sofa, not always to his profit, the splendours of French
poetry—the heroic figures and thrilling verse of Hugo, the quiet
melancholy of Lamartine, the inspiration and historic sense
of de Vigny—have been only the treasure of a few. We have
named three of the early masters : they stand at the head of a
glorious succession. The growing union of French and English
minds at which we are now assisting, will never go very deep,
until the noble stream of French poetry which has flowed in
swelling volume throughout the century, finds a public here,
comparable at least to that of the French play or novel. It has

a disciplinary value like that of the best Latin verse. Its music and its pleasure-giving power may be felt by all who have once taken the trouble to turn the key. And as the years of our age of hope roll on, it comes more and more into contact with those deep problems of life and thought which Wordsworth has taught us are the proper subject of poetry. Indeed when we think of Cazalis and Sully Prudhomme—to name no others—it may appear that France has done more even than England in our century to promote that union of poetry with science and philosophy which the English poet indicated at its commencement as the task of the future.

But Victor Hugo is not only the dramatist and the leader of young France in song, he is also one of the greatest writers of prose romance. In no one else is the kinship so strongly marked between poetry in the strict sense and the novel, which is the prevalent type of imaginative literature in the nineteenth century.

What are the causes of this growing predominance of the novel, which coincides with Scott's own change of method from the poetic narratives of his early years to his main life-work in the novel ? Since then the novel has largely displaced the essay, the sermon, the epic, the narrative in verse. It has become the leading form for literature in the modern world.

As in so many other changes we must go back to the eighteenth century for its first clear manifestation. There, in Goethe's *Wilhelm Meister*, we have the exemplar of the modern novel, the book in prose which interweaves reflections on modern problems with the development of a leading character amid typical scenes and events. Perhaps it is mainly the complexity of modern life and the growing analysis of science which have engendered the novel as we have it. But there are powerful subsidiary causes which have assisted the process. The novel is much easier to write and to read than the poem. Carlyle, not without fury, saw men reading Scott's novels 'all their lives upon the sofa'; and, as to writing, compare *Les Misérables*, poured out volume after volume, or the torrent of Scott's and Balzac's novels with the *Légende des Siècles*—epic on the grandest scale, but slowly chiselled in a few short and finished poems. The novel, too, gives the author a double chance, much more difficult to secure either in the drama or in verse. He can express his views freely and at length, and he can describe the social background with adequate fulness and detail.

Of the two French writers who lead the century, Victor Hugo's novels belong to the earlier and more romantic stage, Balzac's to the later and more analytic. Victor Hugo has four great novels which will survive—*Les Misérables*, *Notre-Dame de Paris*, *Quatre-Vingt-Treize*, and *Les Travailleurs de la Mer*. But one wonders already whether he has that band of faithful followers who read him through once a year, as people in England read their Scott or Jane Austen. He gives you magnificent rhapsodies and long, interesting, but unnecessary digressions, such as the account of Waterloo in *Les Misérables*, or the growth of his own mind in the person of Marius, from the simple and passionate loyalism of his youth to the larger vision of freedom which he achieved in later life and foresaw in the future. Yet *Les Misérables*, the longest and most diffuse of his books, has been the most read, and a modern gospel to many a man in his youth.

Balzac, the better observer, the greater artist in prose, never brought a gospel to any one. He is the bridge between the romantic and the realistic school, and it is not the business of the realistic novel to inspire. He was born in 1799 and died in 1850—the year of the death of Wordsworth, and Peel and Louis Philippe. Much was passing away just then,

of thought as well as of life, at the turning-point of the
century.

Balzac was outlived for thirty-five years by Victor Hugo, who
pronounced his funeral oration. His special quality, as Hugo
then said, was to combine a high degree both of imagination
and of observation. It is thus that he serves as a link between
different schools of novel-writers. A strong admirer of Scott,
he began with historical romance in direct imitation of him,
and unintentionally he followed Scott also in his revolt against
the legal career which had been chosen for him by his father,
and in his lifelong struggle under a burden of debt. The historical sense remained with him throughout, and prompted him
again and again to such revelations of the inward eye as—'*l'histoire de France est là tout entière*', of a street in Saumur. But
whereas Scott's absorbing interest was in the past, Balzac lived
in the present, the life of France, and especially of Paris, in the
early decades of the nineteenth century. This life he saw with
an intensity of vision, a realism, which makes him a pioneer in
the psychological school which bulks so largely in later years.
With Balzac, as with so many writers who practise this acute
analysis of characters and action, the resulting picture is sombre
and often poignant. He sees his world black, and can only
console us with an occasional '*l'homme ne fait pas mal toujours*'.
Sometimes we refuse to believe the perversity of wickedness
which he describes, as in that story of *L'Auberge rouge*, where
two apparently innocent, light-hearted young men, just off for
a walking-tour, are tempted to murder a genial old German
merchant who had lain down to sleep beside them in the inn with
a great box of gold under his pillow. One of them cuts off the
merchant's head and escapes, to reappear in a later story. The
other, who nearly succumbs to the same temptation, is deserted
by his companion and left to die on suspicion. This prevailing

darkness Balzac attempted deliberately to lighten from time to time with a *tour de force* of virtue, as in the *Médecin de campagne*, or of religious mysticism as in *Séraphita*. But more affecting and convincing are the glimpses we have in nearly all the novels of deep human feeling in the midst of a world of horrors. There is the unshakable, extravagant affection of *Père Goriot*, prose-brother of Lear, stripping himself of all his property for his two daughters, who leave him to die in misery while they pursue an almost equally unhappy life of selfish luxury. There is the quaint genius and kindly weakness of *Cousin Pons*, who, to get good dinners, bears the snubs of his wealthy connexions and is stript of all his treasures on his death-bed by a crowd of harpies, feebly kept at bay by an old German friend, exquisitely drawn, and a dissolute ballet-dancer. There is the quiet love and suffering of *Eugénie Grandet*, who bears every hardship from her miserly father, and thanks and kisses him when for selfish motives he releases her at last after months of solitary confine-ment for having lent a few gold pieces to her needy cousin. These things have the Shakespearean ring, and they are told with a wealth of wit and aphorism as biting and brilliant as Voltaire's. But at the end of it we ask ourselves whether the picture is on the whole a true one, whether any great society can really be compounded of such a mass of selfishness and jealousy, the worship of money and the obsession of sex : and beyond this, again, whether the greater artist is not the man who sees the better things in human nature more clearly than the worse, and whether, as he must select by the very nature of his art, there is not a place, the highest place of all, for the artist who, while preserving the general truth of his picture, yet idealizes in such a way as to inspire by the beauty of goodness and the hope that goodness may at least survive.

This short chapter gives, of course, no scope for the discussion of the aesthetic principles of the novel. But a few comparisons of its leading exponents will give some material for an opinion on a question as important as it is difficult. The life-story of Tolstoi, the greatest novelist in the latter part of the century as Scott and Balzac in the earlier, is a personal illustration of the issues involved. The Russian, like his great French and English fellows, had imaginative power of a high order. In observation he is more akin to Balzac than to Scott. In geniality and breadth of sympathy and hopefulness he is nearer Scott, but nearer than either to the ideal novelist we have suggested. In mid-career he was arrested by the problem of the right use of his art, and set himself to work on lines of deliberate edification. It is no condemnation to call it this ; but it leaves us only to surmise what the full harvest might have been. Yet Tolstoi and his somewhat earlier contemporary Turgueniev approach perhaps more closely than any other novelists of the century to our ideal. They have both the wide sympathy and imaginative power which make their characters live : they both tended, without falsifying their picture, to that idealization of goodness which is essential if the new art is to take rank beside the great art of the past and help to build up the humanity of the future.

In the future, as in the past, there will be tempers like Virgil's and tempers like Juvenal's, and each will see the world with somewhat different eyes. But the subject of their pictures is the same vast whole,—human life developing through the ages into the infinitely varied and complex forms which we have around us in the modern world. It is with this complex and changing scene that the modern novel mainly deals, and it is so full of new and interesting sights that the novelist is mostly devoted to acquainting his readers, confined to one corner of the bustling fair, with the doings—real or imaginary—of their contemporaries who are hidden from them in the crowd. But we believe that one day the tumult will subside, and the new life become a more settled and better ordered thing. As Wordsworth anticipated the absorption of science in poetry, so we may look forward to a society which has at last assimilated the triumphs of mechanical power, enlightened as to the laws of its own nature, reverent to the past, open-eyed to the ideal. Then we may see in romance as well as drama an imaginative art beside which the current novel would be as a film picture to Velasquez or Michelangelo.

Russia, France, and England—Goethe apart—have been throughout the century the leaders in novel-writing. We have seen how some of the Russian writers, developing rather later than those of the West, have approached nearest to the ideal by a combination of knowledge and sympathy with creative power and inspiration. France has throughout the period maintained a steady flow, with work always penetrating, lucid, and polished, and with occasional figures of giant power such as Hugo and Balzac. What of England ?

In volume the English novel, including that of the United States, must be far larger than that of any other country. It is the chief reading of a large part, perhaps the majority, of people who read anything at all beyond the newspaper. It would be marvellous therefore if this mass of work were all, or even mostly, of the highest quality. To a sane judgement it will appear a great achievement that there are so many people who can write so well. But let us compare the better part of our English novels with the better part of the French, and draw our examples mainly from the earlier half of the nineteenth century. The comparison fits in well with our review of the joint work of France and England in developing the ideas of the revolutionary age.

Jane Austen and the Brontës, Dickens and Thackeray, and, in the next period, George Eliot and George Meredith—we should all agree that these are the greatest names which follow Scott. They are the writers whom it is usual to call Victorian or Early Victorian, sometimes with the suggestion that their style is out of date, and their books, like venerable maiden aunts, upon the shelf. Well, there are three main points about them which will strike any impartial critic in a general survey. The first is their strongly individual character, the mark of English genius in art. Jane Austen and Charlotte Brontë, Dickens and Thackeray, couples always to be named together, are yet so different that their rival merits have exercised the argumentative wits of their admirers ever since they wrote. Jane Austen, the earliest in date, beginning to write before the end of the eighteenth century, and describing the placid orderly society of English country life before the steam-engine, the bicycle, or the motor-car had disturbed its quiet pleasures and its routine, yet describes it with a humour, a realism, and an acute analysis of character which make her in some ways the most modern of them all. Charlotte Brontë, with the new industrial life bursting into her wild Yorkshire valleys, is yet more absorbed by personal passion than all her contemporaries, and idealizes the love of man and woman more vividly than any other novel-writer of the age. Dickens, the philanthropist and humanitarian reformer, is the most typical of the times, for he began writing as the first Reform Bill was going through, described the new middle-class in England, the class of little culture and much (if ignorant) benevolence, and created for that class types of eccentric vigour, generous humanity, and perverted strength which have become part of our English being. Thackeray, the most delightful, the man of widest education and most European outlook in that early group, has, next to

Scott, made more of our history live again than any other writer of romance, and has given us the permanent picture of the Victorian upper middle-class with the satirist's touch and the humanist's pathos. So varied are they and yet all so typically English. That is our second main point ; we can group them all together, in spite of their differences, by certain characteristics in which they are unmistakably divided from other national groups, and perhaps most clearly from the French.

French art and knowledge are more complete and penetrating. They often tell us more of the realities of life and thought than our English writers. They send flash-lights into dark, sometimes horrid depths, while English writers spread a dimmer light more equally around. Compare the genial amateurishness of Thackeray discoursing on painting in the *Newcomes* with the master-touch of Balzac in *Le Chef d'Œuvre Inconnu*. The French seem so often to be grown-ups by the side of children. Their form is nearly always better, which is the reason of their triumph in the short story, from Balzac downwards, and our comparative failure. Our countrymen ramble on, believers in Scott's doctrine of the plot, that it is only justified by the good things that you can hang upon it. Good things and a good heart : these are the strong points in the English novel, if it is not too proud a boast to claim them. There is no doubt less naked truth in the English writers, but there is more kindliness and humour. Think of the hosts of men and women whom we wish to remember because they were themselves well-wishers to their kith and kind, the Caleb Balderstones, the Monkbarns and the Nicol Jarvies of Scott, the Mr. Woodhouse and the Miss Bates of Jane Austen, the Colonel Newcome of Thackeray, the Cheerybles and Aunt Trotwood of Dickens, all people with patent oddities and foibles, but all lovable because of their essential goodness and kindliness of heart. These are the glory of English fiction. We have, too, in the English novel another standard of love, and picture-galleries of women and children that are almost wholly wanting in French fiction.

There is of course deliberate reticence in the Victorian novel, and the avoidance of certain topics. On this matter there was a revolution in English taste which coincides broadly with the end of the eighteenth century and the revival of religion. But the difference in the view of woman and the standard of love between the typical English novel and the typical French in the nineteenth century goes much farther and deeper than this. Love is the main theme in both, but go back as far as you will in the century, take the women of Jane Austen, living in the narrowest circle and with the smallest mental equipment, they are free women, choosing their husbands and weighing their fate, compared with the women of Balzac. In the typical French novel there is no assumption that marriage is the consecration of love, a partnership in all joys and sorrows entered into with full consent by both parties. Marriage is rather a matter of business, and ideal love rather more likely to be outside it than within. That they are acting on another theory is the strength and the supreme grace of the English heroine, of Di Vernon and Dorothea Brooke, of Elizabeth Bennet and Shirley Keeldar. Herein they triumph and herein their social order led the world in the early nineteenth century.

It is surely no idle fancy to connect this with the prominence that children and young people hold in English as compared with French novels. They are the pledge of love and the hope of the future, and in this forward glance, this self-restraint in the present for the sake of the greater good to come, we find the third main feature of the school—that aspect of English fiction in which it has most strongly served the ideal tendency of the age.

The little lonely woman who poured out her soul in the parsonage at Haworth had a dim but true inkling of this when she addressed herself to Thackeray in the preface to the second edition of *Jane Eyre*. ' I think ', she says, ' I see in him an intellect profounder and more unique than his contemporaries have yet recognized. I regard him as the first social regenerator of the day—as the very master of that working corps who would restore to rectitude the warped system of things. No commentator on his writings has yet found the comparison that suits him. They say he is like Fielding : they talk of his wit, humour, comic powers. He resembles Fielding as an eagle does a vulture.' Unjust to Fielding, she is true to the main current of English fiction. She spoke of what she knew in her own passion and her own ideal, and she points the way to those who were to continue the work with fuller knowledge in a later day. *Middlemarch* and *Beauchamp's Career* are higher flights by wings akin to hers—the wings of hope and of love for our fellow-men.

Thus we have seen in the new literature of the early century all those thoughts moving which we had traced as the legacy of the Revolution ; the love of nature, strong in Scott and Byron, in Hugo and Lamartine, a religion in Wordsworth ; the sympathy with common human nature which speaks to us in Burns and Béranger ; the passion for freedom of which Shelley's is the purest voice. To these we must add that ideal of perfect beauty which Keats gave us in the short life which ended in 1821. This stream of poetry, flowing broadly through the century, unites with the greater volume of prose romance to make one of the world's greatest ages of imaginative literature. And by its side we have to place the equal effort of the Western mind to recreate its past, the work of the historians. From Gibbon to our own day this has been growing, and later science, the discoveries of biology and archaeology, have given it fresh substance and fresh direction.

But in all these writers one note may be detected, deeper than the rest and linking all the rest together. It sounds in the history of Carlyle, as in the poetry of Shelley, in the novelists as clearly as in the philosophers. A new order is being born, in which mankind is all to share in a life of greater freedom and beauty, worthier activity, and more unselfish happiness than the world had known before.

IV

THE BIRTH OF SOCIALISM

' Social regeneration ' was the final note of that new spirit
in literature which we have just described. Charlotte Brontë
discerned it beneath the glamour of *Vanity Fair*. Dickens
made his art an engine to force social reforms. Balzac por-
trayed a *Comédie Humaine* as terrible as the lower circles of
the *Divina Commedia*, and laid the blame for its horrors on the
greed of money and the selfishness of competition. The poets
were all awake to usher in a new and brighter day. We have
now to look at the same problem from another point of view.
Side by side with the new literature and the new industry,
another impulse of thought and effort was issuing from the
same spirit of progress, aiming directly at the redress of social
inequality, at curing the diseases of poverty, at substituting
co-operation for competition as the master motive in human
life. Our task in sketching the early stages of this movement
is to isolate the relevant facts sufficiently to appreciate them,
without separating them entirely from their context. We have
primarily to consider Socialism in the narrower sense in which
the word was first applied to Robert Owen and his nearest of
kin, without forgetting the looser sense in which, as Sir William
Harcourt said ' we are all Socialists ', and in which we have
become much more Socialist since his time.

In this wider sense we may trace back Socialism to Christianity, to the teacher who told us that ' we are all members one
of another ', or to Plato and the *Republic*, or even to the earliest
thinkers who realized that every human society exists by

co-operation and prospers by the welfare of all its members. But to do this would be to lose sight of the finished and individual organism in the study of its undifferentiated germ. In the egg all creatures are alike, and in general benevolence and in taking joint action to meet an emergency all men are Socialists. To gain an intelligible definition of modern Socialism we must connect it with the development of the capitalist system which first became prominent in the eighteenth century. The Industrial Revolution gave Socialism birth, and its first home was England.

Socialism implies in this stricter sense the possession, or at least the complete control, of capital and all the means of production by the community, in the interests of the whole body of workers. We cannot go back to the ancient world for comparison because of slavery, and in the Middle Ages, though class distinctions were clear enough, they were not based primarily on wealth or on the possession of the means of production, but on status. The small man as well as the big had his rights to the land, the small man as well as the big had his own tools and made his own clothes, furniture, or weapons for use or sale. It was the merging of all these little things in great concerns which made the industrial revolution and industrial classes—great wealth, and by its side masses of level poverty. This was the world in which Socialism was born.

To put the social position of England at the end of the eighteenth century as briefly as possible, we should say that man's powers of production and of controlling nature had outrun his moral powers and his social organization. 'The steam-engine had been invented too soon', as one writer phrased it; or, as we may say in a less debatable form, the steam-engine worked more quickly to transform industry than man's mind worked to absorb its product and reorganize society. For the moment the machine controlled the man. Hence two sharply contrasted views of the social conditions of the time were thrown up which it is our business, if possible, to reconcile. On the one hand we have the easy optimism of a man like Macaulay, who saw nothing but progress in the growth of wealth and population, the power of machinery over nature, the improvements in commerce and communication, the triumph of England in the continental war. On the other hand, less articulate but more widely and deeply felt, was the depression of the labourer, the helpless poverty and deadened life of the new manufacturing and mining towns, the unthinkable cruelty to the children. Both aspects are true; but it was from the latter, the cry of suffering, the demand for justice, that Socialism arose.

There is another contrast which will command our attention, after the procession of principles which have passed before us in preceding chapters. Freedom was one of the chief of these. It figured in poetry, in politics, in social life. It was the breath of life to most of those whom we have sought to honour. But in this region of industrial competition, freedom seems at first sight ill at ease and drooping to death, an eagle which soars majestically on the mountain, but is singularly out of place in the coal-mine and the factory. For freedom had been invoked in the early days of the factory system by its promoters, and sometimes for good ends, but on the whole for evil. It was good in the name of Freedom to abolish mediaeval restrictions on apprenticeship and rates of wages, and the rule that paupers were relieved only in their proper parishes. It was good to grant the labourer 'freedom' to choose any place of work which he thought fit. But in practice the latter 'freedom' was only nominal. And it was altogether bad in the name of Freedom to allow the employers to impose any conditions of hours, wages, fines, housing, sanitation, protection from injury, which the labourer would accept. And in practice the evils of the new liberty far outweighed the relief from the removal of the old restrictions. For in practice only the minimum could be secured which would sustain the worker's life, and it was often even less than this. During many years, for instance, the death of miners by accident in Durham and Northumberland was so common, and so easy to hush up, that inquests were not held upon them. Freedom, to be a real good in this sphere, implied the mutual dealings of equals, and equality was impossible between one man who possessed all the instruments by the use of which a livelihood could be gained and another who had to use them in order to live. Still less was it possible in the case of children, who were sent as chattels to the mill by the Guardians of the Poor, and taken habitually by their parents as soon as they could be of any use at the machines. In 1833, the great year of political reforms, a fifth of the 200,000 persons working in cotton factories were under fourteen years of age, considerably more than a third were under eighteen.

Before, therefore, freedom in the higher sense could be enjoyed, the attitude of complete *laisser-faire* had to be abandoned by the State, and fresh restrictions introduced on 'free' contract between employers and workpeople in order to secure for the latter the minimum conditions of decent life. From the end of the eighteenth century onwards, small measures began to be passed for the protection in the first place of children and then of women. But each step was sharply contested. There was the socially conservative group, in which both Whigs and Tories might be included, who would interfere as little as possible and trust to the working of normal causes—competition, the ordinary means of relief, the progress of enlightenment. But in most of such conservatives there was too little knowledge of the facts, too little sympathy with the mass of unrealized suffering, or interest in its causes or its cure, to make their opinion weighty.

There was a great gulf between this class of opinion and the next, the school of Godwin and Place and Bentham and James Mill, the radical reformers who aimed first at justice. This school did not desire the intervention of the State, least of all in owning or controlling the means of production. But they were profoundly convinced of the iniquity of the existing social order. They revolted against the complacency which saw in the British Constitution the last word of political wisdom, and in the parson and squire the twin pillars of an ideal community. They aimed at more equality, and hoped to gain it by curbing the unequal working of existing institutions and by raising the whole body of the people through self-government and education. The fight over the Combination laws, mentioned in Chapter I, was typical of their policy. The masters had always been practically free from any check in combining against their workpeople, and formed all kinds of tacit agreements to keep wages down and refuse better conditions. But the workmen were indicted and severely punished for any attempt at united action to improve their own state. This was the typical injustice which the radical reformers attacked, and by their partial success in 1824, completed in the emancipation of the Trade Unions in 1868, they contributed their share, and a large one, to the later rise of the working classes in welfare and power. But by the side of this class of reformers, and in some cases emerging from it, came the third group, at first small, a few scattered individuals in England, France, and Germany, who looked for a much wider and swifter redress of social grievances, and had no theoretical objections to invoking the State. These were the pioneers of nineteenth-century Socialism, and, as with our other origins, we go back to the eighteenth century for its beginnings.

Robert Owen for England, St. Simon for France, Karl Marx for Germany, these are the obvious founders in the three leading nations of the West. St. Simon was the oldest, born in 1760, Owen was contemporary with Scott, born in 1771, just after the famous year of Wordsworth, Hegel and Beethoven. Marx was wholly of the nineteenth century.

Owen was one of our fertile and persuasive Celts. He combined high practical ability and the power of moving men with a rich fund of useful notions and a burning zeal for the good of his fellows. He was born at Newtown in North Wales, the son of a man who was the saddler, ironmonger, and post-master of the little town. Beginning, after a few years at the village school, as a shop assistant, he became in his twentieth year the manager of a cotton-mill in Manchester with five hundred workpeople under him. This was just after the steam-engine had been introduced into the mills. Owen was one of the new men who seized the opportunity for making money rapidly, but, unlike most of them, he never swerved from his purpose of using his power and money for the benefit of those who worked under him. Before the new century began he had married the daughter, and acquired the business, of Dale of New Lanark. Here all his social and educational experiments were tried, and his reputation founded.

His aim in dealing with his workmen was primarily an educational one. He believed that a virtuous and unselfish temper could be created by removing temptations and sur-rounding people, especially the young, with pleasant sights and healthy occupations. And of all the virtues, harmony and the love of others took the highest place. His rules for New Lanark deserve to be commemorated, for the last hundred years have been spent in securing for everybody what Owen secured for his workpeople at once. No children were admitted to the mill until they were at least ten years old, and he was prepared later on to advance this age. Schools were founded on Pestalozzian principles. Gymnastics for the boys, household work for the girls formed part of the curriculum, and no prizes or punishments were (officially) allowed. The workrooms were made as clean, healthy, and attractive as possible, and a co-operative shop was open on the premises where good things could be bought cheaply. Pension societies were started for sickness and old age, and when in 1806 a business crisis threw a number of hands (for a time) out of work, Owen paid them their wages as usual. In fact, you have in miniature most of the social programme which the State has been carrying out in the last three or four decades at the public expense and with armies of officials. If this had been done generally by manufacturers, either as individuals or in groups, we should have had Patriarchalism instead of Socialism ; nor would Robert Owen in his early years have objected to this. He would probably have preferred the manufacturers to take the initiative, expecting that as the workpeople became educated, they would by degrees have taken the management of their various interests into their own hands. The might-havebeen is an attractive vision, and Owen's ideal may some day yet be reached by one of history's circuitous mountain paths.

But Owen was no impracticable theorist : he always hunted his quarry to the death. As his fellow-masters did not follow him, and as the bulk of the employers were immersed in money-making and the employed in misery, he turned to the State. In 1815 he tried to gain support in his agitation for factory-reform by tacking it on to a movement for repealing the import-duty on raw cotton. This repeal was supported by all the manufacturers. As soon as peace came, it was possible for the Government to begin remitting taxes, and the cotton trade was first in the field. To Owen the repeal of the duty was only a preliminary to the better treatment of all those, especially the children, employed in the trade. The manufacturers snatched at the jam but left the pill. Owen failed with them at a meeting he summoned in Glasgow, and his failure made him turn to the press with a burning denunciation of the factory system. We had founded our wealth and our power on a system which for the first time had treated children not as human beings but as machines, and subjected all employed persons to dangers and evils unknown in earlier times. Were we to demand free-trade in cotton, which would give a further extension to the system, and pass a sentence of death on thousands of our fellows? Better that the whole industry, and the power of England with it, should go to the ground, for the system was worse than American or African slavery. But we could remedy the abuses to some extent by regulations such as those which had been in force at New Lanark—no labour for those under twelve, a working-day of ten hours and a half, including intervals for meals, compulsory schooling up to twelve, hygienic rules enforced by inspection.

The older Peel was more open to reason than the body of the manufacturers, and in 1819 the first general Factory Act was passed, based on Owen's proposals though falling far short of them, nine instead of twelve for the age of work, twelve hours instead of ten and a half for the working-day, and no inspection.

After 1815 Owen began to turn to a wider public than his fellow-manufacturers in the North, and extended his programme. He attended congresses in London, and he went abroad to interview leading men in France, Switzerland, and Germany. His report to the Parliamentary Committee of 1817 on the Poor Law gave the gist of his ideas, to which he remained faithful throughout. Poverty and the want of employment were the result of the industrial system and were capable of cure, but the cure must be applied by those responsible for the system, the manufacturers, or, failing them, the whole community which profited by the gains of the trade. The old methods of poor relief were insufficient and unsuitable to the purpose. Provision for unemployment thus becomes a public responsibility, and the way was opened to the National Workshops of the Second French Republic. To Owen the remedy for social evils was to be found in a reorganization of society in communities similar to that of New Lanark, and instituted either by individuals or local bodies or the whole State.

The patriarchalism of his original attitude gave way as he became more and more conscious of the selfish and unyielding temper of the manufacturers, and as the working-class leaders rallied round him. This change took place about the year 1820. At that time his principles, which had begun as the expression of his own ideals and the result of his own experience, were taken up by one wing of the advanced labour movement, and the internal fight developed which it was the special object of Francis Place to avoid. The Chartist movement contained both elements, those who put political reform first, and those who, inspired by Owen, were working for a socialistic or communist State. Place succeeded in keeping the political programme in the forefront, and Owen, disappointed of immediate regeneration in England, turned to North America. He bought the Rappite Colony of New Harmony in Indiana and emigrated in 1825. It had been founded a few years before as a religious communist society by a German called Rapp, and was extended under Owen's influence to about a thousand members; but after two or three years it broke up, and Owen returned to England an impoverished man, to spend the rest of his life, till 1858, as the head of a propagandist organization, spreading the principles of Socialism and Secularism by means of lectures, pamphlets, and books. The successful business man of early life failed when he attempted a wholesale reorganization of society without regard to its religious and social traditions. His failure was the prototype, in the more stable conditions of England, of the failure of the Second Republic in France. Both efforts were symptoms of that ardent spirit of hope and confidence which arose at the end of the eighteenth century and reckoned on sweeping the world clean by one determined drive. Right, as we now see them to have been, in their main contention, and high as was their purpose, they failed at the time from want of judgement and from exaggerating one aspect of social progress. They misjudged the future, as the greatest reformers of all ages have been apt to do—the Platonic Socrates, dreaming of his 'Fair City'; the early Christians looking for the Second Coming; Dante calling for the regeneration of Italy; Comte announcing the establishment of a Western Republic. If men, they thought, can only realize what is clear as day to us, they will at once enter on the better way. A hundred years of wars, obstruction, conflict, and delay have proved how slow and difficult is the approach to the most glorious goal. The aspect of progress on which they, and especially Owen, laid undue stress was the influence of the environment on the individual will. 'Man', said Owen, and Socialists have as a rule approved his saying, 'is but the creature of his antecedents and his surroundings. Let us, or let the State, put the surroundings right, and the desired end will follow.' If we could grant this of the present environment—and we clearly cannot—the whole weight and driving force of antecedents, that is of history, would still remain unaltered.

The life of Saint Simon, the founder of French Socialism as Owen was of English, is an interesting parallel to that of his fellow-worker. The Welshman was primarily a business man, drawn to reform by the sight of the actual evils around him and the proved effectiveness of his own measures to redress them in his own immediate sphere. The Frenchman arrived at very similar conclusions from an opposite starting-point. He was a younger member of an old and famous family, and at the same age at which Owen was acting as shop assistant, he was fighting for the Americans in their War of Independence. But he was full of reforming schemes from his earliest youth, and studied in books rather than in life for the right principles of social action. He tended, as life went on, to a religious rather than a practical point of view, but the sect he founded contained many men of weight. Buchez, President of the Assembly in the Second Republic, was one of his followers. He died in 1825, before Socialism became a revolutionary force. His doctrine was that we needed to reverse, or at least to supplement, the course of the French Revolution by a constructive policy in which the supremacy of labour should take the place of the supremacy of military chiefs in the old feudal system. The Revolution had destroyed the feudal system, but so far had put nothing in its place. The industrial chiefs of the new order were obviously the successors of the war-lords in the old, and in the place of the Catholic Church of the Middle Ages, we had now the leadership of men of science. The parallels are exquisitely neat and suggestive : they are in fact very largely true. But there are fallacies in such historical analogies which the nineteenth century has not failed to demonstrate.

In the first place, the military system is by no means extinct, though it becomes more subordinate as modern countries become industrial and free. We have seen its desperate efforts a hundred years later in a country which in some respects is the most highly organized on the industrial side as well. And in the second place, the patriarchalism in which St. Simon agreed with the earlier attitude of Owen has not become the dominant type of social reorganization. The State in all countries has been compelled to take the lead, while enlisting as far as possible the co-operation of the industrial chiefs.

The comparative fortunes of the two movements, in France and in England, offer an even more instructive study than the lives of their chiefs. Both come to a climax in 1848, the next great revolutionary year in Europe. Chartism in England and the republican-socialist movement in France were analogous products. Both were inspired by industrial discontent; both aimed at strong measures for immediate redress; both, after the mid-century, were gradually absorbed by the policy of progressive social reform which we shall have to sketch later. But the differences in the early years, before our present notions of constitutional government and orderly reform had gained full sway, are highly instructive and characteristic of the two countries.

In England as in France the Reform movement of 1830–32 put for a time the more far-reaching agitation into the background; but in both countries it was soon discovered that the advantages which Reform had promised to all, and to which all had given their support, were in practice to be enjoyed almost exclusively by the middle class. This was admittedly the case with the franchise, which in each case had been granted only to the fairly well-to-do. But this could never last. That industrial chiefs should hold sway, as St. Simon and Auguste Comte had proposed, might be arguable, if they had given evidence of their general probity, competence, and high purpose. The many might conceivably consent to be governed by the few who held important posts through merit, and justified their position by its general success. They could not possibly acquiesce for long in the rule of those whose only claim was that they were able to pay a little more rent for their houses. Why, that was what everybody wanted for himself, and a vote into the bargain! Hence the political grievance was a leading element in the new agitation after 1832 on both sides of the Channel. But poverty and social misery were at the bottom in both cases.

In England the Chartist movement contained two sections avowing their respective preference for the social and the political side of the programme ; but, thanks to the stronger political instinct of Englishmen and the organizing skill of Francis Place, the radical and parliamentary section held the field. The ' People's Charter ' reproduced the six points of C. J. Fox and the Westminster association of 1780 '—manhood suffrage, the ballot, annual parliaments, the abolition of the property qualification for members, payment of members, equal electoral districts. It was drafted by Place in 1838—and it only added to these a demand for equal electoral districts. The fact that it was possible to hold together and extend, during ten years of agitation and great social discontent, a working-class movement, numbering at one time some 40,000 members, in support of such remote and abstract objects, is striking evidence of the political training of the nation. The special distress of the year 1848 and the example of France led to the final scene on the 10th of April. But it was not a conspiracy to overturn the Government and proclaim a republic behind barricades. The culminating act of the Chartists was a demonstration on Kennington Common, whence hundreds of thousands were to set out for Westminster to present a giant petition to the Parliament which they desired to reform. How far this crowd would have remained faithful to their peaceful and constitutional programme can never be known, for the procession was forbidden and a large force of special constables enrolled to prevent disorder. The mustering of these and their concealment under the bridges on the route were among the last acts of the Iron Duke. One of the constables was the future Emperor of the French, Louis Bonaparte, who was soon to take the crowning part in the suppression of the corresponding movement in France.

Contemporary events in France and on the Continent make an interesting and, on the whole, an encouraging study for Englishmen. The capital difference was that in England we had a much more stable political system than anywhere else in Europe. There was never an appreciable chance of a revolution with us, and a formal Republic or a Socialist State always remained in the ideal region of pure theory. But it was otherwise abroad. In Italy and Germany there was yet no national government at all, and the revolutionary movement which soon broke out all over the Continent took in those countries the form of insurrection to obtain the first elements of a national freedom. France was in outward seeming much more like ourselves. She had obtained, just before our Reform Bill of 1832 a constitutional monarchy largely modelled on our own. As we have seen, it rested, like ours, on a limited middle-class franchise, and had, especially in its earlier years, passed many measures of moderate reform. But there were differences which led to the Revolution of 1848 and the subsequent reaction. One was the unstable foundation of the monarchy itself; another, the presence and influence of a larger class of advanced writers and thinkers than with us; a third, the greater spread of the doctrines of revolutionary Socialism. In France, then as always, pure intellect held more sway than with us, and it was working there in an atmosphere of less restraint and livelier passions, without our solid structures of immemorial custom and real, though limited, liberty.

The English political system, stronger in itself than the French, was further strengthened in the Victorian period by the fact that a woman was on the throne, who was loved and revered, and, being a woman and reigning so long, fitted well into a constitutional order which demanded continuity and reverence for the past, while allowing free play to party conflicts and changing currents of opinion. In France the head of the State at this time, though estimable personally, did not inspire enthusiasm or even general respect. Louis Philippe could not rely either on the historical sanctity which surrounded the legitimate branch of the Bourbon House, nor on the glory of the Napoleons, nor on the strength of his own character. He had always against him the ardent convictions of a powerful republican party, and he weakened his precarious position by playing, feebly but obstinately, for his own hand. He was constantly coming to Parliament for large money grants for his children, and, as his reign wore on, he leant more and more on Guizot and the extreme right, whose policy was to resist reform and preserve the interests of the capitalist middle-class. The crisis came, significantly enough, after an estrangement from England. The normal policy, both of Louis and of Guizot, was to keep on good terms with England. 'Entente Cordiale' and 'Socialism' first appear in our common political vocabulary some time in the 'thirties. In their amicable intentions Louis and Guizot had cordial sympathy from Sir Robert Peel and his Foreign Secretary, Lord Aberdeen. But with the fall of Peel in 1846, after the repeal of the Corn Laws, Palmerston returned to the Foreign Office. He was then in his second and aggressive manner, which, as we saw, superseded his earlier and wiser way of making a good understanding with France the 'pivot of his policy'. He now held the dangerous, though in this case happily unjustified, belief that a war with France was sooner or later inevitable, and in the French Chamber Guizot's lifelong opponent, Thiers, was constantly feeding the same flame by attacking the French Government for its weakness in dealing with England. The competitive world-expansion which plays so large a part in the later years of the century was already beginning to throw its sparks over a wide area—Tahiti, Morocco, the Gold Coast. But the actual estrangement came over the marriage of the young Queen of Spain. Was her husband to be a Coburg and thus akin to the English throne, or a Bourbon and thus allied to the reigning house in France? The unfriendly attitude of Palmerston and the reciprocated suspicion in France at last incited Guizot and his sovereign to a distinctly hostile act. Two Spanish marriages, of the young queen and her sister, to a cousin and a son of Louis Philippe, in violation of his undertakings, were forced through, and destroyed the Entente. This led Guizot into more reactionary ways. Breaking with England, he had to find his friends among the three great absolutist Powers of the North and East—Russia, Austria, and Prussia.

This was in 1846. In February 1848 the French monarchy had fallen, and Louis Philippe was in retreat to England. Guizot's stiffer and stiffer resistance to reform of any kind and his general incompetence in administrative work destroyed any prestige that his Government had gained by the dynastic success over England. It is poor comfort that your king, himself on sufferance, should marry two of his kinsmen to royalties in another land, if you have no voice in the government of your own. Only 200,000 citizens had a vote—those who paid over £8 in taxes; and on this point the prejudice of the king, if less religious than that of George III against the Catholics, was equally obstinate. During the winter, political banquets had been held all over France, demanding parliamentary reform. The last of these, fixed for February 22, was arranged by its promoters, the leading reformers and journalists of Paris, to take the form of a public demonstration and procession. It was prohibited by the Government, and a popular rising immediately followed. Guizot was dismissed. In a collision with the troops, thirty-five people were killed and many more wounded. The corpses, carried in procession throughout the city, aroused a flame of passion which within forty-eight hours had swept away the king and all his family.

Nearly four years elapsed between the fall of Louis Philippe and the *coup d'état* of December 2, 1851, which installed Louis Bonaparte as Napoleon III. This is the period of the Second French Republic, and its story is second in interest only to that of the First. The similarities and the contrasts between the first and the second occasions on which France, and especially Paris, were for a time given up to social and political anarchy are as instructive as the comparison between England and France from which we started. We cannot pursue either topic far, as we are passing on to consider the part which Socialism played—perhaps the most considerable in the drama of the Second Republic. On both occasions there was a marked want of governing capacity shown by the middle-class intellectuals thrown into power by the force of events. In both there was a sharp and sanguinary conflict between the moderate incapables who first headed the movement and the extremists, aided by the Parisian mob, who disputed authority with them. In each case leaders and led were exalted by oratory above the careful study of the dangers which were undermining their position, until it was too late to arrest the downfall. But the Second Republic, in spite of these likenesses, bore many marks of fifty years' experience and a change of mind.

Among these we note a much greater appreciation of public order. The first governors of the new Republic were, it is true, incompetent men, but their most anxious thoughts throughout were for the reconciliation of parties and the preservation of social peace. They had lived in the shadow of the Terror, and though the most bloody civil conflict ever known in Paris—the insurrection of June 1848—took place in their time, they were all free from complicity in it. Even in that moment of disaster there was more tolerance shown and more humanity than can be traced in the horrors of the First Republic. The place that Lamartine occupied in the early months of the Second Republic is significant of the spirit to which France then aspired, though she was not to reach it for many years. The tender poet of harmony, the man of moving eloquence and perfect language, held for four months, during the most dangerous crisis, the post of President of the Executive Council. He had neither governing capacity nor experience in governing. The contrast is conspicuous with the England of Wellington on the one hand and the France of the First Republic on the other.

But the point which specially concerns us here is the invasion of the new Socialism into this troubled order.

While, after the abdication of Louis Philippe in February, a Provisional Government was being appointed by the National Assembly, with Lamartine at its head, another list of new governors was being drawn up at the office of the most powerful reforming newspaper. This consisted of extreme Democrats and revolutionary Socialists, including Louis Blanc, and was thrust upon Lamartine and his colleagues when they left the National Assembly to take possession of the Hôtel de Ville. The Hôtel de Ville was the necessary stronghold of every revolution in France, and to secure it, and with it the support of the more advanced section of the Parisian population, Lamartine and his friends admitted the rival Government to a share of their power. It was this section, or the failure of the majority to consolidate and control them, which led to the catastrophe. Within two days the majority had made the fatal concession to the Socialist extremists of the decree granting the 'Droit au Travail'. The Government's admission of the Right to Work was followed by the establishment of the National Workshops, which led ultimately to the insurrection of June. The Revolution had shaken credit and led to a large reduction of industry all over the country, and this was the moment taken to open Government workshops and yards, and guarantee a franc a day to every registered workman. The result was of course inevitable. Small as was the wage offered, it was better than destitution, and crowds poured into Paris from all over France. At the maximum, just before the workshops were closed down in June, there were over 100,000 men collected, with nothing for them to do but to plant ' trees of liberty ' in rows. The growing drain upon an empty treasury, the demoralization of the people, the sedition hatched by idle and half-starving workmen, at last convinced the National Assembly that a step backward must be taken. But it was too late to take it without disaster. The proposal in the middle of June to disband the workshops and find work elsewhere, if possible, for the workmen was the signal for the most serious rising which the Second Republic had to face. During four days the greater part of working-class Paris, the East End, and especially the St. Antoine district in the north-east, was held by a determined body of forty to fifty thousand men, starving, desperate, and skilful in defence. Forty to fifty thousand regular troops with the bulk of the National Guard, all under the direction of General Cavaignac, were needed to reduce them, and at last all the barricades were levelled and order returned to desolation. Cavaignac had been given absolute powers to suppress the insurrection, and he resigned them loyally when it was over. The Republic, its supporters said, had gained its most signal triumph and was now firmly established in the confidence of a re-united nation. But the bells of triumph were really ringing the death-knell of the Republic.

The reaction from the chronic uncertainty and spasmodic violence of the spring and early summer was overwhelming. Men longed for peace and order and the security of property. Meanwhile the old gang were impenitent to the last, and when, in

September, the question of the National Workshops was finally debated, they all agreed to defend the disastrous experiment, which had in the first instance been forced upon their better judgement by Louis Blanc. Lamartine's concluding speech on the subject was a brilliant exhibition of the good hearts and weak heads of the republican junta. '*A une époque de sinistre mémoire*', he cried, '*Danton disait : De l'audace ! de l'audace ! et encore de l'audace ! Et nous, nous dirons : Du cœur ! du cœur ! toujours du cœur pour le peuple ! et le peuple en retour vous donnera le sien.*' The Assembly, however, was inexorable. It disbanded the workshops, suppressed the '*Droit au travail*', and substituted, not even the '*Droit d'assistance*' which was at first proposed, but the '*Devoir de bienfaisance*'.

General Cavaignac, who had conquered the insurrection, proved himself in the end not strong enough for the dictatorship which the country craved for. He made enemies on both sides, while Louis Bonaparte (nephew of the first Napoleon), who after the fall of Louis Philippe had been working his way back to France through many adventures, succeeded in capturing the goodwill of all parties except the strict Republicans and extreme Revolutionists. He corresponded with Proudhon and Louis Blanc, and showed enough but not too much sympathy with Socialism. He supported the temporal power of the Pope to please the Catholics, and wrote a *Manual of Artillery* to please the army. In June he was elected to the reluctant National Assembly as member for five departments. Once in the House, he continued a policy of reserve, conciliation, and secret propaganda until in December, at the first general election for a President of the Republic, he was returned by an enormous majority (five and a half millions to one and a half) over Cavaignac, the only other serious candidate. From the President of 1848 to the Emperor of 1852 was an inevitable progress. It meant personally the success of a good-hearted, clever, but unstable adventurer, who profited by a great name and the confusion in affairs to seize the helm. It meant, as a milestone in history, the close of the first period of nineteenth-century reform and the beginning of a period of new men, new ideas, and comparative reaction. To France it was a wound self-inflicted and, in the end, disastrous.

But we are thinking mainly in this chapter of the early days of Socialism; and the fall of the Second Republic in France, coming soon after the Chartist fiasco in England, marks truly and clearly a definite change from the early, hasty, and unscientific spirit in dealing with the social problem to the later, more careful and scientific approach.

The history of Karl Marx and the contemporary attempts at revolution in Germany coincides exactly with what we have seen of the French and English movements. Marx was born in 1818, and mixed as a student with the group of young Hegelians in Berlin. He gained from this a more complete and philosophical view of the social revolution than any other Socialist leader ever reached. But for action he turned to France. There he found, early in the 'forties, in full activity, those men whose influence counted for so much in the inception and the downfall of the Second Republic—Proudhon, Louis Blanc, Pierre Leroux, and the followers of St. Simon. In them he thought he saw the pioneers of an approaching social regeneration for all Western Europe as well as France, for ' the day of German resurrection will be announced by the crowing of the Gallic cock '.

The famous saying had been already verified, not only in the first French Revolution which had brought into Germany the strong hand of Napoleon and the subsequent revival, but also in 1830, when the July Revolution had led to constitutions being granted in several of the German States. It was again to be verified in 1848, and verified not only in a general uprising but in a speedy reaction. The French Revolution of February 1848 was followed by risings all over Germany and in Hungary, Bohemia, and Italy. Metternich was overthrown in Vienna. Frederick William IV of Prussia granted a constitution, and marched through the streets of Berlin wrapped in a German tricolour. A national Parliament for all Germany began its meetings at Frankfort. Self-government and national unity were the leading motives in all these movements, but the Socialist element was not wanting. Marx had returned to Germany soon after the Revolution broke out. He had made friends in Paris with Engels, the son of a German cotton-spinner, who had come to Paris to meet him after two years of work with the Owenites and Chartists in England. A close and lifelong friendship was the result of this meeting, and they went together to Cologne in May 1848 and set up a revolutionary socialist-democratic paper to take advantage of the upheaval. But in November the King of Prussia dissolved his National Assembly, and Bismarck's policy began. Marx and Engels advised armed resistance and the refusal of taxes. In the state of siege which followed, their paper was suspended, and Marx was next year expelled from Prussia and finally settled in London for the remaining thirty-four years of his life, which he spent in writing and organizing the International Association of Working Men.

One sees how closely connected the Socialist movements were in the three leading nations of the West. One sees also the sources of Marx's special strength. Born a Jew, and brought up as a Protestant Christian, he added to a legal training a long and systematic study of history and philosophy. Then, by his sojourn in France and his knowledge, through Engels, of the English industrial system, he was able to put all this dialectical training at the service of labour, to turn ' upside down ', as he said, all the theories he had learnt. He ' saw things whole ' from his own angle of vision, and did not attempt, as most of the Socialist leaders had done, to separate the political revolution from the social. He preached the use of political means to gain socialist ends, and in this the later movement has followed him, with the difference that, where he was revolutionary, we are Fabian—the Fabian of wise delay. On the other side of his teaching there is an equally significant likeness to the general current of modern thought and an equally significant difference. He presented his socialist gospel as the last stage in an historical evolution. The capitalist organization of industry had followed as a necessary stage in the evolution of great societies, and must be followed in its turn by the complete reversal of this order and the organization of industry by and for those who create its values, namely the workers themselves. In this appealing to the force of historical sequence, Marx appealed to one of the strongest beliefs of the nineteenth century, but his premises, when examined, have been found too narrow to bear his conclusions, even by his professing followers. As they have become more Fabian in practice, so they have become more evolutionary in theory. The modern exponent of Marx, a man like Edouard Bernstein, finds his theory marred by too great simplification, by undue emphasis on the opposition of classes, above all, by seeking the mainspring of human progress in a materialist impulse and not a spiritual. Herein the doctrine of Hegel, which Marx turned upside down, was nearer to the truth than his own.

The *coup d'état* in France, the failure of the Frankfort Parliament to achieve a constitution for a united Germany, the suppression of all the revolutionary movements in Europe, combine to mark a wide and real reaction in which England also had her share. It was less marked with us, partly because the previous tendency to revolution was less strong ; but it will be noticed that, although the Liberals were in nominal power, no considerable reform was attempted until the second Reform Bill of 1867, which was carried as the result of the two great parties playing for power. Till 1868, when Gladstone came in with a large majority and a definite programme, it was a time of party strife at home and war abroad—the Crimean War in which we were engaged with Louis Napoleon in the doubtful enterprise of propping up the Turkish Empire, and the Indian Mutiny, in which we were imposing a more effective rule on our largest dependency. In each of these cases we were imposing, for the time and for what seemed to us then inevitable necessities, an alien and repressive *régime* upon people struggling, according to their possibilities of action and by foul means as well as fair, to be free. Both cases will call for fuller treatment later on.

But from the European point of view, the two critical points were the rule of Napoleon III in France and the policy of Bismarck in Prussia. Militarism was the result of each ; and the good which was accomplished—in some points great good—was achieved, not by the methods of discussion and free decision—which was the ideal of the earlier reformers—but by diplomacy and the strong hand and the play of competing Powers. Bismarck's famous speech after the failure of the palavers at Frankfort was typical of much more than the unification of Germany ; and when we read his conviction that ' the German question would not be settled by speeches and parliamentary decrees but by blood and iron ', our minds revert to the teaching of the great popularizer of German thought in England, Thomas Carlyle.

In 1839, when the Chartist agitation was at its height, Carlyle published his book on *Chartism*, and its motto was : ' It never smokes but there is fire.' In 1850, after the set-back, he wrote *Latter-Day Pamphlets*. Both are unmistakably the work of the same mind, strong, poetic, prophetic : both are as clearly marked by the impress of contemporary events. They are so full of instruction, both as to the genesis of Socialism and the lines of its development, and their author has counted for so much in the history both of England and Germany, that we must examine their teaching for a moment and see how it fits in with the general course of things. Carlyle's was not a systematic mind, like that of Marx or St. Simon or Comte. He had no practical experience behind him to suggest reforms like Owen's. Of all his predecessors in social reform, he was most like a Hebrew prophet. He saw the flagrant evils around him, and he had a passionate sense of human suffering and human worth. But he was impatient and intolerant, impatient of slow methods as well as of what seemed to him corruption and pretence, intolerant of those who differed from him, either in their views or way of life. Hence the profound good he did in shaking the current optimism of the British mind ; hence also the serious evils and dangers which he provoked both at home and abroad. He saw the fatal cleft between the ' Two Nations ' in English life, which the industrial revolution had deepened, and he saw it with an intimate and prophetic vision and not with the suave detachment of the author of *Sybil*. To Carlyle the ' Condition of England ' was the supreme question, to which the easy-going reformers of the Whig Parliament were ludicrously, criminally blind. This is the burden of *Chartism*, and he lashes the complacency of the governing classes with every thong—sarcasm, invective, humour, pathos. The new Poor Law had just come into force. ' To read the Reports of the Poor-Law Commissioners ', he says, ' if one had faith enough, would be a pleasure to the friend of humanity. . . . Let there be workhouses, and bread of affliction and water of affliction there. It was a simple invention ; as all truly great inventions are. . . . A still briefer method is that of arsenic. Rats and paupers can be abolished.' It is the fiercest and most telling diatribe against *laisser-faire* that was ever penned—a call for government and for work. Even the starveling Poor Law is a step in advance as a recognition of the need for work. He passes on to the state of Ireland, just ripening for the horrors of the potato-famine in 1846. 'Has Ireland been governed and guided in a " wise and loving " manner ? A government and guidance of white European men which has issued in perennial hunger of potatoes to the third man extant.... All men, we must repeat, were made by God, and have immortal souls in them. The Sans-potato is of the selfsame stuff as the super-finest Lord-Lieutenant ... with Immensities in him, over him, and round him ; with feelings which a Shakespeare's speech would not utter ; with desires illimitable as the Autocrat of all the Russias.'

There speaks the fellow-peasant, the fellow-countryman, the fellow-democrat of Burns. Within twenty years of the writing of these words, the population of Ireland had been reduced by famine and emigration from eight millions to less than six.

But when we go on to what he says about the French Revolution, the weakness of the other side of his position begins to appear—the want of any definite constructive ideas by which this gospel of government and work can be put into effect. The French Revolution appeared to him merely as a great destructive portent, the clearing away of corruption and shams, bringing home to mankind the severity of the naked truths of life. The French Convention, the first experiment in self-government by a large modern community, had, he tells us, to cease being a free Parliament before it could so much as subsist. ' Democracy, take it where you will in our Europe, is found but as a regulated method of rebellion and abrogation. ... Not towards the impossibility, self-government of a multitude by a multitude, but towards some possibility, government by the wisest, does bewildered Europe struggle.' And in the *Latter-Day Pamphlets* of 1850 he abandons himself narrowly to this vague or, at the best, Utopian ideal, and denounces without restraint all the methods and actions of democratic government, especially as he saw it at work in his own country. Sympathy for the claims of the oppressed and hopes for their future are now in the background, and he is rapidly descending the slope at the bottom of which is the defender of Governor Eyre in Jamaica, the denier of freedom to the Irish. ' Free men,' he tells them, ' alas, had you ever any notion who the free men were, who the not-free, the incapable of freedom. The free men, if you could have understood it, they are the wise men; the patient, self-denying, valiant; the Nobles of the World; who can discern the Law of this Universe, what it is, and piously *obey* it.'

Such is the other side of the picture, brought into vivid prominence by the force of reaction playing upon a passionate and impatient mind. But for the sake of historical truth, especially on the subject of the present chapter, we must be careful not to allow the impression of this last phase of Carlyle's teaching to efface the rest. He was the strongest influence towards Socialism, in the wide sense of the word, among English writers of the nineteenth century, the first great writer to appreciate the supremacy of the social question and to burn it into the public conscience by eloquence and profound conviction. It was for others, in various degrees of socialistic tendency, to consider the problems in detail and apply the methods of patient study which Carlyle swept so impetuously aside. Among these thinkers the most important of all his contemporaries was John Stuart Mill. Mill was an actual living link between the old radical reformers of whom his father was a leader, the world of triumphant science of which his teacher and correspondent Comte had just appeared as the prophet, and the Socialists whom he carefully studied and whose ideas influenced him more and more throughout his life. His *Political Economy*, the book which shows best the convergence of all these streams, was published in 1848. A more cautious and steadier mind than Carlyle's, though without his inspiration, he admitted with reservations the interference of the State in industrial matters. It was to be gradual, and so far as possible avoid weakening the vigour of individual effort. ' Government aid,' he says, at the end of the *Political Economy*, ' when given merely in default of private enterprise, should be so given as to be as far as possible a course of education for the people in the art of accomplishing great objects by individual energy and voluntary co-operation.' Here is a definite principle, difficult no doubt to apply but easy to understand, a definite preference indicated for trying to do things in one way rather than another, while still admitting the rightness of exceptions if the general good appeared to demand it. In Mill's view the highest form of social good would be for the whole people voluntarily to do great things, and grow by co-operation and service. Mill's voice is also one of the boldest in the century for hope. ' All the great sources of human suffering ', he tells us, ' are in a great degree, many of them entirely, conquerable by human care and effort.' Some of the efforts we have witnessed in this chapter. The ' care ' involves the orderly and prescient, i. e. scientific, use of the intellect, the results of which we are now to consider.

MECHANICAL SCIENCE AND INVENTION

THE soil on which Socialism had sprung was Western Europe, prepared by the industrial revolution, and this industrial revolution was the result of the application of science and larger organization to some of the fundamental occupations of mankind. The forging of metals, the transport of goods, the weaving of garments, these and many more were transformed some hundred and fifty years ago by new methods which enormously increased production, brought vast masses of men together in mushroom cities, knit up the world by mechanical means, and threw into the spiritual and political arena a new and dominating problem of which we studied the first attempts at solution in the last chapter. We propose in this chapter to give some account of the process from its scientific side, to see by what channels science entered the industrial sphere and became linked with invention. The science we have to consider in this connexion is physical and chemical, and in the early part of the development largely mechanical. The movement culminates, practically, in the triumph of the railway in the 'forties; theoretically, in the establishment of the principle of the conservation of energy in 1848. It had its public glorification in the first International Exhibition of 1851, held appropriately enough in England, the first home of the industrial revolution. At that point we shall stop in this chapter, and take up the further development of physical science later on. Now our first consideration is ' Tools and the Man '.

Man has always used thought to improve his tools, from the first moment when he parted company from the other arboreal primates. The history of any flint implement gives ample proof of this. But the application of science in a modern machine goes so much farther that we are bound to treat it as something different in kind. Take for comparison two great typical inventions, the wheel and the locomotive steam-engine, one born in primaeval times of practical intelligence and necessity alone, the other the result of scientific intellect combining with practical necessity and intelligence. Both inventions have a similar purpose, the facilitation of transport. Both made epochs in human history, the wheel the epoch of migrations and conquering empires, the locomotive the age of world-communication and colossal engineering. But the differences are so great that they obscure the resemblances. The simple wheel, the common element in both, is overlaid by a complex mass of new machinery, involving adjustments of the most elaborate and finest kind and many scientific principles, the fruit of age-long thought. A new motive-power is added, superseding animal assistance and immensely extending human agency, and a new steel-way is laid, an indispensable part of the whole machine, and itself composed of many parts carefully thought out and gradually adapted to the general purpose. The simple wheeled vehicle, developed in milleniums from logs, wagons, carts, chariots, and coaches, was due to successive modifications of external objects as given to us in nature. The locomotive engine propelled by steam had its genesis in man's thought exploring the secrets of nature and applying the results to new ideal purposes of his own. Now this examination of nature to find rules of her working not obvious to the passer-by is scientific thinking, and the Greeks were the first people to show us how to do it.

How was it that the transformation of industry on scientific lines did not follow immediately on the discoveries of the Greeks? Why had the world to wait two thousand years for the harvest ? The answer rests mainly on social grounds ; it is a warning to all who are inclined to anticipate a speedy triumph for some progressive cause from the achievements of the *élite*, without reference to the general conditions in which the *élite* may be working. For the Greeks were by no means backward in mechanical invention. They made many applications of their abstract science to instruments of peace and war. Archimedes, their greatest man of science, was chiefly famous in his own day for ingenious inventions involving applications of his scientific discoveries, the lever to raise the laden ship, the water-screw for irrigating the fields of Egypt, the giant catapults for harassing the invading Romans. And Hero of Alexandria, some three hundred years later, towards the end of Greek science, describes scores of instruments based on some scientific principle, one for land-surveying like our theodolite, and more than one involving the expansive force of steam, prototypes of machines that have been in use for minor purposes ever since. But there were at least two grave reasons which prevented any industrial advance following on these discoveries at that time. One was that industry itself was despised by the intellectual class. Not only Plato and Aristotle—the types of intellectual aristocracy—but Archimedes himself, most fertile of inventors, considered such work as unworthy of the man of pure science, who dwelt, or ought to dwell, in a higher sphere. In consequence of this the arts of life were left to slaves or base-born men, between whose activities and those of the philosophers a great gulf was fixed. Moreover, at the time when Greek science was making strides, the whole social condition of the West was so unstable that no great industries could have taken root. War was desolating the world until the short span of good government and comparative peace under the Antonines, and by that time the scientific and inventive genius of the Greeks had flickered out.

More than a thousand years elapsed before science made a second and a more permanent appearance in the world. In the interval the social order of the ancient world had been so far transformed that in the leading countries of the West labour was free and strongly organized in guilds and town-communities, holding their own against the feudal lords who had succeeded the Romans. Thus science came for the second time, into a world where domestic and industrial slavery had disappeared, and at her second coming she began to rule the earth.

The first achievement of modern science was the building up of the mechanical laws of force and motion which we connect with the names of Galileo and Newton. The pioneers of the sixteenth century had gone back faithfully to the Greeks, but by the seventeenth century the new mathematics had secured a momentous advance. Laws of motion had been added to the simple conceptions of equilibrium which were the summit of the mechanics of the Greeks. And to achieve this, the mechanics of the heavens had been called in by Newton to confirm and generalize the mechanics of the earth. Means of measuring, too, incomparably superior to those of the ancients, were introduced by the logarithms of Napier and the calculus of Newton and Leibnitz. The way was being made plain for the modern steam-engine. The first essential was the extension of mathematics, including both mechanics and better means of measuring. Close on this came the earliest discoveries in modern physics. The most relevant to the coming invention were Boyle's and Mariotte's law of the expansion of gases and Black's investigations into the nature of latent heat. They are in the direct line of the steam-engine's ancestry. By the middle of the eighteenth century this necessary scientific work had been accomplished, and it is worth noting how near was the succession of the pioneers. Newton was born in 1642, the year of Galileo's death. He died in 1727, the year before the birth of Black, whose collaboration with Watt led to the invention of the condensing steam-engine. Boyle was the contemporary of both Galileo and Newton, and published his law of gases somewhere between 1660 and 1670.

About these modern men of science there was a healthy symptom which distinguished them from the Greeks and promised well for the advance of industry. Like the Greeks they were full of inventions, but, more enlightened than the Greeks, they were proud of them. Boyle, while agreeing with Archimedes and the Greeks that the acquisition of knowledge is the supreme end of science, yet interested himself in many practical devices. He invented an improved air-pump, and experimented on the transmutation of metals in the course of founding chemistry. As soon, of course, as men get interested in the working rules of the world around them, they begin to improvise methods of altering its arrangements to their own advantage. The seventeenth century is full of new science and fashionable inventors. Napier, the father of logarithms, invented a warlike machine much like an infant Tank. Kings and nobles loved to dabble in laboratories and make new scientific toys. The Marquis of Worcester, a rather older contemporary of Newton's, invented a sort of steam-engine a hundred years before Watt. It is described in his *Century of the Names and Scantlings of such inventions as at present I can call to mind to have tried and perfected.*

The Marquis describes, but without much detail, two simple engines for raising water by the expansion of steam. The raising of water was, in fact, the purpose of all the early steam-engines, including Watt's own first invention. Savery, Denis Papin, and other inventors down to Newcomen were all concerned with a simple steam-engine of perpendicular movement for raising water. It was while repairing a model of Newcomen's engine that Watt fell upon the capital improvements which made his invention the turning-point in the industrial revolution. The occasion was so modest, but yet so carefully prepared by circumstance and thought, that it deserves our close attention if we are to understand the conditions which made it a great event.

James Watt was a man of good general education, well trained on the mathematical side, and he was established in 1760 at Glasgow as mathematical instrument-maker to the University. He was on intimate terms with Joseph Black, the lecturer on chemistry who had just discovered the principle of latent heat, and with John Robison, the professor of natural philosophy. It was an ideal combination of Homo Faber the smith and Homo Sapiens the man of science. They frequently discussed the possibility of improving the steam-engine, which was just then in great demand for the pumping of coal mines. Watt tried several experiments in the early years of that decade, and in 1764 a model of Newcomen's engine in the college museum was given him to repair. Watt noticed that the steam being condensed by water in the cylinder itself, under the piston, between each stroke, occasioned such a loss of heat that the machine could never on that principle work economically. The consumption of fuel was too great. Then came the illuminating flash : Keep the piston always at the same high temperature by condensing the steam in a separate chamber, to which it would be led after each stroke. This idea created the ' condensing steam-engine ' which gave Watt his chief title to fame and became the chief mechanical agent in the industrial revolution. It converted the old, cumbrous toys and curiosities into a commercial success. Watt's other improvements, important and ingenious as they were, are comparatively minor matters. The straight, perpendicular action of Newcomen's engine had to be converted into circular motion before the machine could be used for general purposes beyond the pumping of water from mines. This was effected by an arrangement of a crank and a fly-wheel. The third improvement worth noting here was the steam-indicator, which draws a diagram during the stroke of the piston, showing the amount of the pressure of steam and its ratio to the volume. It was important commercially as enabling the engineer to estimate and control the work, and it is interesting scientifically as a typical example of mathematical methods applied to physics.

Watt became a successful man of business in partnership with Matthew Boulton of Birmingham. In 1785 one of his engines was installed to drive a cotton mill in Nottingham; in 1789 one began in Manchester. The industrial revolution was installed in England at the same moment as the States-General in Paris.

It is quite as necessary to study the general conditions of the times as the personal factors which led to Watt's success. Industrial changes were taking place all round him as he worked. The manufacture of iron [1] was being transformed and extended by the use of coal in smelting. The more abundant iron was available for Watt's engines, which in their turn had been first needed to pump out water from the coal mines. There was thus a circle of co-operation. The changes in agriculture fortified the same movement. Larger holdings were being formed by enclosure, and numbers of country people were displaced and driven into the towns to find work. Here they became the 'hands' of the new factories, the unincorporated citizens of the new mining and manufacturing towns. The steam-engine was thus the offspring as well as the creator of the new epoch, the age in which 'manufacture' ceased to mean a thing 'made by hand' and came to mean 'made by machine'. The age of organization had begun, in which machines, created by mankind for their own ends, too often assumed the mastery of those who had to work them, and the whole of industrial society seemed

[1] Steel comes into general use for machines after Bessemer's and Seimens' discoveries in the nineteenth century.

to become for a time a huge machine destroying the initiative and lowering the vitality of the great mass of the workers.

The installation of the steam-engine and the attendant factory-system are, strictly speaking, antecedent to the period of which we are speaking in this book, just as the French Revolution, with its clearance and its new plantings, was antecedent on the political side. But it is necessary to go back to it here, because all the sequel is truly a development of the conditions which were established before the nineteenth century began. Organization is the leading note, organization of society parallel to organization of thought, and the flagrant evils which meet us in our course can only be overcome, as we shall see, by assimilating the new state of things and rising superior to it. There can be no turning back. The human mind, to gain a step forward, has to accept the work that it has accomplished in the past and use it for still higher purposes in the future.

The inter-dependence of action and thought in human progress is well illustrated when we compare the order of industrial scientific inventions with the natural order of the sciences themselves. Mathematics, physics, chemistry, biology have their accompanying applications in that order. Mechanical science, and in the first instance the mechanics of masses, was the first achievement of the men of the Renaissance, taking up the work of the Greeks. This was almost immediately followed by some of the elementary laws of physics. Look now to the earliest practicable applications of science to industry, and you will see that they depend on these earliest generalizations of the simpler kind. The steam-engine, based on these elementary laws of mechanics and physics, comes first of the inventions based on science. Its sequel in the locomotive, and a thousand other applications, follows close. Then comes the first-fruits in practice of a more obscure branch of physics, the telegraph based on the earliest laws of electricity. Chemistry, which, as the more abstruse, was the later-organized science, has its practical results after these : we seem only now to be entering on the full harvest of chemical inquiry. In chemistry the earlier results with inorganic, as compared with organic substances, is reflected in the derived processes ; while the whole science of living things, biology, including organic chemistry, has hardly yet begun to exercise its due effect upon our action. But the latter part of the century gives evidence of its growth in numerous medical theories, in experiments on the best methods of cultivating useful plants, in the ideals of eugenics, or the best physical methods of cultivating ourselves.

Thus the order of practical inventions bears out what we should have inferred from the nature of the sciences themselves, and there are two other general considerations worth noting before we return to the course of the story itself. One is that the sciences have, broadly speaking, become applicable to useful ends, in proportion to the degree in which they have become exact. Mechanics was constituted as a science, and became applicable to industry, when motion became measurable and predictable ; and so on with all the rest. Lavoisier, by rigidly applying the balance to chemistry, created another branch of exact science, and biologists are now constantly extending similar methods to the infinitely more complex case of living things. The other, that practical applications of science have become more and more abundant in proportion to the mutual aid of the sciences among themselves. The greatest output of practical results in recent times has been due to the combination of physical with chemical inquiry, especially in the case of electricity. The analysis and synthesis of various materials by electricity, the production of useful substances in larger quantities and purer forms by artificial means of this kind, is perhaps the most striking application of science to industry in recent years. In all cases this has involved exact quantitative methods, i. e. the infusion of mathematics, and also to an increasing degree the breaking down of the barriers between the separate sciences—autonomous a hundred years ago, autonomous no longer.

But we must return to the sequel of Watt's capital invention. We saw that one of the conditions and one of the objects of the steam-engine was the improvement and the increase in the smelting of iron and the making of steel. Down to the end of the seventeenth century most of the smelting took place in the south of England, especially in Sussex, where wood was abundant, and where such names as 'Hammer Pond' still recall the ancient industry. Gradually the fine old forests began to be exhausted, and the industry itself, by the beginning of the eighteenth century, was leaving England in favour of Sweden and Russia. Then, by the middle of the eighteenth century, the experiment was tried of ' running iron-ore with pit-coal '. It was first done successfully at Coalbrookdale in Shropshire, where the coal and the iron were found lying conveniently close together. This new step meant the transfer of the industrial centres to the coalfields where iron was also to be found : it meant the rise of the North, the Midlands, the South of Wales, and the Lowlands of Scotland. It also meant the necessity of pumping the new coal-pits which came quickly into use. We saw that the first steam-engines were called for to pump the mines, and the early connexion with coal is clearly marked at every stage of the industrial revolution. The great industries grew up within easy reach of the coal and iron, and the first experiments in steam-transport took place in connexion with collieries.

The application of the steam-engine to transport was the most momentous extension of Watt's machine. He had himself thought of a steam-locomotive, and left some drawings among his papers. But he became conservative in his old age, and did not press even his own new ideas. It was not till 1804 that the first locomotive was made and used by Richard Trevithick near Merthyr Tydvil. Between this and George Stephenson's final success in 1825 various experiments were tried, some with cogs and rack. 'Puffing Billy' hauled coal from the Wylam colliery near Newcastle in 1813, and in 1814 Stephenson made an engine which drew a train of 30 tons up a gradient of 1 in 450 at four miles an hour. The decisive success, however, he won with the Stockton and Darlington Railway by which, in 1825, passengers were conveyed, and the price of coal reduced in Darlington from 18s. to 8s. 6d. a ton. This led to the Liverpool and Manchester Railway of 1830 for which the 'Rocket' was invented, the first locomotive of the modern type. It drew a train of 13 tons at forty-four miles an hour.

England was the pioneer of the railway as she had been of the steam-engine. Within a decade from the birth of the 'Rocket', railways were being made all over England, and were beginning to be seen in the United States and in most parts of Europe. Only the more backward countries, such as Turkey and Greece, delayed till after the middle of the century. By 1844 railway promotion was at its height, and the over-speculation had some share in the financial crisis of 1847 and the troubles of 1848.

The first harvest of the steam-engine was now being gathered in, and it is curious to note how the stages of its progress kept pace with the general political movement. The first steam-propelled cotton-mill was started at Manchester in 1789, the year of the outbreak of the French Revolution. The first railway ushers in the Reform Bill and Louis Philippe. The failure of the Chartists and of the Second Republic in France follow immediately on the failure of the railway boom. Some reaction seemed general, but the First Universal Exhibition of 1851, in London, gave a formal and cosmopolitan stamp to the industrial revolution, and was followed shortly afterwards by the corresponding Paris Exhibition of 1855. Le Play, who visited our Exhibition in 1851, had a leading share in organizing the Paris sequel, and his work in studying the conditions of working-class life all over the world, with a view to its amelioration, is the introduction to a later period of social reform.

Transport by water has been, from the earliest days, at least as important to mankind as transport by land. Nature's provision in ocean, sea, river, and lake was supplemented by man from the time of the ancient empires of Egypt and Assyria onwards. The Romans, as well as the Chinese, made canals, and Charlemagne planned a great system of waterways connecting the Danube with the Rhine. But the invention of locks, which was not accomplished until the fifteenth century, was essential to give canals a wide extension. Locks were invented either by the Dutch or the Italians, and by the beginning of the seventeenth century, the French had taken up the work and made full use of it. In this matter they anticipated us and have always maintained their lead. England did not seriously begin the construction of canals until the latter part of the eighteenth century. Then James Brindley, working as engineer for the Duke of Bridgewater, built the Bridgewater Canal connecting the Duke's collieries at Worsley with Manchester. Again the use of coal was the motive. Brindley's work was followed by others, and England bade fair to have as useful and complete a system of canals as continental countries. But with us the railways won too complete a triumph. The canals were cheap competitors, and the railway companies saw their interest in buying them up and otherwise obstructing their use.

But water, like fire, if a dangerous enemy, is one of man's surest and most available servants. There were no landlords to buy out on the ocean, and no costly legal bills in fighting their claims. Hence ocean transport by steam, which was an easier adaptation of Watt's invention than the railway, made quicker strides than steam transport by land. A usable steamboat was floated on the Forth and Clyde Canal in 1802, and a regular service with the *Comet* began upon the Clyde in 1812. In the interval an American inventor, Fulton, following up the experiments of Jouffroy in 1783, had started in 1807 a paying steamer on the Hudson, with engines made by Boulton and Watt.

Next to steam-locomotion, the telegraph is probably the most powerful mechanical agent invented for promoting the unification of the world. Their joint effect on the life and thought of mankind is beyond our calculation, and it may be that the rapid transmission of thought which the telegraph has effected has been really more potent than the transport of men and things due to the railway and the steamer. The two inventions marched side by side from the eighteenth century onwards. In the middle of that century, when the Leyden jar was the greatest curiosity of electric science, the transmission of signs by current began to be discussed. All the later discoveries in electricity—the identity of magnetism and electricity, the cells of Volta, the dynamos of Faraday—were turned to account by experimenters, who finally produced a working machine about the year 1836. The possibility and the main principle had long been clear. The difficulties turned on the details. How was the current to make intelligible signs? Should you have a separate wire to move separate pieces of paper marked with the letters of the alphabet—this was the first idea—or, if not, how could you make a sufficient variety of signs by using only one, or a very small number of wires? Morse in America in 1835, Cooke and Wheatstone in England, first solved the problem in a practical way. They were the Stephensons of the telegraph, and the telegraph wires were first laid along the newly-constructed railways. The London and North Western Railway had them in 1837, and the Great

Western Railway opened the first public service from Paddington to Slough in 1843.

The beginning of oceanic cables followed shortly after. It is an exciting chapter in the story of man's struggle with nature. The first cable of all was laid between France and England in 1851, and marks the year of the first International Exhibition, held in Hyde Park. But the fight took place in making the connexion between the Old World and the New. Storms, accidents, mistakes, filled up most of 1857; but skill, largely on the part of Lord Kelvin, and perseverance, on the part of English and American seamen, succeeded at last, and messages began to go through in 1858. During the 'sixties several cables were got to work between both England and France and the United States. By the end of the century 162,000 nautical miles of cable had been laid, of which 75 per cent. were British.

In all this earlier application of science to industry, England took the leading part and the lion's share in the profits. France kept close to us, often anticipating us in a new idea, as in the case of the canals and of Montgolfier's beginnings in aeronautics at the end of the eighteenth century. But it was not till the latter part of the nineteenth century that our clear pre-eminence disappeared, and this, as we shall see, was mainly in one sphere demanding the patient and well-organized labour of hosts of experts. Here Germany outstripped us, and founded the art and industries of synthetic chemistry within the last thirty or forty years.

The great inventions which we have sketched, together with many improvements in munitions of war, gave the West its undisputed material primacy in a world just awakening to a sense of oneness. The story suggests one or two reflections of a general kind which it will be well to note before we pass on to other aspects of the industrial evolution.

Note first that the inventions which we have so far studied

were in the main applications of the governing principles in mechanical and physical science which had been established by the men of the seventeenth and eighteenth centuries. And just as the laws had been built up by careful observation of fact after fact, fitting one into another through consecutive toil, illuminated by occasional flashes of synthetic vision, so the machines were the growth of innumerable adaptations of innumerable details, governed by the main idea of doing a particular piece of work more economically than it could otherwise be done. Every valve and rivet in the engine, every bolt in the permanent way, is the result of special study, the adaptation of some previously existing means to a new end. Thus in a machine man has projected into space an embodiment of his thought, which works out his will more powerfully than his own limbs could do. The steam-engine, especially the locomotive, is the great type of this result. It was the fruit of abstract thought applied to practice, and, in its turn, paid back its debt to science by leading to the greatest and most fruitful generalization which had yet been reached. This was the principle of the conservation of energy, arrived at in 1848.

Before the end of the eighteenth century, a general truth had been observed which may be regarded as the first sketch of this principle. This was the idea of the conservation of matter, which arose from the analysis of the air by the early chemists. Lavoisier, by the use of the balance in all his work, showed that nothing was lost in weight by any chemical reaction. The products of the combustion of the candle in the bell-jar are exactly equal in weight to the substances concerned before they enter into combustion. The action of the steam-engine carried the question a step farther. By the burning of a ton of coal in the engine work was done. The heat generated was, by the expansion of the steam, converted into motion, first the motion of the parts of the machine, then of the dead-weight of passengers, goods, and carriages moved along by it. The indicator which Watt himself invented was an instrument of thermodynamics, the science of the relations of heat and work. Sadi Carnot, son of the organizer of victories under the First Republic, is the next name in the story. Dismissed from political work after the Restoration, he devoted a keen and indefatigable mind to science, and, in particular, studied the action of heat in the newly popularized steam-engines. By this study he was the first to arrive in 1824 at the law of the equivalence of heat and work which was established in a general form later on by Mayer and Joule. He saw that the passage of heat from a hotter to a colder body does work, just as the falling of a body may do work—the waters of Niagara, for instance, as they drive the dynamos which create to-day millions of pounds of artificial graphite. And the work done by the engine is exactly equivalent to the heat communicated. Mayer was a German who approached the problem twenty years later from another and extremely interesting point of view. He was a doctor in the Dutch service in Java, and noticed, on the occasion of a bleeding, that the venous blood of the patient was unusually red. This suggested to him that the organic combustion of the body was less than normal, and he connected it with the greater heat of the climate, which caused less loss of heat in the body. All the actions of the body must, considered physically, result from the energy of this combustion, and he thus arrived at the same equivalence of heat and work in the organic machine as Carnot had reached in the steam-engine. Joule argued to the same purpose from an electric battery. The consumption of the zinc reappears in the heat generated, and this may be recovered through the conductor, and made to do work in the decomposition of water, or absorbed in friction. Here again material consumed is connected with heat generated and work done. In 1847 all these results were summed up and described by Helmholtz in a decisive paper on *The Conservation of Energy*, read to the Physical Society of Berlin. Thus the middle of the century saw the establishment of the greatest generalization of science, extended now beyond the limits of inanimate nature to all energy. All physical changes being measured by the mechanical work done as the result, and this measure being called energy, then the sum of all energies is a constant quantity. The later work of Clerk Maxwell and others, by which the equivalence of heat, light, and electricity has been further elucidated, and the different lengths of the waves of motion calculated exactly, merely unfolded in accurate detail further implications of this simple governing conception reached by the middle of the century. Beginning with the obvious effects of combustion, seen first in the expansion of gases and then in the work done in a machine propelled by this expansion, the fact was traced further in the subtle and marvellous phenomena of electricity, until its presence was discovered in the light of day itself, coming to us from the common source of light and heat.

And so man's primitive worship and dependence on fire came home again. It was his earliest distinction and his earliest boon. He recognized its greatness from the first moment when he reflected on the laws that ruled his fate. Fire, he then thought, had a superhuman source, and he deified the man who stole a spark from its heavenly owners. The history of science has given the cult a fresh and deeper meaning. It was by fire that the mediaeval alchemist tested his elements in the crucible. The burning of a candle led to the discovery of the elements in the air and the foundation of chemistry. The combustion in our bodies which follows respiration started the scientific thinking which constituted physiology. The oft-observed effect of fire upon the most familiar of liquids gave men ultimately the most important of machines. In our own day the equivalence of all forms of physical energy — the greatest generalization of science—has been evolved from the study of the effects of heat.

It would be well for the world if the unification of scientific theory had had its counterpart in the unification of sentiments and aims in life. But progress in inventions, and especially in the use of fire, has been as fruitful in producing more and more effective ways of destroying the life and work of man as it has been in protecting and promoting them. One hopeful fact, however, may be recorded. Nearly all the achievements of science in fabricating weapons of destruction can be converted with little change into constructive channels. The process of manufacturing the most deadly explosive is near akin to that of producing the most effective fertilizers of the soil. Dynamite prepares the way for railroads as surely as it levels forts. And the skill of the engineer, which adjusts the bearings of the ·75 gun with the admired perfection of the French, can, when occasion offers, be applied with equal ease to fitting telescopes.

The earlier developments of applied science rested mainly on mechanics and those branches of physics which deal with matter rather in the mass than in the molecule. And they tended on the whole in a very marked degree to the unification of the world. Steam-ships, steel-rails, and telegraph-wires were the chief agents, and later improvements, the turbine engine, the internal-combustion engine worked by oil, wireless telegraphy, are all developments arising directly from foundations laid before the middle of the century and all tending in the same direction. The inhabited world thus moves on clearly to a common goal just as the members of the solar system are all one in their concerted movements round the one source of light and heat and motion.

After the middle of the century the centre of interest for industry and the main source of new industrial inventions was transferred to chemistry, which aimed at penetrating farther and farther into the constitution of matter. But here again, for the beginnings we have to refer to times before the nineteenth century began. Of the atomic theory, in its ancient origins and its modern expansion, we shall have to speak in a later chapter ; but the figure to which we naturally turn as the chief founder of chemistry applied to the arts of life is Sir Humphry Davy, one of the great band of men of genius born just before the French Revolution began. His greatest discoveries were made in the sphere of the chemical agency of electricity. For the first time he prepared potassium and sodium by electrolysis, and thus opened the way to the chemical isolation and preparation of substances which have played so large a part in recent industry. In 1806, while the French war was going on, he won the medal and the money prize which Napoleon offered for the best improvement made each year in the construction of electric batteries. The reward was handed over in spite of actual hostilities at the time. No Defence of the Realm regulations proclaimed him a traitor ; no national jealousy prevented the French emperor or the French public from doing him honour. In 1813, the war still raging, he lectured in Paris, taking Michael Faraday with him as assistant. But the simple application of a scientific experiment which has made his name a household word took place in the year after peace was re-established. In January 1816 he explained to the Royal Society the use of wire gauze as a protection for miners' lamps from the explosion of fire-damp. The temperature of the flame within the lamp was lowered below ignition point, as it issued into the air outside, by the introduction of a substance able rapidly to carry off the heat. This invention, simple as it was, was his crowning glory, recognized by the coal-owners, the miners, and the Government alike. It enabled light to be thrown without danger to life in one of the vital spots of modern industry.

The early nineteenth century saw the beginning of many kindred inventions for making artificial light and heat more accessible to man. Friction producing heat was the immemorial method for making fire. The savage, with his two polished sticks, our grand-parents with their tinder-boxes, were all employing this primitive means. Chemical inquiry now disclosed fresh substances which would easily ignite when combining with the oxygen of the air. White or yellow phosphorus, the most inflammable, the most poisonous of these, was also the most common. It was an instance like so many more—like poisonous gases or bombing aeroplanes in war—of the dangers which, side by side with benefits, beset the application of science to industry. It began to be used for matches in 1833. It took more than half a century before protective modifications were insisted on by law to save the workers, who had contracted horrible diseases from handling and inhaling it. Safe phosphorus is now practically universal in the civilized world, and in the course of its production wide experience has been gained of the oxidizing powers of other substances. The same story might be told of a hundred other things, the story of wider and wider investigation, deeper and deeper penetration into nature. Candles, soap, oil, fuel of various kinds, glass, and many foods were all improved so materially as often to be entirely re-made by the science of the nineteenth century. A French chemist, Chevreul, in 1823, gave us the modern candle by the chemical treatment of fats and oils. A Scotchman, Murdoch, who worked in Boulton and Watt's factory at Birmingham, first developed an illuminating gas by heating coal in closed vessels away from the air. This was at the end of the eighteenth century. Gas came into general use within the next twenty years and before the invention of matches. It was from Scotland, too, that mineral oil first came for illuminating purposes. The shale beds in the Lowlands preceded the petroleum wells of America, Russia, Rumania, and the Persian Gulf.

The larger scope of chemistry which has dawned recently upon mankind, especially in its relations with electricity, belong rather to a later period than we are considering here. But the one supreme physical problem which has begun to possess men's minds in our generation arises so directly from what we have been reviewing in this chapter that we cannot pass it by. Long ago men learnt that matter was indestructible, and chemistry has been, of late, discovering a growing multitude of fresh means of disengaging and re-combining the elements, of forming and converting common substances. On this side the vista seems illimitable. And on the other? Energy we have also learnt is constant and indestructible. But in the forms available for man's life it may disappear. Can we, by transformation, again make available the energy that we need—we, the living organism of thousands of millions of separate organisms inhabiting this globe? Here again, though our progress has been less, there seems no necessity to limit our hopes. It is true that the familiar storehouses, on which large inroads have already been made by the industrial revolution, will be soon exhausted, as the universe might reckon time. Coal-fields, peat-mosses, and oil-wells must have a comparatively early end. Hence men are looking more and more to other sources of available energy, and exploring the constitution of the world more deeply to be able to recover both energy and matter for their ultimate security and greater use. Light comes on many paths of this endeavour, and the future will disclose things not yet dreamt of. Electricity—one form of universal motion—is inexhaustible. Oil and fuel of other kinds than those immobilized in the earth's crust will always be obtainable so long as vegetation lasts; and to promote vegetation the sun's light and the stores of nitrogen held in the air are practically endless. One of the latest scientific ventures is the fixation of the atmospheric nitrogen, and in this the Germans have preceded us with success. With an abundant vegetable kingdom, supplies are accessible of carbon compounds of infinite variety and illimitable uses. No possible want of food or power while this grey world is green ! And here is but one source of untapped power. The sun's light and heat fall on us largely unemployed and often harmful. One day this too will be husbanded, and we shall use too the almost untouched energy of wind. The force of gravity, moving the incalculable masses of the world's water in tides and water-falls and rivers, will play its part. Already at Niagara and a thousand other falls it drives industrial dynamos. And in the constitution of the atom, reservoirs of force have been discovered which surpass conception and stagger our imagination by their unfathomable depths.

So towards the future the world, at least the material world, looks bright. Its resources are illimitable, and man's powers of dealing with them have grown in the period of our review beyond all previous attainment. We shall see later on how far these powers have been employed during the same time to make the life we live a fuller and a fairer thing. But be the answer to that question what it may, the fact of mechanical power, that man has within the last hundred and fifty years multiplied his resources a thousandfold, brought land and air and water and the hidden stores of nature into subjection to him, is a stupendous one. It gives us the pride of creation, amazement at our infinitely expanding strength, and a weight of new responsibility. Our past achievements are there, in the mammoth steamship, in the tunnel which pierces the mountain-chain, in the canal which makes a new passage between two continents, in the engines which have added a thousand million ' hands ' to our production. These works are permanent, to be extended and employed for the sustenance and the further building-up of the myriads of fresh inhabitants which the same process has added to the population of the globe. The past therefore becomes from this aspect, more perhaps than from any other, an object of surpassing interest, of inspiration, of guidance, and of warning.

We may quite justly put first the inspiration, for it is in these achievements that man has found himself as the continuous creator. His thought, growing from age to age, has linked itself in the work with his active and inventive powers, and gone on adding strength to strength. It is the application of his knowledge which proves to him both its foundation in reality and his own capacity for using these realities for his own ends. From this comes confidence and a vista of fresh conquests awaiting him in the future. The guidance comes from reflecting on the conditions which have made this progress possible. The thought lying at its basis is a collective thing, not limited by any national boundaries, but spreading freely wherever it finds congenial elements, just as a Frenchman, an Englishman, and a German co-operated to establish the law of the conservation of energy. The fact that such co-operation is often unconscious is the strongest evidence of the inherent likeness in the workings of all human minds and of the common process which unfolds itself continually throughout the world. Unconscious and obscure as the first workings of this thought may be, when once announced and applied to the world of facts it proceeds to create an organization of life as complete and unbreakable as the links which bind the thoughts themselves together. This is the patent and most significant result of the triumph of applied science in the last century, as true and striking as the social nature of the science itself. Society has become, in all those countries where industry has been organized and developed by science, a far more united and stable thing than it was before, or than it is in other regions less advanced in this respect. Later chapters will illustrate the point more fully both in regard to social and to international progress, but lest we may seem to be chanting an indiscriminating paean of the factory and the steam-engine, we must add here the limiting condition which contains the warning. The organization and closer union which result from the application of science to industry and life are only to be considered good—satisfactory, that is, to the ideal which we are tracing in these pages—if they express themselves ultimately in a fuller and nobler life on the part of all the individuals who are enmeshed in the system and made to work as wheels, and parts of wheels, in a great machine. That it has not done so yet, the slums of any industrial city, the banks of the Congo, or the jungles of Putumayo are there to tell us. But just as the humblest worker in a great observatory may feel some glow in the revelations of the telescope above him, or the fitter on the railway bridge reflect that his work is vital to the lives of thousands and the welfare of a continent, so we may believe that all organized industry is capable of inspiring this feeling and giving the worker this foothold in a universal scheme. The human problem aroused less interest in the early stage and was met with less determination than the mechanical. Its solution, therefore, lagged behind. But it was not insoluble. The same period which gave mankind the triumphs of the mechanical arts which we have sketched contained also in germ the principles of the humane sciences, the belief in foresight, the instinct of brotherhood, which were to bear fruit in later times.

VI

BIOLOGY AND EVOLUTION

In the last chapter, when dealing with physical science and its applications, we were constantly referring to the seventeenth and eighteenth centuries. In this, which is to treat of the sciences of life, our sources will be mainly in the nineteenth. Great as were the achievements of mechanical science in the last century, its foundations were firmly laid before the century began. Physics had felt the touch of Galileo, Mathematics of Descartes, Astronomy of Newton, Chemistry of Lavoisier. But in the sciences of life it was not so. Aristotle, 'the master of those who know', was, it is true, a biologist; but his knowledge, though marvellous, was too inaccurate, and his generalizations, though profound, were too vague, to serve by themselves as a basis for a scientific structure. The actually operative conceptions in biology and in all the kindred sciences—anthropology, psychology, sociology—were a birth of the nineteenth century, its supreme and characteristic fruit.

The climax of the last chapter could be fixed at about the middle of the century, for 1848 saw established the doctrine of the conservation of energy, and in 1851 the first international exhibition was held, which was the official apotheosis of science applied to industry. For this chapter the following decade may well be taken as the turning-point, for 1859 saw the publication of *The Origin of Species*. That publication will always remain a landmark, not because the teaching of Darwin was final, but because it put for the first time in a clear and realizable form a theory which had long been floating vaguely in men's minds, because it gave an unparalleled stimulus to research, because it fitted in with other contemporary movements in thought and action, and thus gave a new direction to religion, a new philosophy to politics, and in its widest sense a new foundation to hope.

The progress made in the exact sciences and their applications was amazing, but when we turn to the sciences of life, the mind is still more overwhelmed with admiration at the changes the century brought forth. The knowledge amassed in the last hundred years in biology, the growth of distinct sciences as branches of the great whole, the insight of new possibilities, the weaving of new connexions between old facts, the ferment of opinion, the conflict between giants of research, the ardour and the patience of the seekers—all these things make the sciences of life not only the most striking intellectual achievement of the age, but perhaps the greatest collective effort of man's mind in the history of thought.

The world of living things thus revealed surpasses in interest and variety and beauty the best that we can conceive of inanimate nature. Splendid as is the rainbow, awe-inspiring the march of the heavenly bodies in illimitable space, marvellous and unfathomable the dance of the infinitesimals of matter, yet when we turn to the world of life, though confined only, as we know it, to our own planet, its wonders outstrip all that the merely physical world can display ; and—greatest wonder— we are here a part, the crowning part, of the scientific structure itself. Now all this thought, in spite of the contributions of earlier ages, in spite even of Aristotle himself, has taken shape in the last century. But this world of wonder, which we build up into science by our thought, has not yet taken, perhaps will never take, the same exact well-ordered shape which we know in physics or mechanics. The process of science in all its branches consists in ordering our knowledge at the same time that it extends its scope. The nineteenth century achieved the crowning triumphs in this advance, so great that some good judges have held that all the science or organized knowledge acquired by man in earlier centuries could not compare in extent or value with that of the nineteenth century alone. And the nineteenth century in science is above all the century of life. Yet the way of advance in the sciences of life, great as it has been, is not exactly comparable in method with that of the physical sciences. For them the railway, one of the most powerful fruits of science, would be a useful type. Like a railway, the physical sciences lay down a permanent way through the territory which they explore. The new branches all connect with the main line, and, though the system may be indefinitely extended and its working quickened and altered in a hundred ways, it is the same system to the end. Newton stands firm. But in the sciences of life, progress follows different lines. It reminds one rather of that other more modern form of communication by travel in the air. There is no permanent way. We travel quickly ; we feel our way and dart hither and thither to escape a contrary wind. But the speed, the exhilaration, the prospect are superb, and the solid world recedes beneath our flight.

It is more difficult in such a changing scene to trace a leading principle, but one may be detected, and it is mainly Darwin's work which has made it visible. It first comes dimly into view at the end of the eighteenth century ; it gathers strength as the nineteenth century goes on; in its philosophic form it is one of the governing principles of the age, and powerfully reinforces the rest ; it will prove in the end, when fully understood, a guiding star to action in the future.

What is this principle, applicable to biology and human history alike, which biology, and especially the work of Darwin, has made predominant in the last century ? It is this : that every organism—and in this broad sense we may treat every human society and mankind at large as an organism—is an historical being, to be explained by its history. We do not understand it, whether the living thing be an amoeba or a vertebrate species or a human institution, unless we know its history, and when we know it we see that every living thing is its own history, embodied and making fresh history.

When we treat Darwin's work as the greatest illustration and enforcement of this principle, we are, of course, deliberately putting in a subordinate place the particular method of development to which Darwin gave his name and his chief thought. '*Darwinismus*' means specially, and above all to the systematic German, the theory that living beings vary naturally in all directions, and that those varieties are 'selected' and tend to survive which give their possessors a superior chance in the universal struggle for existence. Darwinism, as we shall see, has in this restricted sense been subjected continuously since Darwin to a more and more close and sceptical examination. But we are as fully justified in treating Darwin as the protagonist of evolution in the wider sense as we were in taking Robert Owen and Karl Marx as types of nineteenth-century Socialism. In each case the man who has impressed the idea on his generation was possessed and carried forward by a conception larger than he was able to express in his own personal categories, and the aspects of the conception on which he dwelt have been found subsequently to have been exaggerated to the point of fallacy. But when flying in the air, we can correct our bearings if the light is good, and such a temporary deflection in our course is but a slight deduction from the gratitude we owe the man who gave us the wide expanse of view and the confidence of flight.

The wider view to which his teaching leads is abundantly present in Darwin's work. He feels himself to be the leading exponent in his generation of the doctrine that all living things are the result of an immemorial development by gradual steps from simpler forms; that they are all akin; that we can speak with as much truth of the growth of a species, and of all species, as we can of any individual being which grows before our eyes. This is, in the broad sense, the historical spirit which has transformed in the last hundred years all the sciences of life, and Darwin was its clearest voice. ' When we no longer look ', he tells us, in one of the concluding paragraphs of his most famous book, ' at an organic being as a savage looks at a ship, as something wholly beyond his comprehension; when we regard every production of Nature as one which has had a long history ; when we contemplate every complex structure and instinct as the summing-up of many contrivances each useful to the possessor, in the same way as any great mechanical invention is the summing-up of the labour, the experience, the reason, and even the blunders of numerous workmen ; when we thus view each organic being, how far more interesting—I speak from experience—does the study of natural history become.'

There speaks the modesty of a master-builder, commending to the world a supreme achievement on the ground of the simple pleasure it has given him to build it ; and the remark itself is of extreme interest as summing up the advance made in the nineteenth century in the conception of life. It indicates the relation of the dominant biology of the century towards the dominant physics and mechanics of the centuries before : they had created wonder-working machines ; the new century was applying its intelligence to understand the most wonderful of all machines which comes to us ready-made. It strikes the keynote of modern biological and sociological thought—the organism is to be interpreted historically as the issue of an infinite process of growth and adaptation, the fitting of the being to the fullest use of its environment. And in the comparison of the living organism to the lifeless and manufactured machine, it suggests the danger of the narrower type of Darwinism which omits the action of the organism in making itself.

We shall develop these hints from the great master, with the necessary criticism, in the few pages which follow.

The nineteenth century can claim all the greatest advances in the doctrine of evolution, but, as so often in other chapters, we find clear finger-posts before the century began. Goethe, who points the way to so many things in the modern world, was profoundly interested both in plant and animal life and profoundly stimulating on their problems. He held the balance, as every competent and open-minded inquirer must, between the two opinions which divide our mind in dealing with the development of life—does function determine form or form function? does the creature make its life, or are its life and its shape imposed upon it by outside forces? Such are some of the eternal antinomies which force themselves upon us in this, the higher sphere of scientific thought; nor can we hope to surmount them fully till we are able to rise above ourselves and above the temporal conditions of which life is built. Goethe, as the poet-philosopher, strove to see things whole, so far as man may, and refused to rest on either side of the dilemma. We analyse the living thing, he tells us, into its elements—and since Goethe's time the analysis has become more and more minute and mechanical—but if then we think we have found the clue, we have only lost it the more completely by the thoroughness of our search. For life is the common action of all these parts, and escapes as they are separated.

In philosophical biology, as in so many other ways, Goethe became a pioneer, through his length of life, his breadth of mind, and his power of work. Backwards he came in touch with men and thoughts and movements from the classical past, and he stretched forward into the evolutionary future. In biology he brought a breath of Aristotle into the new science which was being built up with the aid of microscope and scalpel. Like Aristotle he looked on living beings as all striving to express an idea by activity from within. And this was true not only of the individual but of the whole world of animate things. The forming power shapes all according to one harmonious plan. He was very near, but just missed the historical link which was to come. Instead of asking, as the evolutionary biologist now does, how did this being come to be what it is, historically, by the process of hereditary growth, he saw with a philosophic eye that certain parts of plants and animals resembled one another in shape and position, and decided that they must be the same thing transformed. Thus, in his morphology of plants, he had the true intuition of leaves, petals, stamens, as all modifications of the original plant-appendage; in the famous case of the skull-theory he held with Oken, though in a detailed sense which later research has not supported, that the cranial bones are vertebrae transformed.

Goethe thus deserves our memory here, both for his insistence on the unity of plan, and for his appreciation that life is an artistic thing, that the creature is also a creator, part-maker of himself.

But for the more strictly scientific founders of biology we must turn to France—Lamarck, Cuvier, Geoffroy St. Hilaire, and Bichat. Lamarck gained fresh glory in the later century as a pioneer of Darwin, and in our own time a third immortality has accrued to him as the prophet of another theory of development which seems now to many biologists necessary as a supplement, if not a preferable substitute, for the general variation of pure Darwinism. But in his original greatness he was the continuer of Linnaeus in the work of classifying the natural groups of plants and animals. Beginning with plants, he went on to animals, and before the nineteenth century began he had recast Linnaeus's orders, and for the first time brought system into the realm of invertebrate zoology. He revived Aristotle's main division of all animals into Vertebrate and Invertebrate, and in the latter sub-kingdom arranged ten classes. He was the first systematic explorer of this, the largest branch of animal life, and his work on the subject, which began to appear in 1801, fitly ushered in the new century. His more famous work, the *Philosophie Zoologique*, appeared eight years later, in 1809, the birth-year of Darwin.

His labours in classifying the invertebrates had shown him the difficulty of separating species, and deciding between a species and a variety. 'The more we collect the productions of nature,' he tells us, ' the more do we see almost all the gaps filled up and the lines of separation effaced. . . . Nature has in reality formed neither classes, nor orders, nor families, nor genera, nor constant species, but only individuals, which succeed one another and resemble those that produced them. Now these individuals belong to infinitely diversified races, shading into one another, and each maintaining itself without change, so long as no cause of change acts upon it.' But Nature has worked upon them all with a plan of organization in her mind, proceeding from the simpler to the more complex.

Clearly, the more we fill up the gaps, the more we realize the kinship of all animate things; and Lamarck, in his early labours at classification, was doing similar work to that of the post-Darwinian palaeontologists who have been finding horses of all sizes between the primitive tiny creature of the American strata and the elephantine cart-horse of to-day. Lamarck found the closeness of contemporary forms, especially of the lower orders, so great that he inferred inherited relationship. The post-Darwinians have been striving to make it actually complete in historical sequence as well as in theory. Lamarck had intuition and a vague philosophy ; his successors in the last hundred years have been accumulating proofs. It is much the same story as in other branches of nineteenth-century progress. The prophets of freedom, equality, and fraternity were not in error ; they were only *trop simpliste*—crude and vague like the child who thinks he can make a flying-machine with a pen-knife and a stick. The intuition was right and inspiring : it remains for maturer minds to work out the thousand details of the truth. It is interesting to note the kinship of Lamarck's biological philosophy with the general currents of revolutionary thought. We find in him, as in Turgot or Condorcet, frequent mention of an inherent tendency to progressive improvement in living things. Nature was compelled, by a law the Supreme Being had imposed, to proceed by the constant fresh creation of the simplest forms, the monads of life which are the only beings directly created. These then develop by gradual steps towards the highest level of intelligence and organization, partly through their own innate tendency to perfection, partly through the force of external circumstances, the variations in physical conditions on the earth and their relations to other beings.

What is this, one may ask, but a short and general statement of beliefs held by a large part of all subsequent thinkers on the subject ?

The difficulties arise when we attack the problems of how these general principles have worked in practice. Lamarck assumes boldly that it is the mode of life, the action of the creature, that have determined its form and its faculties, subject of course to the supreme consideration that a universal perfecting is going on.

Take the case of web-footed creatures, such as frogs, ducks, or otters. They were not made web-footed in order to swim, but, coming to the water in search of food, they stretched out

their toes in order to swim more quickly, and as they kept
stretching them out for generations, the skin acquired the
habit of extension, and the new broad membranes were formed.
So with the giraffe's long neck and the light agile bodies of the
antelope or the gazelle.   Lamarck imagined that the stretched-
out skin was transmitted from parent to child and continually
became more stretched-out until the final form was reached
which suited best the animal's needs ; variations acquired
during the lifetime of the parent could be transmitted to
the offspring : and on this, as we know, a keen and unsettled
controversy has raged and is raging still.   But for our present
purpose it imports most to note that Lamarck had achieved the
capital point of regarding the organism as an historical being.
He brought decisively into biology the category of time.   We
have talked and thought since then of man learning to walk
upright, of his brain growing backward to take in more of the
spinal cord, of vertebrates acquiring backbones, or birds gaining
wings, not merely as individual acts, still less as injunctions of a
supreme authority once immediately conveyed, but as age-long
processes in which each creature has been approaching its final
nature by an infinite number of intermediate steps, transmitted
or accumulated from generation to generation.   Historical
progress, which man had begun to trace in his own social
existence since the later Greco-Roman Age, could now be
studied as one instance, though the highest, of a universal
movement, identical with the nature of life itself.

It happened, however, that at the time when Lamarck was
excogitating his theories, French armies were for four years in
occupation of Egypt, and with them were men of science who
disinterred the mummies of consecrated animals embalmed in
the tombs.   Multitudes of cats, dogs, bulls, apes, and crocodiles
were found perfectly preserved, as well as wheat and other
useful plants.   It was observed that all these were as much like

contemporary specimens of the same species as the human mummies were like contemporary men. Cuvier, the greatest anatomist of the day, declared, on this and other grounds, against the supposed evolution of species, for some of these animals, such as the cat, have been transported since Egyptian days to every corner of the earth and every variety of climate : yet they remain practically unchanged. Lamarck had his answer ready, and palaeontology was beginning to furnish evidence to support his views. In Egypt it was clear that climatic conditions had varied so little since the days of the rock-tombs that there was no reason to expect any change in the animals. The animals transported to other climes were mostly living in special domestic conditions, and, in any case, the time available was a mere clock-tick compared with the geologic time in which Lamarck began to look for the setting of evolution. 'If the physical geography, temperature, and other natural conditions of Egypt had altered as much as we know they have done in many countries in the course of geological periods, the same animals and plants would have deviated from their pristine types so widely as to rank as new and distinct species.' [1]

Here was the key to the solution of the doubt, the first hint of the correlation between earth and life, geology and biology, Lyell and Darwin, which was ultimately to win universal assent for the doctrine of evolution.

The influence of Lamarck, indeed, led up to Lyell as well as to Darwin. Since the Italian school of geologists at the end of the seventeenth century, men had been learning to connect the fossil remains in the earth's crust with the formation of the strata in which they are found. Lamarck, in a work on geology published about the same time as the beginning of his *Philosophical Zoology*, threw himself strongly on the side of those who

[1] *Philosophie Zoologique*, 1809.

L

contended that the strata of the earth's crust have been slowly formed by causes which we still see at work, the weathering of rocks by wind and rain, the erosion of valleys by rivers and of the coast by the sea. Here was an evolution of another order, slow, steady, unresting, without the element of life, but able to be put side by side with the evolution of life for their mutual elucidation. It was indeed the presence of fossil shells lying, as they had lived, in strata laid down by the sea, that convinced Lamarck of the continuity of the geologic process : and it was the discovery in the strata of the remains of bygone species, forming unbroken series and leading up to the types of to-day, that finally convinced all thoughtful men of the broad truth of evolutionary biology when Darwin threw down his challenge to the world half a century later. The two series of changes illustrated one another, and it was early noticed, by Lamarck himself among others, that the forms of animals and plants preserved in the rocks were less like those now living just in proportion to their remoteness in time. True, we know now that it is only with many exceptions and reserves that we can subscribe to his theories, but we know also that he was far nearer the truth on the whole than men like Cuvier or Linnaeus, who had treated species as substantially fixed and geologic changes as catastrophic. He was in advance of his age, but not alone. There were torch-bearers leading on to Darwin, and Lyell in the later editions of his *Principles of Geology*, when he had become Darwinian, tells us how Geoffroy St. Hilaire, the contemporary of Cuvier and Lamarck, used to point to the rudimentary organs found in so many animals as evidence of the transmutation of species. Geoffroy discovered the teeth in the foetus of the whale, and held that these and all such organs must once have been serviceable to a distant ancestor and had disappeared, or been reduced in size in the adult, through disuse.

The argument is now taking us into embryology, but, before we follow it there, we must turn for a moment into another channel of biological thought.

As in classification, as in the morphology of Goethe, so in the cell-theory, discovery spread from plant to animal in the unfolding of the mysteries of life. Bichat, a contemporary of Lamarck, had compared and contrasted plant and animal life in his *Recherches Physiologiques sur la Vie et la Mort* (1800). The plant lives within itself having only relations of nutrition with the outside world : the animal adds to this vegetative life a life of active relations with surrounding things. The plant is the framework or foundation of the animal, and one might say that to form the animal, it sufficed to cover this foundation with a system of organs fitted to establish relations with the world outside. Hence we have in the animal two quite distinct classes of functions. By the first class it maintains its existence within itself, transforms into its own substance the molecules of surrounding bodies, and rejects those that have become useless to it. This is the organic life in which the animal and the plant are akin. The second class of function brings the animal in further contact with the outside world, enables it to perceive its surroundings and respond by will to outside stimulus. This is the plane on which the animal rises above the plant, and Bichat notices the striking differences which distinguish the special organs of the animal from those of the life which it shares with the plants. The organs of the animal life are all symmetrical and intermittent in action, while those of the organic—the visceral muscles and connected nerves—are irregularly arranged but continuous in action. And while the organs of the organic life do their work perfectly without training or use, the purely animal functions require an education and are governed by habit. In all this Bichat was developing with more fullness and precision some root-ideas of Aristotle, but in his study of the tissues of the body he was breaking new ground. He distinguished in each organ of the body different tissues—bony, muscular, nervous, and so on—and turned attention to these as the proper home of life. Each tissue had its own form of life, and we must study these if we would understand the nature of life in the whole. This was the preliminary step to the study of the cell which was to follow in the 'thirties.

The cell-theory must be put side by side with evolution as among the greatest scientific discoveries of the century, and it owes most to German men of science. It began with plants. In the seventeenth century cells had been discovered in cork and pith, but their discoverers had not regarded them as living units building up the structure. In this matter, as in evolution, it was left for the nineteenth century to grasp the real significance of the fact and make it operative in thought. It was Schwann, a pupil of the great Johannes Müller, who first applied to animal-tissues the same methods of analysis which others, and especially Schleiden, had been applying to plants. He showed, in 1838, that yeast was a mass of living cells, and turning to animal life he chose the most plant-like of cells and compared them in point of structure and of growth with the plant-cells which Schleiden had described. Then he pushed on into the very germ and origin of animal life. Is not the egg itself a cell ? And he concludes that ' the whole ovum shows nothing but a continual formation and differentiation of cells, from the moment of its appearance up to the time when the foundation is given for all the tissues subsequently appearing : we have found this common parent of all tissues itself to consist of cells.'

Thus we must now go farther than the tissues of Bichat. All tissues originate from cells, and our task is to see how these cells have been modified to form the various kinds of tissue which Bichat had distinguished. Schwann described five of these. There were the simple, isolated cells such as the corpuscles of the blood. Then there were the groups of contiguous cells, not fused together but lying side by side ; such we find in the epidermis, or the lens of the eye. Then come the cells joined by their walls but keeping their cell-cavities intact. These form the bone and cartilage. The most specialized are those forming nerve and muscle where walls and cavities are all continuous, and a fifth class forming all the fibrous tissues of the body.

This was the first systematic attempt to apply minute analysis to the body. It was the result of patient dissection and the use of powerful microscopes, and it has given a permanent bent to all subsequent research. We shall not attempt here to pursue the details of cell-division and cell-growth, but wish rather to point out the assistance offered by study of this order towards the establishment of a general doctrine of evolution. Life was now seen to be not only continuous in time, by the unbroken process of generation with change, but also at any one time—similar in texture throughout, plant with animal, organ with organ, species with species, man with the beast. A statical view of the community of life aided the dynamical view which had been dawning on the minds of Lamarck and the early evolutionists. The discovery of the cells showed a real family of all living things : evolution was to demonstrate its advance through time, in complexity, unity, and power.

The work of the embryologists fits in exactly between the two. This branch of the science of life is, like the cell-theory, largely the result of German labours, and while Schleiden and Schwann were investigating the cell, Pander and von Baer were building up the history of the embryo. But all the nations of the West have borne their part, and to an Englishman there is a special and pathetic interest in passing from Harvey at one end of the series to Francis Balfour at the other. Both wrote descriptions of the stages of development in an incubated egg. Harvey, in 1651, described the young chick with magnifying glasses of such low power that he could see no change in the embryo before the thirty-sixth hour. Balfour, in that manual of embryology which he took with him to correct on his last and fatal journey to Switzerland in 1882, gives us also a picture of the growing chick ; but so much greater was his knowledge, so vast the improvement in the instruments of research, that he can portray the changes in the embryo from the earliest hour till the sixth day, when, on the appearance of the beak, he is able to say ' we can now for the first time see the bird '. The remaining changes till it breaks the shell were by his time so familiar that he dismisses them in twenty pages, while two hundred are devoted to the earlier history when the body layers are being developed and the organs are appearing in their primitive folds.

But von Baer is the greatest figure in this branch of science, and we look to him both for some of the most important contributions to our knowledge and also for wider views, which have linked up his study with other aspects of evolution. Like all the greatest men of science, his wide intellectual activity was held together by a master interest, the evolution of the adult being from its primitive cell. He was leader of an Arctic expedition as well as Professor of Anatomy at Kant's University of Koenigsberg. While Schwann was analysing the structure of cells, von Baer discovered, in 1827, the true mammalian egg, and could thus trace throughout the parallelism in the embryonic growth of all animals alike. His greatness lies mainly in this achievement, and in appreciating the importance of embryology for all the sciences of life, and even for philosophy as a whole. His work was one of the greatest factors in building up our subsequent knowledge and interest in questions of development. Largely through him the biologist endeavours and is able to trace the history of every living thing from the egg upwards, and in the egg all animals agree. Von Baer's discoveries in the developing egg gave fresh force and fullness to the division which Bichat, following Aristotle, had drawn between the animal and the vegetative organs. What Bichat had surmised from a consideration of the form and functioning of the adult body was now laid bare in the actual segmentation of the growing germ. The first division of the germ is into two distinct layers, of which the inner develops into the plastic body-parts of the embryo, the outer into the animal parts. Von Baer then went farther and distinguished four layers, two in each. The plastic or vegetative layer he divided into a mucous and a vessel layer, and the animal layer into the skin and nervous layer and the skeletal and muscular layer. Then came the fundamental tubes from which the separate organs afterwards arise. He showed that in their earliest stage all animals and even all plants are alike, but with the division of the germ the main types of animal organization soon begin to appear. These von Baer divided into four—the vertebrate, the annulate, the mollusc, and the radiate. Any creature in one of these classes is from an early stage distinguishable in the embryo from those of other classes, but develops at first in a very similar manner to the other members of the same class. The Vertebrates, as they include ourselves, have naturally absorbed the greater part of the attention of biologists, and von Baer tells a story illustrating the likeness of all vertebrate embryos. He had two specimens preserved in spirit which he had forgotten to label, and he found himself quite unable afterwards to distinguish them. 'They may be lizards or small birds or very young mammalia, so complete is the similarity in the mode of formation of the head and trunk in these animals.' It is on this fact that von Baer's principal law depends, and it is important to note how far it departs from the law of 'recapitulation' with which it is often connected. Von Baer did not hold that every adult animal passes in its own life through all the stages of the development of its species, but that it resembles at earlier periods the embryos of other members of the same class, and the farther back you go in its embryonic history, the closer the resemblance to the general type of the class. The development of each creature is from the more general to the more special features of its kind. It was this aspect of his teaching which led Herbert Spencer to say that von Baer's law is the 'law of all development'. It was the strongest reinforcement possible of the doctrine which we have found to dominate all modern teaching about the nature of life, that every organ is an historical being. 'Every organ becomes what it is', he tells us, 'only through the manner of its development, and its true value can be recognized only from its method of formation. . . . The developmental history of the individual is the history of growing individuality in every respect. . . . One creative thought rules all the forms of life, and this thought is nought else but life itself, and the words and syllables in which life expresses itself are the varied forms of the living.'

Von Baer was pre-Darwinian, and he did not accept the doctrine, which Lamarck had made current, that species originate by gradual change due to hereditary growth. Indeed it is a curious and noteworthy fact that embryology, which gave such powerful aid to the theory of evolution at a later stage, did nothing to initiate it. It was the naturalists and geologists, men like Lamarck and Lyell, Wallace and Darwin, interested rather in the habitat and modes of life of varying species and their adaptation to their environment, who made the doctrine prevail. And of this class Charles Darwin was easily the greatest by perseverance, openness of mind, and, we may add, nobility of character. He was born in 1809, the year of the publication of Lamarck's *Philosophie Zoologique*. He had a tradition of evolution in his family through his grandfather Erasmus, and from his earliest years, in spite of the distractions of the traditional school and college course, he remained faithful to his tastes as a field-naturalist. The voyage in the *Beagle* from 1831 to 1836 was the decisive event in his life. He wrote in 1842, that while in South American waters he was struck by the remains of great fossil animals covered with thick scales like armadilloes, and noticed how one species succeeded another as he passed southwards down the continent. He saw too in the Galapagan Islands how the species differed slightly in one island from another, and he began to reflect deeply on the causes of these variations. It was precisely the same kind of evidence which had impressed Lamarck. The conclusion was irresistible that these were cognate species modified by the working of some unknown set of causes. These causes he drew later from the effects of the deliberate selection of breeders to produce a given variety. If man can in a few generations produce a new variety by conscious selection, cannot Nature do the same, and more also, by a process of selection acting steadily for countless generations ? But what is the cause in Nature which thus acts by selecting individuals who approximate to a new type more suitable to its environment ? Here the old facts newly expounded by Malthus, of a rate of animal and vegetable reproduction vastly exceeding the possibility of sustenance and survival, came in to complete the chain of proof. He read Malthus in 1838, after his return from the voyage on the *Beagle*, and found in him the link which he required. The natural cause, which seized on favourable varieties and created new species as the breeder creates varieties, was the struggle for existence. In the struggle of multitudes of creatures for means of subsistence quite inadequate for them all, it was the favourable variation which enabled its possessor to survive. 'It is the doctrine of Malthus', he tells us of his own theory, 'applied with manifold force to the whole animal and vegetable kingdoms.'

Darwin wrote a first sketch of the *Origin of Species* in 1842, but, like Newton, he refrained from publication for several years. At last an essay by A. R. Wallace, sent to him for criticism in 1858, containing conclusions exactly similar to his own and also inspired by Malthus, decided him to publish, and the *Origin of Species* appeared on November 24, 1859.

A public controversy followed which is one of the turning-points in the century : we will consider its main issues in a moment. But among men competent to judge and make use of it, the theory spread at once, for it was seen to give fresh meaning and a firmer basis to all the leading ideas in biology which had been gaining currency for a hundred years. The unity of plan in animals of the same class which Goethe had proclaimed before the century began, Geoffroy's foetal teeth in the whale, von Baer's identity of the embryos in kindred orders, all these fell into place when the comprehensive truth was once envisaged. And Darwin had foreseen these bearings of his theory when he first sketched it in 1842. 'The affinity of different groups, the unity of types of structure, the representative forms through which the foetus passes, the metamorphosis of some organs, the abortion of others, cease to be metaphorical expressions '—when we believe in descent with modifications—' and become intelligible facts.'

The organism in fact, in all its parts and with all its instincts, was for the first time seen fully as an historical being.

That all things, and especially all things living, had come to their present form by a long process of change was of course an ancient thought, old as the Greeks or older. But these modern men were suggesting a mechanical cause which seemed to cut away the element of purpose, especially of divine purpose, from the world. Hence the outcry, hence to many a thoughtful and aspiring mind agony and depression of spirit. There were two broad issues which thus affected the thinking public. Was this variation, on which Darwin and his followers built their scheme, a mere haphazard thing, reducing the universe and all its highest hopes to a fortuitous concourse of atoms? And was it true that Man, the glory of the world, a little lower, as we thought, than the angels, was himself only one of the animals, deriving body, thought, and instinct from bestial sources, lower and not higher than himself? These were the two main issues, and Darwin's two books which followed the *Origin* dealt with them in that order. *The Variation of Animals and Plants under Domestication* appeared in 1863, and *The Descent of Man* in 1871. It is the first of the two topics which, as time has gone on, has absorbed more and more of the attention of biologists. The differences in the initial variations and the ultimate causes of all variation—these are now the leading questions. We are beginning to believe that while some variations may be so slight as to have no effect on the making of a species at all, others are profound and decisive : to these the name of 'mutations' has been given. This may prove an important step in the development of Darwin's theory, who started from the assumption of indiscriminate small variations, some of which, if favoured by natural selection, would accumulate in the course of generations and give rise to new species. This accumulation of variations and their transmission is a problem of infinite complexity and doubt, on which Weismann, Herbert Spencer, and a host of others have spent incessant and still unconcluded labour. Whether the changes that any individual may acquire during his lifetime can be transmitted to his descendants is now in doubt and very generally denied. Nor have we yet attained the answer to that fundamental question which Aristotle raised but could not solve, what causes life to vary at all, and how we can reconcile the general resemblance of every offspring to every parent with the latitude of variation which, as we now believe, results in the course of many generations in a being so unlike the ancestor that it is only the eye of faith and science that can trace the lineage.   But the opinion seems to gain ground that something like purposeful effort lies behind the variations of life.

But the most striking problem which Darwin's work thrust on the public mind was that which he treated more fully in his third book, *The Descent of Man*. Was man himself but one branch of the animal tree, and, if so, what was his descent ? On this Darwin himself is sound and cautious enough.   He applauds the ingenuity and knowledge of Haeckel, but admits that the farther we attempt to trace the genealogy of the Mammals, the greater is the obscurity which surrounds us.   But on the main issue his answer was not uncertain.   Man is close akin biologically to the other Primates, the various families of apes. He was once a hairy beast, both sexes having beards, and his ears were once pointed and capable of movement.   His foot was once prehensile and his progenitors arboreal, frequenting some warm and forest-clad land.   He had a tail and many muscles which now only occasionally appear.   At an earlier stage still, his progenitors must have been aquatic, for our lungs are plainly only a modified swim-bladder which served as a float, and the clefts of our ears and our embryo neck speak of ancestral gills.   On all this side of his work Huxley supported and popularized Darwin's conclusions, and dealt decisive blows to those who would maintain any essential biological difference between the ape's brain and our own.

The immediate successors of Darwin tried to fill out his cautious sketch, for the wonders of embryology had excited speculation to the farthest flights. Men were engaged for many years in drawing imaginary family-trees for all the Vertebrates. These all ended in Man himself and started in some simple worm-like form in which the notochord, or early sketch of the backbone, could first be traced. The battle raged, and is still unsettled, between the partisans now of the Amphioxus, now of the Ascidian, now of the Balanoglossus, the worm which seemed to its supporters the nearest to the ancestral type of all the Vertebrates, and hence of Man. Wild as were some of the guesses and hypothetical many of the links, it was an enthralling thought to picture, in unlimited time and with unbroken steps, the march of life from the first cells to the elongated worm-like forms in which the notochord appears, and then on to the double-symmetrical type which gives us the Vertebrate. And the history could be followed, at least in outline, by any one who dissected an embryo chick or the embryo of any vertebrate animal. There in the early hours of germination the two fundamental tubes appear, in one of which the head and nervous system are to blossom forth and the other which is to produce all the organs and limbs of the trunk. Man becomes chief of creation because his nervous system is most developed and his head, growing backward has taken in more and more of the spinal chord.

Here is the eternal procession of spirit, from the first raucous sound of the amphibian emerging from the waters to the Chorus of Handel, from the worm to the Athena of Pheidias.

But there may be a fallacy in the application, and we saw

in Darwin's own summary how it may arise, if we interpret the story in terms of merely mechanical or physical advance. Even the animal, as Goethe had seen, is part-maker of his own being, and in the case of man a fresh order of conscious factors comes into play, to which Darwin hardly gave sufficient prominence and which many of his followers have ignored or denied. The effort involved in all life becomes with man not only conscious but ideal, an effort to reach a higher state which he deliberately thinks out and places before himself. Huxley in later life, in the Romanes Lecture which he delivered at Oxford in 1894, dissociated himself strongly from the purely naturalistic view, and maintained that moral, aesthetic, or social progress could not be explained by a mere struggle for existence or any process of mechanical causes. There were, in fact, two natures in man, and the higher had to fight not only or mainly against external nature or hostile animals, but against the lower nature in man himself. This was to be brought into subjection to a higher purpose, and this purpose, though it may be traced backwards in the growth of a larger and stronger brain in the animal series, can only be achieved in the present and the future by a painful and persistent effort in conscious co-operation with fellow-workers in the same task. It is this effort which adds to the Descent an Ascent of Man. It is needed every day to elevate our personal nature and in every generation to effect social reform, and it is reflected biologically in the growth of the higher functions of the body.

No other part of science, therefore, no other episode in the story which we have to trace, affected so powerfully as did the theory of evolution the development of the historical spirit which we distinguished at starting as one of the characteristics of the age. The body of a man is like every social institution, history incarnate, and to Darwin more than to any other the world owes its overwhelming bent for the historical point of view, the desire to know the origins of things, the conviction that it is only by studying their steps in change and growth that we can arrive at a true comprehension of their nature. How far this conviction now pervades all science, a glance at any encyclopaedia, or any work purporting to give a full account of any subject, will assure us. Round the doctrine of evolution are now grouped a mass of special sciences, of which the mere titles would fill pages. Archaeology, the sciences of religion, of law, of economics, of language, have all received a new direction from this potent influence. And if we ask how this new spirit compares with that belief in progress which we saw triumphant in the French Revolution and which speaks to us still in the kindling words of Condorcet or of Kant, Darwin himself can supply the answer. He, and his fellow workers on the doctrine of evolution, transformed the old simple faith in human perfectibility by two additions. They gave a body of facts, a set of operative causes to fill out the vague and somewhat empty formulae which satisfied the first enthusiasts. And they supplied the other complementary term which any sound notion of progressive life requires, the idea of the environment upon which the developing organism acts and which reacts upon it. To Condorcet, to the enthusiasts of the Revolution, the future was a vision of ' mankind marching with a firm tread on the road of truth, virtue, and happiness ', a road on which ' we could see no limits to our hopes '. To Darwin, to any one who had studied the facts of life from the new perspective, progress was no less real, it was a palpable and concrete thing, but its reality could and should be measured by the adaptation of the living being to its environment, including in its environment those fellow creatures with whom it lives. 'The ultimate result', says Darwin, in the sixth edition of the *Origin* (p. 97), 'is that each creature tends to become more and more improved in relation to its conditions. This improvement inevitably leads to the gradual advancement of the organization of the greater number of living beings throughout the world.'

In this broad sense Man shares the common lot of all animate things : but he has drawn the great prize and all the expectations.

VII

NATIONALITY AND IMPERIALISM

In our first chapter we attempted to fix a point in ' modern history ' at which true modernity might be said to begin. Amid the maze of views which such a question suggests, we seemed to find some clear directions pointing to the latter part of the eighteenth century : it was then that men now alive might have begun to feel at home in the Western world. But from the present chapter onwards—from, let us say, the publication of Darwin's book[1]—we touch the life-work of men and women still alive. Most of us must have known or seen some man who fought with Garibaldi. The middle-aged will all remember the thrills and tension of the Franco-Prussian War. Many an old cotton-spinner in the North took his share of the privations of the American Civil War. These were the public portents of that momentous decade from 1860 to 1870, and the details can still be supplied by living memory. When Darwin wrote, united Italy was still a dream ; Germany was still a mass of unassimilated kingdoms and duchies under the nominal leadership of Austria. Napoleon III was conducting to its inevitable close his career of fleeting good intentions and impotent ambition. The slaves of *Uncle Tom's Cabin* were still in thrall. After 1870 these things had ceased, and the Western world had begun to work out, in more detail and with more knowledge, the great problems which the revolutionary age had handed down—self-government, social reform, international relations, and world-control. Far as we seem still

---

[1] *Adam Bede* and *The Ordeal of Richard Feverel* were also published in 1859.

M

from our goal, the last half-century has advanced us incomparably further in appreciating both the possibilities and the difficulties of these problems than the half-century before, and for good and evil we begin to see our own handiwork.

If the question of national unity stands out most prominently, as it does at once in Italy, Germany, and the United States, yet a glance back to our introduction will show that in all these cases the other moral and intellectual forces we noted were also at work. In Italy the national cause was also equally the cause of freedom and self-government. The alien and absolutist Government of Austria in the North, the brutal repression of King Bomba in the South, gave the active stimulus which drove the patriots of the Risorgimento to march for an ideal Italy, free and undivided. The lack of freedom and of honest government in France made the throne of the third Napoleon totter and strain with every foreign adventure and fall at the first grave reverse. The desire of domestic prosperity and well-ordered development, as well as the need of unity, conspired with the prestige of foreign success to put the Hohenzollerns in the seat of power.

England in this decade takes a less conspicuous part than she had done fifty years before in the events touched on in our second chapter. Her co-operation with France, which played so large a part in the 'thirties, had slackened, though it was revived for a time in the Crimean War, to which we shall refer in a moment. During the 'fifties, apart from the Crimean War, the mutiny in India had absorbed most of the public interest in external events. In the 'fifties Mr. Gladstone's series of reforming budgets commenced; the first was in 1853. They inaugurated a period of Victorian peace and non-intervention. England was entering on a time of quiet expansion and growing wealth, though she looked with an interested and benevolent eye on the struggles for freedom and better government which went on abroad. Keen competition, first with France and then with Germany, was to follow before the century was out; but England had already begun that movement towards wider democracy and social reform at home which has gained impetus at every step. Looked at from the angle of world-influence, her faults at this time were rather of omission than of commission, of inertia in thinking about public issues, of complacency with her past triumphs and her present prosperity. But she was storing strength and knitting her people together for the great trial which was to come.

The story of nationalism and empire which we have to sketch in this chapter begins, as so many great things in the modern world have begun, with Italy. In the actual outburst of national liberation in the nineteenth century, Greece had come first of the old political units which were to be reconstituted as modern nations by the revolutionary spirit. But Greece was freed almost entirely by others, Italy mainly by herself. In each case the force of an ideal past was at work to recreate a better future. Greece was, as her past deserved, the idol of Western poets and prophets of freedom, and it was the intervention of the West which enabled the Russians, hostile to Turkey and spiritually allied to the modern Greeks, to detach the first limb of disintegrating Turkey. But in the case of Italy it was her own national soul that made her one and set her free. She too had claims, religious as well as political, on Western enthusiasm. She had a longer and far more glorious record of European power than Greece. Sympathy and good wishes were not wanting for the Italians in their national struggle, especially from England, and Italian statesmen did not fail to make the fullest use of these and of the competing ambitions of their powerful neighbours. But, while giving due weight to outside influences, the impartial student of Italy's resurrection will yet admit that she justified the proud boast of one of her protagonists and ' made herself '. The ' Heart ' of the Risorgimento, as George Meredith sang, was Mazzini, the ' Brain ' was Cavour, and the ' Sword ' was Garibaldi. Divergent as were the ideals and temperaments of the three, bitter and frequent their personal conflicts, yet the spirit of a true nation held them together, backed by the pertinacity of the House of Charles Albert and Victor Emmanuel.

A glance backward is necessary to understand the crucial events of the 'sixties. The first Napoleon had conquered Italy. He would have been glad, as an Italian in blood, to make Italy a nation, though he did not wish her, any more than Germany, to be too strong. In both countries his devastating blast brought also purification in its wake. In the three Italian states—all directly or indirectly under himself—into which he divided the conquered land, he introduced personal and religious freedom, equal and common laws. The *Code Napoléon* became the law of Italy, and, compared with what preceded or what immediately followed it, the Napoleonic *régime* was liberalism to the Italians. After the Congress of Vienna in 1815 the old territorial and legitimist sovereignties returned. The House of Savoy and Piedmont came back from Sardinia, the Bourbons from Sicily to Naples. Lombardy and Venice again went under the Austrian yoke and the Popes resumed their temporal sway of the Papal States. This, with various little despots in the duchies north of the Papal States, was the political status of the peninsula in the 'twenties and 'thirties, when the ferment of nationalism and political revolution began to work again throughout the West.

Perhaps of all the prophetic figures in this new movement the most striking and universal in his appeal was Mazzini, born at Genoa in 1805. We saw him, at the end of Chapter II, an exile in France, sending out his passionate gospel to all the democracies of the West. Without him we can hardly imagine the wave of popular enthusiasm which carried the ship of Italy into port. But with him alone, and his immediate followers, the voyage must have failed. In 1830 he was exiled by the Piedmontese Government as a Carbonaro, an active conspirator against the existing order. In 1831 Charles Albert, educated with leanings to Rousseau and national freedom, succeeded to the throne of Piedmont, and Mazzini, though an ardent republican in theory, addressed a public letter to him from Marseilles, urging him to take the lead in the coming fight. In its immediate object the appeal was futile, for Piedmont and Italy were not yet ready nor was Charles Albert the man. But it added fuel to the patriot fires, and, though Mazzini remained under the ban, Piedmont began to set her house in order and Italian hopes to centre round her. In 1846 Pio Nono succeeded to the Papal throne—a 'liberal Pope'. Again Mazzini published a letter, this time to lead the Pope to take action. With a quondam liberal king at Turin and a supposed liberal Pope at Rome, the cause seemed nearly won. The Gallic cock, who wakened so many echoes throughout Europe, had crowed in February 1848. Sicily had actually anticipated him by rising for freedom in January. On the 18th of March the revolt took place in Milan which Meredith has immortalized in *Vittoria* for all readers of English. Charles Albert was induced to march against Austria, but only to meet disaster and the loss of his crown. He was succeeded by his son Victor Emmanuel, destined one day to lead the forces of Piedmont and Italy into Florence and ultimately into Rome. But at this time, in 1849, the rising in Rome was a forlorn hope. It brought Mazzini and Garibaldi together in the defence of a glorious if short-lived Roman Republic. Pio Nono, who had found the desires of his people went far beyond the reforms which he was willing or able to grant, had fled before the storm. But the Roman Republic was suppressed and the Pope brought back by Napoleon III with the support of reactionary France. French bayonets henceforth defended the temporal power of the Pope until the war of 1870; and Italian freedom made no further advance until the war of 1859. Mazzini left the Holy City after its surrender, on the 30th of June, 1849, and took up his long refuge in London. Garibaldi, after his noble address of farewell, left through the mountains, pursued in vain by the armies of France, Austria, and Naples. ' I shall return again ', he prophesied, ' in ten years' time.'

But the intervening decade prepared the ground by other means ; and the capital preparation was in the kingdom of Piedmont. Soon after his accession Victor Emmanuel called Cavour to power, and Cavour remained prime minister and practically ruler of the country nearly all the ten years which passed till his death in 1861. Before he died he saw all Italy except Rome and Venice united under the crown of Sardinia and Piedmont. A career which bears so much resemblance to that of Bismarck will come into our minds again when we reach the work of the first German Emperor's Chancellor. Both men were country gentlemen with considerable knowledge of foreign states. Both knew England, and in a different spirit admired her. Both achieved the same work of unifying a nation. Both were masters of a type of diplomacy admired in the past, questioned in the present, needless, as we hope, in the future. But Cavour differed essentially from his German successor in aiming at real self-government at home on the English plan, and in seeking no conquests abroad. He more than once sought war, but he sought it with a single eye to freedom and united Italy. ' A free Church in a free State' was his master-motto. While working for Italy in the ten years which preceded the triumph, he was strengthening the resources and improving the Government of Piedmont. The financial and commercial forces of the country were increased, and the army put on a better footing to meet its next trial, which was not long delayed.

In the Crimean War, Piedmont, soon to be Italy, took her side by the Western Powers, England and France, in prosecuting an object which was held to be of common interest to all Europe. The appearance of young Italy, both on the battlefield and at the council table of Europe, was Cavour's first striking achievement in European politics. He had to deal with Napoleon III, unstable adventurer, tied hand and foot to the clerical reactionaries at home, but at heart nationalist and progressive, ex-Carbonaro and half-Italian by race. And he had to deal with England, just then in a non-interventionist mood, but full of sympathy and holding some ardent friends. The Italian contingent fought well, and at the congress table in 1856 Cavour could speak for Italy as a coming Power.

In England, too, opinion was ripening fast. All parties among us have always admired a fight for freedom, and above all a fight against odds. Here was little Piedmont making headway against the giant but ill-compacted Austria to the north, and with her comrades of the south groaning under the savage and stupid tyranny of the Bourbons at Naples. On the latter a brilliant searchlight had just been thrown by the rising English statesman whose budgets had been the feature of domestic politics from 1853 onwards. It chanced that Mr. Gladstone was travelling through Italy in the autumn of 1850 with his wife and daughter, and was present at the trial of Poerio, a distinguished man and a political prisoner in Naples. He heard the corrupt and worthless evidence on which the prisoner, not long before a minister of the crown, had been sentenced to twenty-four years in irons. He visited the prisons and saw political prisoners chained in double irons to common felons two and two, and he watched them in their sickness, dragging themselves upstairs to see the doctor because their dungeons below were so foul and loathsome that doctors could not be expected to enter them. Next year in two 'Letters to Lord Aberdeen' Gladstone denounced, for the whole world to hear, a state of things which was a ' negation of God erected into a system of government '.

After his success in the Crimean War Cavour began quietly to work with the revolutionary forces throughout Italy. He discouraged and disavowed the forlorn hopes which many of the pure idealists were constantly provoking. He privately abetted enterprises of promise such as that initiated by Mazzini, which finally led Garibaldi in triumph to the Papal States. In January 1858 a curious accident brought Napoleon once more within the orbit of Cavour. An Italian conspirator called Orsini made an attempt in Paris on Napoleon's life, and the bombs, though they missed the Emperor, killed several people in his suite. It was the revenge of one Carbonaro on another who had deserted the cause, and, strange as it seemed to contemporaries, the dying appeal of the condemned man decided Napoleon to do something for the Italian cause. In the summer of the same year he had a secret meeting with Cavour, and arranged a joint war on Austria which was to free Italy, from the Alps to the Adriatic. All northern Italy was to form one state under the crown of Sardinia, Piedmont, and Savoy, though Savoy and Nice were to go to France as the price of her intervention. The war took place, as arranged, in 1859, but half-way through the nerve of Napoleon gave way and a premature peace was patched up at Villafranca, by which Lombardy alone was gained for Piedmont, and Venice still remained in Austrian hands. The exasperation of Cavour, the sense of betrayal in all Italy, prepared the way for Garibaldi's great adventure. Early in 1860 Tuscany and the smaller states north of the Rubicon rallied to the Parliament at Turin, and Garibaldi's immortal Sicilian expedition was prepared and tacitly allowed.

This was the romance of the Liberation, conducted to its

happy issue by the greatest hero of all romance. A sailor from Nice, who had learnt his business as a leader of men in guerrilla fighting in Brazil and Uruguay, he led 1,070 men in two paddle-steamers to assault the two Bourbon kingdoms of southern Italy and in six months had them at his feet. There is no episode in history so thrilling in incident, so inspiring in heroism and skill, so enchanting in its atmosphere of free nature and free men, as the story of Garibaldi's advance across Sicily. As it was Sicily which first rose in 1848, so now it was the conquest of Sicily which won the war. ' General, I fear we ought to retreat,' said Bixio, his gallant second in command, in the desperate moment before the last attack at Calatafimi. 'Here we make Italy or die,' replied the chief. That battle, which was to all appearance only a desperate skirmish between a few hundred Red Shirts and Neapolitans on a grassy, stony slope, was the real moment in the making of a nation. The famished, half-clad, and exhausted band, which struggled up the hill against twice their own number, well-drilled and well-found except in faith, carried in their poor kit that spark of spirit whose triumph over matter is the true history of man.

The original landing at Marsala on the west Sicilian coast in May 1860 was effected before the greater Powers could get their slow train in motion. Cavour knew and connived. Two British men-of-war which lay in the harbour looked on with friendly eyes. But in August, when Garibaldi, as Dictator of Sicily, was waiting at the Straits of Messina for the first chance of crossing, the whole world was awake. At this point Napoleon's divided mind was against rather than for the further growth of united Italy. To add Naples to the new kingdom would make it too powerful, and threatened the incorporation of Rome and the antagonism of the clericals, always the main support of the imperial throne. So he was prepared for naval action opposing Garibaldi, if England would agree. But England, governed at that moment by Lord John Russell, Palmerston, and Gladstone, refused co-operation. A secret envoy from Cavour reached Russell at dead of night and conveyed the real, as distinguished from the official, wishes of the Government at Turin. Garibaldi was allowed to cross, opposed only by the Neapolitan cruisers, which he eluded by one of his most skilful manœuvres. He found the population on the mainland well disposed. Forty years of brutal and senseless oppression, followed by a forced conversion at the eleventh hour to a liberal *régime*, left the kingdom of Bomba's son an easy prey to the most famous knight-errant in the world. On September 5 King Francis and his queen departed by sea for Gaeta, and on the 7th Naples received the Liberator with delirious joy. By October he had succeeded in holding up the counter-attack of the returning royalists, and then, not strong enough to advance himself on Rome, he wisely decided to await the coming of the man who was to be the Italian king.

At this moment Cavour struck the boldest and most successful blow in his career. With Sicily safe and Garibaldi holding out before Naples, he moved the north Italian army southwards through the Papal States to meet the Liberator and reap the harvest of a united Italy for the House of Savoy. Garibaldi had already of his own motion written to invite Victor Emmanuel to Naples and to place his conquests in the king's hands.

As soon as the junction of regular and irregular forces had taken place and the Bourbon troops were finally defeated, a prompt plébiscite was taken of the peoples of the Two Sicilies. Were they, or were they not, in favour of union with the northern kingdom ? Union was voted by majorities of more than a hundred to one. Meanwhile the autocratic Powers— Austria, Prussia, and Russia—had met in conference at Warsaw, in the heart of dismembered Poland, to concert measures to prevent the union of dismembered Italy. Napoleon was feebly supporting the banished Bourbon with a French fleet at Gaeta.

England was united for united Italy and enthusiastic as she had never been, and Lord John issued one of our most famous and most welcome foreign Notes. To Cavour it appeared ' as good as an army of 100,000 men '.

' It is difficult ', said this dispatch, ' to believe, after the astonishing events that we have seen, that the Pope and the King of the Two Sicilies possessed the love of their subjects. Her Majesty's Government can therefore see no sufficient ground for the severe censure with which Austria, France, Prussia, and Russia have visited the acts of the King of Sardinia. Her Majesty's Government will turn their eyes rather to the gratifying prospect of a people building up the edifice of their liberties. . . . The Italians are the best judges of their own interests.'

Thus the Warsaw protest remained as futile as the fleet at Gaeta. The last two stages in the making of Italy are bound up with the conflicts of other Powers. When the kingdom was proclaimed, in 1861, three portions of true Italy remained un-redeemed, Venice, Rome, and the Trentino. Venice was won in 1866 as the reward of Italian support of Prussia in her war with Austria. Rome, the object of every patriot's desire, and of Garibaldi's first Italian expedition in 1849, was still with-held from the new kingdom by Napoleon's troops, till after his defeat in 1870. The withholding lost him his ' one ally ', and possibly altered the fate of that war and of all subsequent history. The Trentino was at issue in the Great War. All three cases are of special interest in this chapter as showing the potency of national feeling in the last hundred years. They illustrate, too, in a striking way the inter-connexion of all European questions.

Cavour died in 1861 when the main work of Italian unity was done, but the coping-stone had not yet been laid upon the building. The want of Rome and the constant opposition of the Pope, prevented the realization of Cavour's ideal—'the free Church in the free State'. Rome was gained, but not the co-operation of the Pope, a few months after the breach between France and Prussia. War was declared on July 13 ; twenty-four hours later the Pope proclaimed the dogma of Papal Infallibility. In September the Italian army invaded the Roman State, and by next year the Temporal Power was gone and a new temporal power installed upon the Quirinal.

But before this the centre of gravity in European politics had changed from France to Prussia. The great but sinister figure which we have compared and contrasted with Cavour had become the strongest man in Europe. The immediate task which lay before the two men was similar, to build from a set of disconnected and often ill-governed states one strong and well-administered nation. Both must be held to have succeeded, and the difference in their methods and in many of the ultimate results must be attributed even more to the different traditions and circumstances in which they worked than to their personal difference. They were alike in having behind them the passionate yearnings of a great people, outraged by centuries of suffering and wrong. They were alike in studying foreign example for their guidance. They were alike, too, in employing for state purposes methods which, as Cavour once said, would be considered scandalous in a private transaction. But, while Cavour admitted it with regret, Bismarck regarded it as the law of nature. He derided ' the English catchwords, " Humanity and Civilization " ' and spoke of a policy of con-ciliation as 'a weak striving after applause'. He was afraid of ' the ultimate discovery of Europe ', and told a correspondent, in 1850, that he ' was a Prussian and that his ideal for one employed in foreign politics was to be free from prejudices and to have the habit of deciding independently of any feelings of antipathy to, or preference for, foreign states '. He was in fact first a Prussian, and after that a German. Had Cavour been asked the same question he would have replied (with a strong French accent) that he was first an Italian and after that a European.

The accession of Bismarck to full power in Prussia soon followed the death of Cavour in 1861. In 1857 the mental health of Frederick William IV, the vacillating King of Prussia, broke down. His brother William I (afterwards the first German Emperor) was made Regent, and in 1861 became King. Shortly afterwards he appointed as his President and Foreign Minister Otto von Bismarck, already a leading man in Prussia.

The events which follow cannot be understood without a glance backward at the conditions in Prussia and in Germany as a whole, which made Bismarck's actions possible, and which his actions were to modify more profoundly than those of any other man in German history, not excepting Frederick the Great himself. Frederick and Bismarck, separated by a hundred years, form in fact a pair of companion pictures, brilliant explosions of force on the continuous thread of Prussian policy, forming and leading modern Germany to her present state.

Prussia had grown in the eighteenth century, largely through Frederick's work, to be the leading Power in the north of Germany among the multitude of small states which since the Middle Ages had acknowledged the nominal and ineffective headship of the Holy Roman Emperor. This emperor, who, in mediaeval theory, was, with the Pope, joint vice-gerent of God on earth, had, after the consolidation of the Western kingdoms, after France, Spain, and England had settled down to a self-contained national life of their own, always been a German. Since the beginning of the fifteenth century these emperors, with two short exceptions, had been of the House of Hapsburg, the heads, that is, of the Austrian dominions. But for two hundred years a rival power to Austria had been growing in the north. Hohenzollerns from Suabia had acquired the Mark of Brandenburg, had added to it Prussia, had become Kings of Prussia, had added other lands to Prussia, had challenged and defeated Austria in the Seven Years' War, and were now ready to supplant her in the leadership of the German race. This rivalry was one of the two fatal hindrances to the unification of Germany on lines such as those followed by the Western states. The other was the vast mass of Austrian subjects not of German blood. Prussia had indeed her Poles, but she was predominantly German. Austria, with greater extent and greater historic prestige, was weighed down by her majority of aliens. She had Magyars in Hungary, Czechs in Bohemia, Slavs in Croatia and the south-east, Poles in Galicia, Italians in the Trentino and Trieste. In these two facts—internal rivalry and the domination of aliens—lay the chief seeds of all the troubles that were to come.

Prussia, after her recovery from the Napoleonic wars, set to work to reorganize and strengthen herself within, and, above all, to strengthen her army. A strong and well-disciplined army and an autocratic king ruling by divine right, these were the two cardinal points in Prussian policy, inherited from the founders of that state in the seventeenth and eighteenth century. They were the chief instruments in the hands of Bismarck, the maker of the modern Empire.

A German Confederation was one of the creations of the Congress of Vienna. It was devised by Metternich, the Austrian minister, as a method of conservation and of defence. It was to conserve the rights and possessions of all the German sovereigns and it was to defend the German world against any future encroachment by France. It was wholly futile, in fact positively obstructive, from the point of view of organizing a strong, united, and progressive German state, The Diet, which was its organ, sat at Frankfort. Austria was in the chair, and for all important decisions a unanimous vote was required. As these votes had to be sought by the delegates, each from his own Government, and there were still 38 of these surviving from the 300 before Napoleon's purge, the prospect of any effective action was small indeed.

But while this was the law of Europe, and while Prussia was strengthening herself within her own borders, the German people as a whole were sighing for a national organization and proper means of self-government. Like other 'unorganized' nations in the early part of the century, like Italians or Poles, or Hungarians or Greeks, they felt themselves a nation and wished this national self-consciousness to be realized in political forms. Like other nations also they made several abortive movements and committed some political crimes. In 1848—the great revolutionary year—the crowing of the Gallic cock waked them to a large and serious effort. A Constituent Assembly met voluntarily at Frankfort to frame a constitution. It arose from a small meeting of Liberals in Baden, and continued to sit with interruptions till the summer of 1849. It was led by able and high-minded men, and after long discussions finally framed the constitution and came to a definite conclusion on the great question which divided all Germany into rival camps. By a sufficient though not a large majority it decided that Prussia must be the head of the new Germany, and that Austria must be treated as a foreign state. By 290 votes out of less than 500 voting it offered, in March 1849, the Imperial crown to the King of Prussia.

To a later speculator on possible history this will appear as the golden chance for unifying Germany on a liberal basis. Would not Austria at this point have accepted the decision without a fight ? And if she had to be fought, and driven out of the Confederation by arms—as Bismarck held—the work might have been done then with all the progressive forces of Germany behind the driving Power. But Frederick William IV, who had succeeded to the throne of Prussia in 1840, was no true friend of popular rights. He was merely weak. He had granted a constitution to Prussia, as we saw in Chapter IV, under the stress of the general rising; but it was speedily nullified by illiberal restrictions. His personal ideals were mediaeval—a divinely appointed sovereign, granting protection and favours to his people, but owing them nothing by right and still less by force. Though ready therefore to accept the Imperial crown, he refused to take it from an assembly of subjects. That would be ' a crown of mud and wood ', he said; ' if any one is to award the crown of the German nation, it is myself and my equals who shall give it.'

The mind travels on twenty-two years to a famous scene at Versailles, when the Imperial crown was accepted by his brother from the princes of Germany who had followed him in the war. But they were not his equals, and the crown was tendered to Prussia across the bleeding body of stricken France.

Bismarck had represented Prussia at the Diet of Frankfort in 1851, and his strong support helped Frederick William to defy the Liberals. In the following decade, the vain efforts of the Prussian Liberals to assert themselves at home and the conflict of Austria and Prussia in the Confederation were the two chief features in the political history of Germany.

William I had no tincture of the occasionally liberal sympathies or the constitutional timidity which had occasionally led Frederick William to make concessions. He was true Prussian, though without the genius of Frederick the Great or of Bismarck; an obstinate man, bent on increasing and improving his army in the teeth of his Prussian Parliament. It was on this point—the traditional policy of the Prussian monarchy—that the decisive conflict took place between the king and the incipient and unorganized liberalism of his kingdom ; and Bismarck's will and skill turned the scale for the Crown. From that date, 1863, he upheld the king while reorganizing his army without parliamentary sanction, and, when the weapon was forged, King and Minister won against Denmark in 1864 and Austria in 1866 the swift and overwhelming victories which turned into friends the hostile majority at home.

The details, which we must not stay to give, are a brilliant record of bold, able, and unscrupulous diplomacy. The duchies of Schleswig and Holstein were torn from Denmark and then used as a means of forcing on the trial of strength with Austria which Bismarck desired. In the case of Denmark, opinion in England was deeply stirred, and one of Palmerston's last acts was an attempt to send the British Fleet into the Baltic to exert pressure on behalf of the Danes. It was over-ruled by the rest of the Government, and after Palmerston's death in 1865 our policy took for many years a line of non-intervention in European affairs, of which we shall see in the Franco-Prussian War the most serious results.

It was the war with Austria in 1866 and the consolidation of Germany that followed which really made the Empire. The war with France and the crowning at Versailles were the completion and public proclamation of a work already more than half done. When Austria in 1866 was beaten and driven out of the Confederation, Prussia proceeded to organize North Germany round herself and on her own lines. The army and the customs' union were the two main instruments. In military matters the Prussian system was imposed in every detail, and all the armed forces of Northern Germany were added to the power of the Prussian Crown. By secret treaties the four southern kingdoms, Baden, Würtemberg, Saxony, and Bavaria, were also bound to come to the aid of Prussia in case of need.

N

Politically, Bismarck introduced universal suffrage for the North German Parliament, but took good care that the Reichstag thus elected should have no real power. This remained, after as before the war, in the hands of the King of Prussia as President of the Confederation and the Chancellor as his agent. There was to be no ministerial responsibility, no appointment of the executive by the elected House—above all, no control of the army. The Upper House in fact, which was modelled on the old Diet of Frankfort, had more real power than the Reichstag. But while Bismarck remained Chancellor, the creator of the State, he was in fact absolute. His mind and hand have made the Germany which we know.

The Treaty of Prague in 1866 ended the war with Austria and founded the present German Empire in fact though not in name. The Treaty of Frankfort, which concluded the Franco-Prussian War in 1871, was from the Prussian point of view a continuation of the same process, the strengthening and development of Germany under Prussian leadership. But from the European aspect the rights of Prussia in the two cases were very different, and the results on the world's peace have differed accordingly. The Austrian War and its immediate sequel were a domestic matter : the Franco-Prussian War thrust the sword into the heart of Europe. Nothing shows this better than the difference in the policy which Bismarck pursued in dealing with Austria after Sadowa and with France after Sedan. He had provoked the war with Austria in the teeth of the German public and with a reluctant king. War once declared, he struck hard and successfully. But as soon as Austria, a kindred Power, was on her knees, he made his terms as easy as possible and the reconciliation solid and enduring. The duchies of Schleswig and Holstein, for which the war of 1864 was made, were of course to become Prussian, with the promise of a plebiscite for the Danes of Schleswig,

which has never been taken.   Austria, the rival head of the
German world, was in future to be excluded from the new Confederation, but no indemnity, no cession of German lands, was
asked from her.   She became in the next four years so little
disposed to alter the arrangement that Napoleon's incessant
intrigues were unable to secure her for an attack in revenge.
Italy, who had received Venetia in 1866 as her reward, also
stood aloof when the greater struggle arrived.   And, Venetia
apart, Napoleon's long-continued support of the Pope's claim
to Rome was a sufficient bar to any co-operation between the
two Latin Powers at the outset of the Franco-Prussian war.
Garibaldi went later as a volunteer, when there was a
threatened republic to defend.

No other tragedy in the blood-stained records of Europe
was ever so wantonly provoked by those who suffered most
from it, so pitilessly pressed home by the triumphant victors.
It was the clash of an age-long rivalry of nations brought to
an issue by an unworthy and unstable leader on the one
side, and the strongest and best-seated champion of the
other.

Napoleon III's career was drawing to an ignominious close.
His attempt to found an empire in Mexico had failed with
disaster to the unfortunate Maximilian of Hapsburg, whom he
had inveigled, and with danger and disgrace to himself.   For
the United States, just freed from the preoccupation of their
civil war, were determined to prevent any such invasion of
the New World by an Old World Power in future.   For that
reason they were never less friendly to France, their old ally
in the War of Independence, than now, a hundred years later,
when she most needed a friend.

Napoleon's position, always unstable, was now precarious.
He had made no friend and gained little glory by his adventures
in Italy.   His adventure in Mexico had covered him with

shame. Meanwhile the most serious rival of France in Europe was gaining strength at every step. The prestige which he needed to secure his throne was, he thought blindly, to be gained by checking the growth of a united Germany, or, if that was impossible, by accessions to the territory of France with the consent of Prussia. Both plans were tried in turn by the shifty and inconclusive methods which he had practised all his life. He had neither the strength at home to fight successfully nor the vision and command abroad which might have enabled him to attain the nobler thing without fighting. He could not see that a strong Germany was in itself a gain that was needed, not to weaken any one but to build up a stronger and more united Europe in which Germany with Italy, France, and England might take her due place. The true Concert of Europe, the ideal which had floated before men's minds from the Middle Ages onwards, was never more wanted than at this moment, and it was never farther to seek. Bismarck, the strongest man in Europe, scouted the idea. Louis Napoleon, who saw it in glimpses, was too weak and selfish, personally too unsafe, to help others in its attainment. England was in her worst fit of national abstraction. 'Belief in the selfishness that dictates our present system of isolation', says Lord Clarendon in 1868, 'has reduced our importance, and therefore our influence, on the Continent to zero. Europe now cares no more about England than she does about Holland, and I have suffered many things on that account during the last two months.'

The immediate occasion and the events of the war of 1870 need not detain us in detail. Bismarck, in his earlier years of power, would gladly have made friends with France on his own terms—the consolidation of Germany under Prussian leadership and no transfer of German lands to France. When in the course of many meetings and negotiations he came to understand Napoleon's character and aims, he anticipated war, and, having anticipated it, he resolved to strike first. The Hohenzollern candidature for the throne of Spain, which would either set up a Prussian bulwark beyond the Pyrenees or provoke France to fight, was his own devising, and at every stage he pressed it in secret with the utmost zeal, while stoutly denying it in public. Napoleon, the Empress Eugénie, and the incompetent ministers whom they had gathered round them, misused the provocation in the worst possible way. England, through Mr. Gladstone, who was then Prime Minister, attempted to assuage the storm. The candidature was withdrawn. The French ministry had the extreme folly to demand an undertaking that it would never be renewed. Then, at the last moment, when a faint hope still remained of a peaceful settlement, Bismarck, by altering a telegram from his master describing an interview with Benedetti, the French ambassador, succeeded in so arousing the anger of the French that the declaration of war came from them. Germany was thus put formally on the defensive, and right in the eyes of her own people and of the neutral world. Right at least she seemed, because the machinations of Bismarck were not yet unveiled. Had they been known, who can doubt the overwhelming wave of indignation which would have swept over the world; and who can doubt, either, that if the shortest space had been allowed for an examination of the *casus belli* by any impartial tribunal, the war could never have occurred ?

War was declared on July 17. The fighting in August was as decisive as the six weeks of the Austrian War. By September 2 Sedan had fallen and Napoleon was in the hands of the enemy. At that point the true character of the conflict changed. With the fall of the chief author of their misfortunes, the French formed a ministry of National Defence, and the war was henceforward a defensive one. Had there been any sense of the ultimate community of interests between the combatants, as there was in 1866 between Austrians and Prussians, or had there been an Areopagus of Europe able to enforce this upon them from without, then, or soon after, peace would have been restored. But the Areopagus was yet to be, and its foundations were in decay.

England was the best hope of neutral action. It was her traditional rôle to intervene in Europe to protect the weak and antagonize the over-strong. But Palmerston was dead; Gladstone, though friendly to France, was closely allied to the non-interventionists such as Bright; the Queen and Court, and a large part of educated opinion, headed by Carlyle, were strongly pro-German. Perhaps the most serious personal blow was the death, just three weeks before the war broke out, of Lord Clarendon, one of our best Foreign Secretaries. Firm, tactful, and assiduous, he was a friend of France and of Napoleon's, and the one of his cabinet with whom Gladstone tells us he could work most easily. He was succeeded by Lord Granville, who showed so little insight that he had quoted with approval, a week before the war began, the opinion that Europe had not known so great a lull for many years, so little promptness that the Provisional Government in Paris, which conducted the defence of Paris through that terrible winter, was not formally recognized by us until February. That tolerable terms might have been arranged in the autumn must be evident to any one who reflects that even five months later, after the fall of Paris, Bismarck was averse from insisting on the cession of Lorraine. The influence which Clarendon might have exercised is well illustrated by the illuminating story which his daughter, Lady Emily Russell, tells of 1871, when she went to Berlin as wife of the British Ambassador. Bismarck was sitting beside her, and suddenly said, ' Never in my life was I more glad to hear of anything than I was to hear of your father's death.'

When she showed her amazement at this speech, he patted her hand and added, ' Ach, dear lady, you must not take it like that. What I mean is that, if your father had lived, he would have prevented the war.' What was wanted, either to prevent the war, or, when started, to conclude it on tolerable terms, was a statesman of long views, bold words, and swift action ; and Heaven had not granted him. Boldness was needed, not to face dangers from abroad, which, with our fleet in command, were at that time negligible, but to face the wide prejudice and wider ignorance which prevailed at home. The bulk of the operatives in the North, who had stood firm for the Union in the American War, were now misled by their dislike of the fallen Emperor, and a majority in Parliament were of like mind. They felt so great a contempt for the part that Napoleon and his wife had played.

Here was scope for the statesman's vision that would have looked beyond these personalities to Europe standing at the parting of the ways, and for the persuasive word which Gladstone might have used so well.

One body of organized opinion must in justice be noticed, which stood for intervention. They were small in numbers, but they said the right word, and did all that a handful of men could do to persuade their fellow-countrymen. These were the Positivists of London, led by Dr. Congreve. He placarded the walls of London with appeals to working-men which may be read to-day with regretful assent by those who know the sequel. For there was true prophecy in them as well as passion, and at those mass meetings of London workmen assembled by Professor Beesly and Mr. Frederic Harrison. They were professing a belief and advocating actions which the bulk of mankind have been compelled to follow after forty years. What was this policy ? To make friends with liberated France, and, in the strength of this friendship, to work for

a united Europe on the basis of freely-governed and independent nationalities.

Meanwhile, between the upper and the nether millstone—
a ruthless nationalism and a discredited imperialism—the hopes
and harmony of Europe were being ground to dust.

Paris capitulated at the end of January after the remaining
armies had been defeated in the field, and in May the Treaty of
Frankfort was concluded which ended the war. France yielded
all Alsace, except Belfort, and most of Lorraine. She
undertook to pay two hundred million pounds within three
years. The money was easily borrowed and repaid. The
loss of the provinces, against the almost unanimous wish of
their inhabitants, has proved so far an insuperable barrier to
the peaceful organization of Europe as a whole. It was to
prevent the erection of such an obstacle that the united efforts
of neutral diplomacy should have been directed, and Mr. Gladstone, who failed to rally the forces required, was fully conscious
of the needs of the case. He wrote on December 20, 1870, to
Lord Granville : ' While I feel more and more the deep culpa-
bility of France, I have an apprehension that this violent
laceration and transfer is to lead us from bad to worse and to
be the beginning of a new series of European complications.'

Granville was against action, and Russia took the opportunity
to affront England and England's allies in the Crimean War by
denouncing the clauses in the treaty of Paris of 1856, which
forbade Russia to build or keep men-of-war on the Black Sea.
This of course added to the difficulties of effective neutral
action on the main issue, and Bismarck showed his accustomed
astuteness by supporting the claim of England for a Conference
on the Russian question. It met in London from December to
March. It paid lip-service to the theory of international law
by affirming ' the essential principle of the law of nations that
no Power can liberate itself from the engagements of a treaty

nor modify the stipulations thereof unless with the consent of the contracting Powers '. It then proceeded to confirm the action already taken by Russia. Meanwhile the aggressions of Prussia, first against Denmark, then against France, were allowed to pass without public action or protest from the other nations, who were in the end to pay so heavily for their want of foresight and common energy. Europe seemed for the moment dead, and by comparison the Congress of Vienna an active agency for public right.

We turn now to the other side of the world, to the third case which we selected at the beginning of this chapter as the most typical and important in the decade 1860–70. The Civil War in the United States was already over before the new German Empire was founded and France smitten in the Franco-Prussian War. But the true meaning of the American War had not yet been read—had been, in fact, quite misread by large classes and many of the best informed men in Europe. We are indeed only now, in the light of the Great War, beginning to understand what the world owes to the great men and the great public steadfastness which fought for human freedom and national unity in the four years from 1861 to 1865, and held together the greatest State in the New World in the time of its mortal peril. The South, through the personal attractiveness of many of its champions, through their heroic defence of a state independence as dear to them as the larger ideal was to the men of the North, touched many fibres in the English heart. But in this cause our working-classes saw the moral aspect right, and stood firm. The northern operatives bore with unshaken bravery the privations due to the cutting off of southern cotton. To them slavery was the real issue, and state independence a doubtful pretext. By 1865 the superb statesmanship of Lincoln and the moral enthusiasm of the North had won completely. Lincoln lived to see the victory just before he fell.

On April 10, 1865, he entered Richmond, the Southern capital, the day after it had surrendered to the Union forces under Grant. On the 14th he was shot down by an assassin in a theatre in Washington.

Slavery, though not the immediate occasion, was the real cause of war. Questions connected with it, and in particular the right of the Union to regulate or abolish slavery in newly-acquired territories, had raged violently and divided the country for many years before the war broke out. Lincoln, though not a pioneer in the anti-slavery crusade,—putting, in fact, the whole question as subordinate to the need of maintaining national unity—became in the end the agent by whom the States were enabled to abolish the evil and yet hold together. He had envisaged the problem in its right proportions from the earliest days of his political work. When standing as Senator for Illinois in 1858, he declared in his address that ' A house divided against itself cannot stand. This Government cannot endure permanently half-slave and half-free, and I do not expect the Union to be dissolved.' He saw the essential features of the problem, and we can now see it fully revealed as a permanent and fundamental issue. Slavery, going to the very roots of politics, in that region where politics and the moral law have common birth, could not admit of compromise or difference of practice in the same nation. It was no question of expediency or the balance of political advantage such as decide on constitutional forms or on the limits of state activity. It was a question of conscience, and if, as we have maintained, the rise of national consciousness is one of the leading features in the nineteenth century, it follows that each national being must, like an individual, have at least the rudiments of a national conscience. The United States, by obeying their conscience, strengthened it, and their national force grew thereby in dealing with other international questions in later years.

They, more than any other Western people, have been dis-interested and scrupulous in their treatment of the weaker races. We shall have examples of this in a later chapter ; and it cannot be without reason that we connect these things with the suffering and effort by which they consolidated their own national existence on a moral basis. They made in their Civil War the freedom and the human rights of every member of the community the cardinal issue *aut stantis aut cadentis civitatis.* Without this sense of personal dignity the nation can have no conscience, and nations without conscience make a world without humanity.

VIII

SCHOOLS FOR ALL

THE American Civil War brought the greatest democracy in the world face to face with the deepest question of human rights. Was every man within the borders of their community to be an end in himself, to call his soul his own ? And the whole community, surmounting the danger of a permanent rupture, decided in the affirmative. We can see now, what many of our most enlightened men could not see then, how eminently wise, as well as heroic, was the decision. The decade following these events may well be taken as the turning-point of another movement which has much in common with the emancipation of the slaves.

Mr. Gladstone's Government of 1868 put its hand to many things. It disestablished the Irish Church, it passed an Irish Land Act, it abolished religious tests at Oxford and Cambridge. But of all its acts probably no one would now question that the Elementary Education Act of 1870 was far the most important. And when we remember that this was followed in 1876 by another Bill enforcing universal attendance at school, that France and Italy were simultaneously doing much the same thing, that the same decade saw the establishment of several provincial colleges which have since become universities, besides the women's colleges at Oxford and Cambridge, and a host of other educational agencies of which we shall speak in their place, we cannot doubt that the educational development of this period is as much the salient feature of the times as nationalism was of that which preceded it. Not only the Gladstonian reforms, but the Beaconsfieldian 'Peace with Honour' which shortly afterwards followed, pale in importance before a movement which was to gain for every citizen a minimum of instruction, and the possibility of more, just as the United States had decided that the basis of their democracy would not be sound unless equal civic and political rights were secured for every citizen whatever his race.

Both movements sprang from principles long since preached by the men of the Revolution, and human dignity, and even religion, were at stake in both. In both, men differed keenly as to the extent to which the State should intervene to attain the end desired, and in both the State found itself at last compelled to do the work, and has been greatly strengthened by doing it.

This however is but one aspect of the educational movement, closely allied with the simultaneous extension of equal education to women. We shall see, as we go on, that the spread of education brings into view again several other aspects of nineteenth century development which we have touched on. It involves the growing realization of that desire for a fuller life for all, which became prominent towards the end of the eighteenth century, and it also introduces into the training of the young the vast stores of new knowledge in science and in history which the awakened mind of the Renaissance had begun to build up. Lastly, it points the way at its highest levels to a new and more permanent basis for internationalism and human unity than the mediaeval discipline had been able to afford.

Of all the eighteenth-century philosophers, Adam Smith perhaps gives the best argument for State elementary education, with that combination of enlightenment and practical wisdom so characteristic of him.

' A man ', he says,[1] ' without the proper use of the intellectual faculties of a man is, if possible, more contemptible than even a coward, and seems to be mutilated and deformed in a still more essential part of the character of human nature. Though

---

[1] *Wealth of Nations*, Book v, c. i.

the State was to derive no advantage from the instruction of the inferior ranks of the people, it would still deserve its attention that they should not be altogether uninstructed. The State, however, derives no inconsiderable advantage from their instruction. . . . An instructed and intelligent people are always more decent and orderly than a stupid one. They feel themselves, each individually, more respectable and more likely to obtain the respect of their lawful superiors. . . . They are disposed to examine, and are more capable of seeing through, the interested complaints of faction and sedition, and they are, upon that account, less apt to be misled into any wanton or unnecessary opposition to the measures of government. In free countries, where the safety of government depends very much upon the favourable judgement which the people may form of its conduct, it must surely be of the highest importance that they should not be disposed to judge rashly or capriciously concerning it.'

Hence he concludes that the State should make elementary education compulsory and a public charge, though recommending also fees and voluntary contributions.

Of course it was a Scotchman who said that, and the Scotch had had universal parish schools since the end of the sixteenth century. But it will be nearer the truth to regard Adam Smith's advice as representing the best opinion of advanced Western Europe in his time, when it was at last recovering from the disruption of the Church in the sixteenth century and beginning to think out afresh the right relations of the spiritual and temporal sides of man's life, the Church and State of the future. For here in education was the crucial point. In the Middle Ages, in Catholic times, education had been universally regarded as the business of the Church. Schools were attached to cathedrals and monasteries, and thus, a little later in England, were to be found ' in every village marked with little spire, embowered in trees and hardly known to fame '. Now the time had come when the State began to recognize that a minimum of instruction was a public concern, above all if government was to be carried on at the behest or with the intelligent consent of the whole body of the people. The industrial revolution made the matter urgent. The mass of the workers were no longer living embowered in trees and near the little spire. They were camped round the pit-head and the factory-chimney, in long rows of mean and monotonous dwellings, too far off and too many for the ministrations, bodily or spiritual, of squire or parson. There was indeed no lack of philanthropic effort. The scattered Sunday Schools, which had been going on for many years in various places, were in the last years of the eighteenth century enormously increased and improved, mainly through the work of Robert Raikes at Gloucester. 'Schools of Industry' were started with the special object of training poor children to be able to earn a wage ; and in the first decade of the nineteenth century Bell and Lancaster founded, with voluntary support, schools on the monitorial system, where large numbers might be taught at small expense by means of other children a little older than themselves.

But all these efforts, valuable as evidence of the need and of a genuine desire to satisfy it, were far too limited in scope, and still more in driving-power, to meet the case. From the beginning of the nineteenth century onwards, Bills were introduced into Parliament to make the provision of elementary schools a public charge. There was the bill of 1802 on the Health and Morals of Apprentices, imposing some slight obligation on employers in the matter of instructing young people whom they employed. Then came Mr. Whitbread's Bill of 1807, the first which sought to make elementary education a public charge. He based his measure on the principle that education was at the root of any plan of Poor Law legislation. He was encouraged by the belief, which Bell and Lancaster had fostered, that an admirable system of education could be established at a cost of about five shillings a head per annum.

He proposed a scheme of two years' free schooling for all poor children between seven and fourteen years of age, to be provided by the vestries or the magistrates, who might levy a rate not exceeding a shilling in the pound. The Bill passed the Commons but was rejected by the Lords; and though Brougham tried again in 1820, and Roebuck immediately after the Reform Act, no Bill was passed until 1870.

But a good deal was done, as we shall see in a moment, without the passing of any Act. In those early days, when the first stirrings of educational activity began in England and a great many schools were started by voluntary effort, the first Napoleon was in power in France, and laying his strong hand on education as on all other factors of the national life. As in law, so in education, Napoleon succeeded to the generous and magnificent schemes of the Convention. Now in education Condorcet had been the moving spirit. He had carried a scheme for complete national education in primary, secondary, and advanced schools, but his death, and war abroad and dissension at home, had prevented its being carried out. Before the end of the eighteenth century Napoleon had gained absolute power as First Consul. In 1802 an Education Act was passed improving the secondary schools or ' lycées ', and in 1808 another Act constituting a new University of France in seventeen Academies all directed from Paris. The contrast with contemporary England is most striking and instructive. We were fumbling away, it is true, with divided counsels, and slow to act. The fervour of the Convention, the master-mind of Napoleon, could strike out a plan, complete from top to bottom, at a sitting. But we were fumbling at the right end of the plant, digging about the roots, and in the right spirit for any one who would work at education, the spirit of the gardener and not of the architect.

Elementary education in Napoleon's plan was, as a matter of

fact, neglected, for the schools were handed over to the communes and left to languish without compulsion or support. By 1806 there were only 25,000 scholars attending all the public primary schools of France, while we had some hundreds of thousands as the result of voluntary effort. And the difference in results corresponds to a certain difference in aims. In our first strivings for public education, philanthropy was the chief motive—the care and salvation of the poor. The rich could look after themselves, and who would have dreamt— except as a nightmare—of a University of Great Britain in seventeen Academies ? To Napoleon, and more or less to France and Germany throughout the century, the leading object in public education was the formation of opinion, the training of an *élite* to carry out the purposes of the Government ; and for this end, organization from the top was the obvious means.

Just at the time when the man whom his contemporaries called Great was essaying the conquest of the world by arms, another man, poor, struggling, devoted, and inspired, was carrying on in obscurity a work of social amelioration which posterity has acclaimed as one of the best deeds of the revolutionary age, a model to all time. Once their two orbits came in contact, and the result is an immortal story. Pestalozzi, a German-speaking Swiss, born at Zurich in 1746, was consumed from his earliest years with the desire to elevate the being and improve the lot of his poorest fellow-creatures by an elementary training based on affection and work. At the age of twenty-eight he began to receive in his house at Neuhof the neglected children of the neighbourhood. He taught them to work on the farm, and in bad weather to spin and to read and write indoors. He and his wife were their father and mother, and in a few months the children were transformed by the régime of love and care, simple living and interesting activity. The fame of the experiment spread abroad, and many more children could have been received in his home had Pestalozzi's resources sufficed. But his powers of managing his little farm were not equal to his powers of educating its inmates. After six years of exhausting labour he abandoned Neuhof for financial reasons, and for the next few years devoted himself to writing about his projects and his methods, which continued to develop on the side of educational theory. In 1798 the French invaded Switzerland in support of the revolutionary party which they had established in power. The town of Stans in the Unterwald was besieged and ruined by the invading troops, and Pestalozzi again became the head of a training institution for the orphans who had escaped from the disaster. This time it was with the support and authority of the Government of the canton. In 1802 he was appointed one of a deputation to meet in Paris and settle with Napoleon the future government of the united cantons. To him education was the first public interest, and he sought as soon as possible an audience with the First Consul. Napoleon sent back word that he had something else to do than discuss questions of A B C. Monge, the mathematician, to whom Pestalozzi was referred, heard him patiently and intelligently, but replied that the proposals ' were too much for them '. One's mind goes on two years to another interview, which Mr. Maclure, from the United States, secured with Napoleon and Talleyrand on a similar errand. After Maclure had explained his work in America, which was of a similar kind to Pestalozzi's in Switzerland, he heard Talleyrand remark to his master, ' It is doing too much for the common people.'

It is refreshing to remember that Pestalozzi's humour and confidence triumphed over his rebuff. On his return to Switzerland he was asked if he had succeeded in seeing Napoleon. ' No,' said Pestalozzi, ' and he did not see me either.'

For France the rejection of Pestalozzi's ideas was a temporary disaster : they have had in later years to make good the neglect of fundamental education for which Napoleon was responsible. Prussia, on the other hand, adopted Pestalozzi, and the revival of the national spirit after Jena is largely due to the care they began then to pay to the education of all. Froebel, too, carried them still further on the true lines, which had been inculcated by many great Germans of an earlier generation. But in later years they have gone through the converse process to that of France, turning away from the fullness and freedom of Pestalozzi and Froebel, and concentrating on the controlled education of the governing class which was the Napoleonic ideal.

England moved on, slowly and tentatively, but on the whole in the right direction. We saw in Chapter II that the Reform Bill of 1832 acted as a strong stimulus to reform of all kinds ; it was in fact the *sacramentum*, or binding oath, which held together for a time the various groups of early reformers. Education, therefore, shared in the general flood-tide. In the first session of the reformed Parliament, in 1833, Mr. Roebuck brought in a motion pledging the House to establish a universal and national system of education for the whole people. His scheme went farther than any educational reformer had yet ventured to go in Parliament. He would have had compulsory attendance for all children between six and twelve, the establishment in every village of at least one infant school and one school of industry, and in towns evening continuation schools for young people over fourteen. The curriculum was to be liberal ; a general as well as a practical education was in his mind. Normal schools were to be opened for schoolmasters. The whole system was to be administered by locally elected committees in school districts formed *ad hoc*, acting under a Cabinet Minister and supported mainly by taxes. It was indeed a fuller scheme than anything we have attempted before Mr. Fisher's Bill of 1917. But it suffered unfortunately from the defect which Monge reported to Napoleon of Pestalozzi, '*C'était trop pour nous*'; it did not even reach the stage of a Bill. But the Government to show their goodwill replied with a grant of £20,000 for the erection of school-buildings. A cynic has pointed out that the estimates for the same year contained an item of £50,000 for rebuilding the royal stables.

The £20,000, however, though less than half what was wanted for really good stables, was far-reaching in its effects. It was followed, two years after the accession of Queen Victoria, on April 10, 1839, by a Government minute establishing a Committee of the Privy Council, with a permanent secretary and inspectors, to supervise the expenditure of public money voted for education. By this side-wind a ministry of education was brought into port in England at the very moment when the country as a whole was protesting loudly against the idea of a state-controlled system. What was the basis of this opposition? It was not confined to the supporters of the old idea that education was the business of the Church. Indeed, in the 'forties the strongest opposition came from those, mainly Nonconformists, who under the name of 'voluntaryists' banded themselves together for 'educational free-trade' and declared that state action in education was immoral.

The motives of this movement were, like nearly all motives, mixed, but a strong element of truth was mingled with the disputable and disreputable elements of party feeling and obstruction. There was the well-grounded apprehension that every extension of state support would be largely to the advantage of the Established Church. The Church held the field. It was the Church which had its buildings embowered in trees beside the village spire. If other religious parties were to contend for the nation's soul on equal terms, they must be prepared for a vast effort, beyond their powers if not beyond their wishes ; and, when it was completed, the field of effort would be encumbered by a crowd of competing agencies, doing badly at great expense what one good broad-minded institution might do well at half the cost. That is the practical root of the ' religious difficulty ', which in one form or another raged and hindered progress down to Mr. Balfour's Act of 1902 and later. But, beyond this, the ' voluntaryists ' had a glimpse behind the practical difficulties of a real and profound truth, which even to the present day the Western world has not fully grasped. They were right in holding that the State, though its inter- vention might in certain circumstances be necessary in matters of religion as well as of education, was not the aspect of com- munity life which naturally turns to things of the spirit, that the State cannot rightly touch these deepest springs of our being if it would, and that, if it tries to form them, they wither and grow misshapen by the act. Napoleon at one end of the century and Germany at the other are proof clear enough.

It is not perhaps surprising that with these lions in the path the Government of England was nearly forty years, after the first Reform Bill, picking its way to the first Education Act of 1870. In what was done, both before and after that date, the two leading political parties both take a share. Of the principal measures up to the present time, the first was passed in 1870 by a Liberal, the second in 1902 by a Conservative Government, and the third in 1918 by a coalition.

Matthew Arnold, who as a school-inspector suffered for many years under the Revised Code of 1862, looked back to the minute of 1847 as a golden age. This increased the grant and employed the new money to encourage the appointment of pupil teachers and to give pensions and better salaries to qualified teachers. It left the inspector free to test the efficiency of the school and to promote intelligent methods by the means he judged best. The Revised Code—the code of 'payment by results'—was passed by a Liberal Government in an illiberal mood. It subjected the schools to a narrow and mechanical examination, limited the subjects of instruction, and actually succeeded in reducing for a time the State grant for education, although the population was then growing much more rapidly than at present. This instrument of repression and commercialized education was in force, with modifications, for over thirty years. One cannot forbear to connect with it that national indifference to great public issues which we noticed in the last chapter. A spirit of greater breadth and more generosity in our national system of education at that time might, one feels, have done much to enlarge the public mind and amend the poor taste in popular art and literature, the want of intellectual interest, all the evils in fact which many critics have found inherent in a democratic age, but which really belong to a democratic education not carried far enough.

But though the work was sadly limited in depth, it was constantly spread out in wider circles. The new science of statistics came into operation. Of Carlyle's two bugbears in dealing with social questions—logic and statistics—this question of national education was clearly not amenable to logic. Statistics, however, continued, as the century went on, to exercise a more and more decisive influence. The first census was taken in the first year of the nineteenth century, in 1801. It was followed by an unbroken series of commissions and inquiries, always fortified by figures, as to the state of the public in health, wealth, and wisdom. Many of these dealt with education. There was a commission, under the Duke of Newcastle, in 1858, on the education of the 'labouring classes': this unfortunately led to Mr. Lowe's Revised Code of 1862. There was a commission on secondary schools in 1865 : this led to the Endowed Schools Act of 1869. In 1850 and again in 1877 commissions were appointed to consider reforms at Oxford and Cambridge. This was the last time, up to our own day, that the State has dealt with our old seats of learning.

The new era of exact and scientific inquiry into social facts had begun to fructify, and the Education Act of 1870 was its most important crop. It was of all our social reforms the least logical in its basis, but the most conclusively dictated by facts and figures. Logically it was a compromise, in the true British spirit, between the views of the National Education Union, centred at Manchester and aiming at denominational schools, with which Mr. Gladstone sympathized, and those of the Birmingham Education League, representing the secular and undenominational parties, which counted Mr. Chamberlain among its supporters. The statistical arguments were overwhelming. The Newcastle Commission had found the attendance even at the inspected schools very irregular, including a mere fraction of all the children over eleven years of age. They concluded that only about one in eight of the whole population was receiving some sort of schooling instead of the one in five which should on a moderate computation be doing so.

The new Reform Bill, passed in 1867 by a compromise between the parties, had brought the question to a head. The democracy had now begun in earnest ; the workmen in the towns had received a vote. And just as the first Reform Act had inspired Mr. Roebuck to his ineffectual efforts, so the second Bill spurred on Mr. Gladstone who came into power in 1868.

But though the State had done little for education in the interval, progress had been made, and many millions spent, especially by the Church of England, in building and maintaining schools. Mr. Forster, on introducing his Bill, was faced by a field imperfectly tilled but very largely pegged out for occupation. Neither he nor his chief wished for a moment to enter on a process of expropriation. They desired to make good deficiencies without destruction or revolution. On the statistical side Mr. Forster gave an even more gloomy view than the Newcastle commissioners. He estimated that there were only two-fifths of the working-class children between six and seven years of age at school, and only one-third of those between ten and twelve. An inquiry of the year before had discovered that only a third of the children in Liverpool between five and thirteen ever entered a school at all. The remedy of the Bill consisted in establishing new education authorities without disturbing existing schools. School districts were to be created all over the country and the deficiency of school accommodation to be discovered. If, after a reasonable interval, no voluntary agency offered to provide the schools required, a school board was to be set up, with power to build and maintain the schools out of the rates and to compel the attendance of all children between five and twelve years of age. Though towards the State, in matters of grant, curriculum, and inspection, the two classes of school—the new board schools and the old voluntary schools—were to be alike, locally, of course, a difference and a rivalry were set up which lasted long and is not yet extinct, even after the Act of 1902 has put both classes of schools on the rates. The distinction has always subsisted that in the rate-provided schools no ' distinctive formularies ' of religion were to be taught, while even in the latest Act the appointment of teachers in the non-provided schools is still reserved to the representatives of the religious body which built the school.

Such was the compromise, as sound on the political side, in spite of the incessant attacks which it provoked, as the Revised Code of 1862 was unsound on the educational side. It has stood the storm, and in 1876, when there were schools for all to go to, an amending Act was passed making compulsory attendance the law of the land.

Thirty years elapsed before the next great attempt was made to deal with elementary education, this time by a Conservative Government. The interval gives evidence enough for a judgement, so far as one can judge at all in so complicated a matter, as to the right direction and success of the policy. The working indeed of all social causes is so intricate and obscure that one will always have some sympathy with the outbursts of men like Cobbett who denounced Brougham and the 'education canters' in 1825 for shifting the causes of crime and evil on to the wrong shoulders. It was food and clothes and a decent life that the people needed, and then morality and education would look after themselves. The educational politicians 'attempt to prevent the evils of the deadly ivy by cropping off, or rather bruising a little, a few of its leaves. They do not assail even its branches, while they appear to look upon the trunk as something too sacred even to be looked at with vulgar eyes.' There is some illumination, though a fitful one, even in Cobbett's jets of liquid fire. The answer, which this book suggests, lies in the convergence which may be traced between reforming efforts on various sides of the social being, all needed and some tardier than others. It seemed to Brougham and the Whigs, as indeed to Mr. Gladstone in 1870, wiser and more practicable to deal first with objects remoter from men's daily action but nearer to the action of the political machine. Franchise, church establishments, school authorities, are such things. Wages, pensions, houses, and public health belong to a later stage of social reform. But it is open to the 'educational canter' to give a good *prima facie* answer to Cobbett and his school. On the figures, there were in 1865 scarcely more than a million children in average attendance at inspected schools. After ten years of school boards this was increased in 1881 to nearly four millions. Meanwhile the criminal convictions went down from nearly twenty thousand in the 'sixties to sixteen and a half thousand in the 'seventies, in spite of a large increase in the population.

But in such inquiries the broader the answer the better. What was the dominant object of the men of 1870 who passed the Education Act ? To give all the citizens of the State, which had just extended its civic rights, that minimum possession of the instruments of knowledge which would enable them in later life to enlarge their knowledge and to act intelligently as the political guardians of the commonwealth. If this was so, it has succeeded, conspicuously on the political side. The enfranchised millions of the last forty years have been in no sense inferior to the few thousand voters who shouted at the hustings in the earlier part of the century. On the great issues which have come up for decision in recent times—protection for native races, avoidance of slavery, self-government for Ireland, India, and the colonies, agreement with France, resistance to German lawlessness and aggression, the extension of education—they have given the right answer, often with less hesitation than the wealthier classes. The social and political advance which is probably traceable to the Education Act seems in fact less disputable than its more strictly intellectual results on the national mind. Nor can one be surprised at this balanced judgement when we remember that all the earlier years of the great experiment were passed under the influence of a system deadening both to teachers and taught, the system of a narrow mechanical test of the attainments of the scholars on which all the Government assistance to the schools was assessed. There we can see English commercialism and want of belief in knowledge and ideas. But on the side of social order and general morals the effect of the schools was all to the good. The mere facts, that within a few years the Government test was being administered to every youngster in the kingdom from the age of seven to eleven or twelve, and that the parents actually paid fees for twenty-one years for the schooling which they could not escape, these things are a triumph for British tolerance and business habits. Side by side with the spread of elementary education has come a vast extension of working-class self-government in trade unions, co-operative societies, friendly societies, and other bodies, in which the habits of discipline and mutual aid learnt at school have found a field for exercise.

Perhaps the strongest testimony to the spirit which the people's schools have inculcated since 1870 came in 1914, a century after Waterloo and nearly half a century since schooling was compulsory. The men of Britain were asked to defend with their lives the nation's cause, which was also the cause of freedom, progress, and international right. In less than two years over three million had joined the colours. Patriotism, therefore, was not in default.

That century since Waterloo has seen indeed few greater changes than in the attitude of all civilized nations towards popular education. The Acts passed in England in the 'seventies were but an acceleration of a process which had begun at the Revolution and which neither Napoleon nor any other reactionary could hinder long. Take as a typical example the action of our Government in the War in the matter of educating soldiers, the classes arranged for them before they go, the Y.M.C.A. hut with all its activities, the stream of lecturers, the supply of books ; and think what the great Duke would have said to any one who had proposed to organize courses on history and social science for the lines at Torres Vedras !

But it would be, of course, a gross fallacy to identify what the State has done in elementary education with the education of the nation as a whole. There were schools before Bell and

Lancaster, and an education wider than any schools. The work done in higher places, more than the efforts of the stray village school, was the dominant factor before the State began in 1833. And in these higher reaches also the State began to use its powers. There was a great stirring from the middle of the last century and especially in the 'seventies.

In higher education, as in social order and in ideals of justice and public welfare, there was a low ebb-tide in England at the beginning of the century. The old mediaeval discipline was then most completely exhausted : the new motive-powers had not come into play. The Revolution abroad which contained the new forces in germ was to us, as a nation, a thing to shun, a portent which in Napoleon—its most fearful birth—we had fought and crushed. And we had allowed the things of the mind to suffer a worse reaction than matters of public justice and international right. In the liberation of nations during the early nineteenth century we might claim a leading share, but in the liberation of our own minds we had to bear the just reproaches of one of our own prophets of education : 'Our middle classes are the worst educated in the world . . . our body of secondary schools the most imperfect and unserviceable in civilized Europe' (M. Arnold). It has been estimated that the condition of our 'public' or higher schools was worse between 1750 and 1840 than at any time since King Alfred. The grammar schools were largely derelict, often scandalous. Sometimes for half a century or more only half a dozen boys might have attended the school at some large centre of population. In 1734 there were no boys at all in the Birmingham school. From 1832 to 1836 one boy at Chesterfield made up the school. A do-nothing clerical master, sometimes absentee, absorbed what endowment there was. The master of Berkhamsted School in 1835 lived in Derbyshire and took the endowment, while the school was entirely empty.

Brougham's Commission of 1818 began the work of regeneration in this sphere. Suits in Chancery and private Acts of Parliament followed to recover the endowments, and in the 'sixties two commissions sat on Public and Endowed Schools. An Act was passed on Endowed Schools in 1869, just a year before the great Act on elementary education, so that the two main branches of education below the university came under state review at about the same time. The Endowed Schools Act enabled a permanent body of commissioners to frame new schemes for old endowments, securing a better educational use of them, and in numerous cases the commissioners were able to carve out a new school for girls. These commissioners were, in 1874, merged in the general Charity Commission which had been in existence since the middle of the century; and at the end of the century their functions were taken over by a Board of Education.

The tendency to unify all branches of education and put them under some sort of central direction by the State is thus clear enough. But it is equally important, and in some ways more significant, to note the differences in the development of the different grades of schools. The extension of primary instruction over the whole population was at the fiat of the State. Local authorities were compelled by law to provide schools, and parents were compelled by law to send their children to them and to pay a fee for the privilege. But the national movement towards a better education was far wider than this legal obligation. The increase in the number of the pupils attending higher schools was at least as large in proportion as that of those attending the elementary schools provided by statute. To take one instance which we have mentioned already and which is typical of hundreds. The Berkhamsted school, founded early in the sixteenth century, had been allowed in the early nineteenth century to become derelict.

By the end of the century it had been revived through personal energy and initiative and grown to over four hundred scholars.

But in this new life for higher schools the State did not at first aspire to more than the position of a legal guardian. It sought to secure that money left for education was expended for that purpose, after making allowance for the changes which had come about in the conditions of the bequest. All the rest—the growth of pupils, the change of subjects, the admission of girls—was the free expression of a new attitude in the public mind.

The education of women is one of the leading strains in this new spirit, near akin, as we noticed, to the democratic instinct which freed the slaves and gave us universal primary schools. There had been learned women before Girton. Elizabeth could argue on theology with her bishops and cap quotations with her ambassadors. But it was an exceptional and privileged thing, not dreamt of, by any one out of Utopia, for every woman as for every man. The elementary school was a weighty factor in producing the change. From the first no one had thought of making any fundamental difference in primary education between a boy and a girl. The girls had a large dose of needle-work, very large in the old-fashioned schools ; but for the rest they learnt all that the boys did. It was one of many cases where reforms have spread upwards, for while in the primary school girls were being taught in much the same way as their brothers, among the wealthier classes the sharpest contrast pre-vailed. The girls were conning Mannall's 'Questions' and learning a little French and music while the boys were studying classics and mathematics and winning battles on the playing-fields. By the end of the century the change had come. Before the background of the early Victorian boarding-school, pictured for all time by Charlotte Brontë, there now stand resplendent the women of Meredith.

There was thus a national movement in education, more, indeed, than national, which we may trace back to the later eighteenth century, and which began to flow quickly about the middle of the nineteenth. The State provision and enforcement of primary education was one part of it; the increased desire for higher instruction, especially for women, is another, the spread of universities a third. The area of national power and enlightenment was being immeasurably enlarged in all Western countries, and the process was soon to be taken up in the East—by Japan in the 'eighties. For us the general movement turns round that date at the beginning of the 'seventies when the State determined to secure a minimum of instruction for every one. Girton was founded in 1869, the year of the Endowed Schools Act, the year before the Elementary School Act. The women's colleges at Oxford came ten years later, Newnham in 1880. The University Extension at Cambridge started in 1872. The Yorkshire College at Leeds, which became one of the constituents of the Victoria University, was founded in 1874. The University itself, embracing Manchester, Liverpool, and Leeds, received its charter in 1880.

A hundred years after Waterloo Great Britain had sixteen universities instead of six, and the old ones were all attracting much larger numbers of students. Oxford and Cambridge were themselves largely remodelled by the two commissions of 1850 and 1877.

A new desire to attain a higher general level of education was beginning to run through the nation : it was part of the larger impulse to secure a fuller life for all. Frederick Denison Maurice excellently typifies this spirit, both in its more general aspect and in its bearing on education, and his death in 1872 falls within our present decade. He was consumed with zeal for social reform, at one with Carlyle that the ' Condition of England ' was the greatest of national questions, and at the same time he left his mark permanently in the foundation of two places for higher education—one for women and another for working-men. Queen's College in London anticipated the Oxford and Cambridge colleges for women; it was founded in 1848. And the Working Men's College in Great Ormond Street, founded in 1854, was the pioneer in the movement which we recognize in our own time in the Workers' Educational Association and the mass of similar bodies now active all over the country.

The streams are abundant and grow in volume, and it is stimulating to note that they have a common fountain-head in the passion for general social reform which first appeared clearly in the reformers of the latter eighteenth century. This resumed its steady flow after the set-backs of Napoleonic ambitions and national unrest; and it is nearly always the same men who are active both for social progress and for education. But education to these men is no longer limited to the Platonic ideal of a complete and scientific training for a small class, the 'guardians' of the Republic, or the knightly training of Vittorino da Feltre or of Milton for an *élite*. Education in this new age, to those who care most about it, is for every man, and though every man may not be able to carry his education to the limits of his powers, yet there should be opportunities for all; and there is a growing feeling, shown by such men as Maurice, Ruskin, T. H. Green, Arnold Toynbee—the new generation on which we enter after the middle of the nineteenth century—that the highest education, like all other great gifts or social advantages, should be held by its beneficiaries as a trust for the welfare of all. The further bearings of this new spirit will occupy us in the next chapter.

But there are some other points about the educational movement which link it up with the general movement of thought and action, and which must be noticed here before we pass on. In each case England, so early in the field with her Sunday schools and schools of industry, and taking, as we saw, a wise, if somewhat dilatory, line with her primary schools, has been behindhand compared with her fellow nations of the West where the higher and systematic training of the mind was involved.

We have seen that the nineteenth century witnessed the greatest extension of scientific thought, the greatest transformation of industry by mechanical science that has ever been. These must have had some reaction on education, but when we come to trace it we shall be surprised that so great changes in the world at large were so slow and slight in their influence on the school-world within.

It may be best to take first the transformation of industry. Before the Industrial Revolution the training of the worker was an individual or at most a sectional concern. The young man was either brought up to his craft in his father's house or apprenticed to another craftsman for a term of years. There were, of course, rules as to apprenticeship enforced by the different crafts themselves on their would-be members, but the State did not regard it as part of its duty to see that its citizens were properly trained for the work of their lives. The young farmer learnt from his farming kin, the smith in his father's forge, the statesman from families in the public service. The industrial revolution upset this old traditional system by two great changes. In the first place there was the huge call for raw ' hands ', and the new labour was massed in factory-barracks, tending machines instead of practising a craft. And in the second place the increasing discoveries of science far outstripped the teaching powers of any individual craftsman. The work of training for industry on scientific lines became infinitely complex and costly, and every modern state has found it necessary to take a large share both in the control and the financing of it. England, pioneer in the industrial revolution and co-pioneer in founding the sciences which were to guide it, was the last of the nations to recognize the need of national effort in technical education or indeed of any technical education at all. Factories and *laisser-faire* had broken down apprenticeship ; and, for the rest, let every man learn by doing what he can, and God save us all. This was our earlier mind.

In this matter the French led the world, and the fineness of their technique and the thoroughness of their application of thought to the details of production are still hard to match. The greatest of Encyclopaedias—the contribution of Diderot and the philosophers to the Revolution—is also the first of technical dictionaries. It is at its best in describing the methods of manufacturing, from gunpowder to gossamer. And the French have lived up to this high standard, and their central schools of art and manufacture in Paris are the oldest and among the best. But it was the example of successful Germany which stirred us from our mental sloth. France had been first in the practical arts, but Germany had learnt the lesson to most purpose. Her armies of 1870 marched to the measures of organizing mind. The same thoroughness and power of combining details was being applied to other arts as well as war, and Charlottenburg was soon to become a sign of wonder and of imitation to the world. The time was coming when every barber's boy in the great cities of the *Reich* was to attend technical classes in the hairdresser's art.

But the Prussian victories began at once to have their reaction abroad. In 1877 the Livery Companies of London, mindful of their ancient origin from the crafts, took into counsel leading manufacturers and men of science, and founded an Institute for the promotion of technical education. It was opened at

South Kensington in 1880. Charlottenburg thus had its
replica on the banks of the Thames, and our decade of the
'seventies saw blossoms on all the branches of public education.

But the largest change remains. The transfusion of all
departments of education by the new spirit of science and the
linking-up of science with other aspects of life and learning
were long processes of which we have not yet seen the full
results or even the full effort. For this involves a profound
mental transformation, and not merely the organization of
institutes or the application of new methods to old arts. The
same period, however, gives clear evidence of what was to come.
The seeds sown for three hundred years, from Galileo to Darwin,
had a first harvest in the material world of industrial science: the
time had now come for their deeper penetration into mental
habits, views of religion, and methods of education. Herbert
Spencer's treatise on *Education*, published in 1863, four years
after the *Origin of Species*, was the manifesto of the new faith.

It is curious to reflect that the cause of science in education
seems, somehow, bound up with success in war. In 1871 the
triumph of Prussia made other nations determine to improve
the organization of their schools : science was the one thing
needed. It was the gospel of the dominant school of philosophers, but had not yet penetrated into the schools of the
young. Then Huxley took his seat on the first School Board for
London, and South Kensington began to examine in Science and
Art. Unfortunately, with our national leaning to patchwork—a
useful habit in governing an empire—we proceeded to cultivate
science by adding on little wings and bays to our system
instead of thinking out the whole problem in the new light.
Elementary schools were allowed their ' specific subjects '—
a little algebra or mechanics or physiology—on which an extra
shilling or two might be earned in grant. Teachers were
allowed their ' science certificates ' on which a pound or two

more might be earned as salary. And the more enterprising Public Schools set up their 'Science Sides' in which boys not quite up to the classical standard might be qualified to improve their chances in a 'practical' life. Thus the first reflection of the new light on the actual world of schooling was scanty and broken; but it was a ray of the coming light all the same.

To follow the leading of this new guide and to discuss its bearing on the other and older parts of the curriculum would take us far beyond the scope of this chapter. But one reflection is suggested by an historical survey of the whole subject, and points onwards to what we shall have to say in a later chapter on international relations. The subject-matter of education in the ancient world was predominantly military and civic. Beside the elements of language and calculation, the old Greek and Roman boy was taught the heroic legends of his mother city, and urged to imitate them; and such religious practices and beliefs as he acquired were similarly derived from the tribal tradition and clung round persons and places in the ancestral story. Even the unity of the Roman Empire made no great change in this spiritual heritage. But Christianity cut deeper, and in the mediaeval system we see the first appearance of a universal element in the matter of education. Other subjects, the grammar and rhetoric of the trivium and quadrivium, were but the antechamber to the supreme subject, the knowledge of God and of His scheme of salvation for man, entrusted to the Church. This was the first spiritual unification of mankind, and up to the present, in spite of all schisms and shortcomings, incomparably the most effective. Then with the Renaissance came for a time, so far as unity went, a falling back. The Divine science of the schoolmen seemed no longer of unbroken texture, and a new form of national training began to press it into the background. The old classical languages entered the service of the new nations which were dividing the Roman and mediaeval unity. Cicero and Plutarch spoke again through the mouths of Milton and Vittorino. But beneath the superficial conflict there was growing from the seventeenth century onwards another method and another matter, the science of Bacon and Descartes, which by the end of the nineteenth century we can see is destined to become the binding force of a stronger international unity.

We shall try in the next chapter to point out how the first negative or anti-religious turn of this development of science was gradually overcome. Just as the pagan deities and legends had seemed to the early Christians to be demons and the work of demons, so, in the first outburst of the critical and scientific spirit, old beliefs and institutions were hotly attacked and desperately defended. But as time goes on, and passions sink and wisdom mellows, it is seen that science in the true sense is not a destroyer, either of life or thought, but a builder-up. Old beliefs are explained, and take their place, in so far as they fortify the human mind, in one vast body of growing and healing knowledge. The idea of evolution comes in to reconcile contradictions and partial views, which seem irreconcilable if we arrest them sharply at each moment of their development. History completes science, and shows it to be as social in its nature and ultimate working as it was in its origin.

Now when, from this point of view, we consider the recent development of education in the most civilized countries of the world, we shall find most significance in the growing community of thought at the highest levels. The learned Societies and the Universities of the world have been acquiring habits of co-operation more and more rapidly with the spread of science, and it would never occur to any professor, either on the physical or biological side, to allow the passions of a national conflict, whether just or blinded, to bias him for a moment in judging of a new hypothesis or criticism. Here we all are, and must be, at one, and on these lines it would seem that science is leading us through our places of education and research into a new unity of thought which will have more permanence than the mediaeval system.

And though the time may be distant when either the nations will be all at peace, or when fuller knowledge shall have reconciled our conflicting theories in history and the human sciences, yet for the educated man there is at once a sure resting-place and an infinite joy. He stands on a solid rock of truth achieved, and he looks out on the growing light of a clearing sky. He lives in the past with those whose minds have built up the high common platform where he stands : he lives in the future with those who will rest on him and make him, too, a part of themselves.

IX

RELIGIOUS GROWTH

DIFFICULT as the task must seem, it would be a fatal mutilation of our subject to avoid some reference to the influence of the other changes in thought and life on the religious mind of the West. Education, science, social reform, all bring us to the threshold of this subject, and we cannot refuse to look in, however short the glance must be, however perplexing and elusive the forms we discern. Moreover, this stage in our story seems the inevitable point, for in the 'seventies Mill had left us, and in the next decade Carlyle, Darwin, T. H. Green, Pusey, Newman, Matthew Arnold, Browning, Emerson, all died, all men of the first importance in framing a new religious outlook, especially in England. A whole generation of formative minds was being gathered in to that great host who rule us from the tomb.

The attentive reader will already have noticed that in the very title of this chapter, and in its first paragraph, a theory is implied which, though perhaps now of general acceptance, would not always have been accepted, and is itself an offspring of the age. To say that religion grows and changes, to include among religious influences names as far apart as Darwin and Pusey, Browning and Newman, attests in itself the force of evolutionary thought. One could not have written so in the mid-eighteenth century, and now one could hardly write otherwise.

But some definition is essential, however rough and tentative, of the subject-matter of this growth. By 'religion', then, we mean, for the purpose of this chapter, the submission, or the accord, of the individual will to what is recognized as the Highest in the world. Perhaps this definition may be found to include everything claiming to be religious, and in any case it will give us some guidance in our quest. It spreads the net wide indeed, but how can we refuse the name of religion to such a temper of devotion ?

Starting from this point we may see at once that certain important conclusions follow. We have seen in the case of the other great concepts with which we have dealt—freedom, science, education, and the rest—that they take on a fuller meaning as we advance in history, and above all in the last hundred years. It is the same with religion. For if it involves the recognition of some Highest thing to which we owe allegiance and with which we should seek to be in accord, then clearly this Highest thing will advance and become fuller and nobler—at least in our consciousness of it—as our own minds rise and expand. Hence we gain the conception of an evolution of religion as part of the general evolution of man ; and the evolution of man is a leading idea, perhaps the leading idea, in the century we are studying.

There is a famous story of Disraeli strolling into a Diocesan Conference at Oxford in 1864. The meeting, like all other religious bodies at that time, was debating the bearings of the Darwinian theory on religion. Were we to believe, the clergy asked, that man is descended from some lower animal type, or even, as some said, from a monkey ? Disraeli took up the challenge in a brilliant speech and declared that 'in answer to the question "Is man an ape or an angel ?" I, my Lord, am on the side of the angels.' But the pointed phrase can be turned against the orator. By all means let us be on the side of the angels, but let us remember that it is the doctrine of evolution which enables us, in the only sense worthy of man, to be on their side. If man was once an angel, and in the course of his descent had become the imperfect, vicious, and erring creature that we know, where would be the basis of our hope? But if, arising from a lower state, he has gradually put on the nobler features which we admire, if, erring as he is, he can be shown to have abandoned still worse errors, and, with wavering steps, to be treading an upward path, then we may claim, without denouncing Darwin, to be on the side of the angels. This is, of course, speaking generally, the point of view that was reached in the latter part of the nineteenth century, and it constitutes a profound change both in philosophy and religion. Turn to any text-book or encyclopaedia on the history of religion, and you will find a host of books referred to, all tracing the upward evolution of religion from simple or savage rites and beliefs to something purer, nobler, and more moral. The authors proceed by collecting examples from all the quarters of the globe, comparing them to find their common elements and their differences, and then go on to show how these primitive forms are gradually transformed, sublimated, and purified in the higher faiths. Examples are needless, for every one who has touched the subject, knows of dozens. All of them belong to the nineteenth century, most to the latter part of it, though there may be an occasional reference to some great anticipator such as Hume.

Now what are the results of this comparative, evolutionary method on the minds of those who look outside the borders of their own creed? Clearly it must be the recognition, in the words of Cardinal Newman, that ' there is something true and divinely revealed in every religion '. So far as the origins are alike in all forms of faith, so far as men have found guidance in any religion from a lower to a higher and more social form of thought and life, so far their practices and belief must be held to draw their inspiration from the same, or at least a kindred, Ideal. Such a position is now so generally held that it may seem almost an unnecessary commonplace to insist on it. But it is in point of fact a new conquest of the human spirit, one of the most signal triumphs of the nineteenth century. Here and there no doubt one may find some earlier thinker who cherished the glorious vision in his breast. So every great discovery has its anticipators. But it was not until the gradual widening process of modern thought set in, and especially towards the end of the eighteenth century, that the truth took solid shape, and became, as it now is, a beacon of hope to all mankind.

Look backward for a moment for assurance of the fact. To the Greek of classical times, foreign beliefs, like the language of the 'barbarous' outsider, were a thing apart, strange, inferior, and not understood. The Roman, with his genius for incorporation, extended a welcome to foreign cults, but it was as a political measure, with no comprehension of their inherent worth or final co-operating purpose. To the early Christian alien faiths were suspect, and often appeared as the work of hostile and infernal spirits. Those who saw them in this light were keen combatants for a new and all-precious thing which was to be justified by the speedy triumph of its believers here on earth. About the middle of the thirteenth century some intercourse began with non-Christian peoples in the East, and Christian missionaries returned with the report that there were other nations inspired apparently to good conduct by religious beliefs and canons different from their own. It was a stray gleam of the universalism which was to come, but the full light did not dawn till after the Renaissance. For with the Renaissance the old ideals of the classical world streamed in again on the West, and men learnt that some of the deepest thinkers and noblest spirits of the world had practised virtue and studied religion from another standpoint. So, even in the conflicts of the Reformation and its obscurity on the main religious problems, there come broad views like those of More in the *Utopia* or of Cromwell in his respect for the essentially good man. A little later the leading Frenchmen of the seventeenth century—Bossuet from an ecclesiastical platform, Pascal from the point of view of a philosopher—proclaimed the doctrine of a universal religious progress, and with the eighteenth century the rationalist thinkers of all Europe, Kant and Herder, Lessing and Goethe, Turgot and Condorcet, agreed in the same gospel. The nineteenth century, the age of historical criticism and of evolution, made good the conquest for all time.

It will have been noticed that most of the names selected are those of philosophers rather than of religious leaders in the ordinary sense. It is impossible in following such an inquiry as this to draw the line, and it is part of our object to show how the views of the philosophers pass over and influence the presentation of religious doctrines by their accredited professors. Newman has been mentioned as representing the greatest of the Churches adhering to the traditional forms, but any other Church would furnish similar evidence. The new spirit, which we are describing, is not the property of any new sect or school of thought, but universal to all thinking men, the reaction of the doctrine of evolution—conceived in its widest sense—on the religious sphere. Newman, ardent Catholic as he became, did not escape it, was in fact full of a deep consciousness of historical evolution. Who else, then, in the less closely-knit Churches, if he opened his mind at all, would be likely to escape? The new movement which Pusey championed, as well as the ancient Church to which Newman gave his adherence, were both deep-rooted in a sense of historical continuity, and the doctrine of development gave them both even more strength than it gave to the looser-knit and more dispersive organizations which arose at the Protestant Reformation.

The new sense, then, of historical continuity in religion and of the gradual evolution of the divine in man must be put among the greatest of the conquests of the nineteenth century. But so far we have considered it rather as the achievement of the thinkers and men of learning and without reference to the religious attitude of the average mind which may not have the opportunity, even if it has the power, for a profound study of the questions involved. It is clearly part of our subject, perhaps the most important part, to estimate the social effects of a change of thought, and later on in this chapter we shall attempt some summary of the recent religious changes as judged from their social and moral showings. But the popular attitude towards the theoretical question must be touched on here, when we have just been assuming that a certain progressive view as to religious truth was commonly accepted from the latter part of the nineteenth century. It is no doubt a minority who reflect seriously upon such questions. But of those who do, few would now question that the lapse of centuries had profoundly modified the meaning of the traditional creeds. So far as this is admitted, the legends of the faith, handed down from more credulous and savage days, are no longer what they were to the first believers. For them the stories of creation or the making of bloody sacrifices at the altar had a meaning and a suitability which they lose with the growth of knowledge and the softening of manners. To recognize this and to see at the same time that the earlier stage fits in to the immemorial process of upward growth, is to apply the principle of religious evolution in our own case.

The new streams of speculation led, in fact, to the breaking of old religious groups, and towards the end of the century four clearly-marked types of serious thought may be distinguished. There are in the first place those who cling to the literal truth of the religious stories and formulae which have come down to them. If there is obscurity or contradiction, it is held to be in the mind of the believer who has not learnt to see aright. There is, secondly, the large class, mentioned above, of those who accept the progressive view of revelation, interpret the Jewish and Christian traditions in accordance with the ordinary canons of historical criticism, but do this as far as possible in communion with the churches which have been the repositories of the faith. This type of mind is what is called in Catholic circles ' modernist '. Then come two groups of more radical thinkers, first those, closely allied in opinion with the modernists, who feel the breach of opinion from the old order to be too great to admit of honest co-operation in religious matters with those who remain within the pale. These work out on independent lines their own schemes of thought, fitting, so far as may be, the expression of their beliefs, or the organizations which they support, to the truth as they can apprehend it. And, lastly, the most negative of all are those who have convinced themselves of the impossibility of reaching any sure conclusion on the fundamental questions—the origin of life and morality, the purpose and governance of the world—and content themselves with the faithful performance of their nearest duties.

It was a striking and a novel prospect, to many minds a terrifying sight. But however we may forecast the issue, one thing is cheering and peculiar to the last few decades. With a wider divergence of opinion than was ever known before, there has come a far wider tolerance, even a deeper unity. Some solution of this paradox we may hope to reach before we close, but the fact of the tolerance is patent and significant. Men of the most varied shades of belief, or of none at all, meet habitually for common work of every kind, without demur, without a question asked. Partly, you may say, through indifference ; still more, we would add, through the growth of other common links which put religious differences in the background. Of these new links, the growth of scientific thought and the increasing hold of practical activities must take first place. This relation, of scientific thought to religion, must now be faced. It is the most profound and difficult aspect of the present chapter. If we look back to the work of any typical mediaeval thinker, say St. Hildegard in the twelfth century or Dante at the beginning of the fourteenth, we shall find that their views of science are embraced in their religious scheme. They received them, they believed, as part of a revelation of the Divine. The Spirit of God declared the vision, and all truth was one. God had revealed and the Church had put its stamp on all alike. The few, like Roger Bacon, who took another road, appealing simply to nature and experiment, were commonly supposed to be in communion with the devil. Now with the Renaissance this other knowledge was vastly enlarged and made a realm apart. The new science was partly recovered from the ancient Greeks, still more of it was built up by the strenuous efforts of man's inquiring and comparing intellect. The new man of science claimed no special channel of inspiration. The road was open to all, and, though most of the great scientists in the seventeenth century were professing Christians, their contribution to progress was a new construction of thought, standing outside the orthodox creed in a fashion undreamt of by the fathers or the schoolmen. The eighteenth century deepened the cleavage. The dominant school of thought, especially in

France, rode high on the crest of the conquering wave, and saw nothing in the old faith or its institutions but an obstruction to the freedom of human reason. With the nineteenth century the tide began to turn. Partly there was a direct reaction. Some like De Maistre and Lacordaire went back to the Pope and Catholic tradition as a guide to belief. But in the wider field the change was not a reaction but an advance to a truer and more comprehensive point of view. The historical spirit, the scientific study of social evolution, gave the link. To this, the only true reconciler, both science and religion appear as necessary and immemorial growths of the human spirit, both arising from common human needs, both diverging here and there, but coming ultimately to a common goal. For their emphasis on this truth the world is under a special debt to Auguste Comte and the school of 'positivists' which he founded in the 'thirties and 'forties of the last century. It was the first attempt to forge a link between those who would base their belief and conduct strictly on scientific grounds and those who adhered to the traditional religious organizations of the Christian West. In this spirit Comte welcomed the reaction of men like De Maistre who defended the Papacy. He sought eagerly for a *modus vivendi* between all parties who aimed at subordinating individual or national selfishness to some higher sanction, and believed with the enthusiasm of a pioneer in the early advent of a reign of peace.

Comte died in 1857. A date twenty years later has been named as the year of most intense rationalist criticism in England. England, as we have seen, while generally ahead in practice, has been correspondingly slow in the purely logical development. In 1877 the *Fortnightly Review* was under the editorship of John Morley, close ally of John Stuart Mill and the most advanced thinkers of that time. It was the moment when the two streams of critical and scientific thought were flowing most strongly together. The influence of Mill, who died in 1873, was still at full flood, critical, agnostic, intensely intellectual, devoted to public ends. And to this was now added the new zeal for evolution which had arisen from the work of Darwin and Spencer, and of which Huxley was the protagonist in the forum of debate. Morley had succeeded Lewes as editor of the *Fortnightly* in 1867, and he held the post till 1882. It was the climax of this review, the high-water mark of the critical, scientific movement in English nineteenth-century thought. The gifts of an editor who combined in a high degree sympathy, acumen, and literary power, achieved the result.

After the 'seventies a change in tone set in. It might perhaps be measured by saying that whereas in the 'seventies the clever boy of seventeen and eighteen would read Herbert Spencer, thirty years later he would read Bergson. No name counts for more in this change than that of T. H. Green. His father was a Yorkshire rector and his mother descended from a connexion of the great Protector and one of his officers. He had thus in his blood and upbringing that combination of piety and sturdy independence which is so marked in all his work and life. His strongest intellectual bias was derived from Kant and Hegel. His greatest intellectual lack was a familiarity with the methods of physical science. This gap was filled by a keen, penetrating, and, above all, an honest mind trying all things patiently and appraising all things generously, so long as they gave promise of subserving the supreme end of the social good, the ideal of humanity. In this last quality, the supremacy of the moral end, there is a real and close kinship between Green and Comte. Both recognized no other canon of right conduct but the moral progress of the human community as a whole.

Mere pleasure, personal or general, is to be wholly rejected as an end. Science, art, and philosophy are of the highest value; but the highest of all is love. Now though the object of our true effort and affection is beyond us, it is easier to apprehend and even to reach than pleasure. We can see it realized in others, and we know that we cannot achieve it without continual self-control and self-sacrifice. A noble creed, looking back with some sympathy to ancient stoicism and mediaeval asceticism, but with a world of new human sympathy between; a doctrine of self-denial, but with a positive content; the losing of one's self, but the finding of it again in the larger self of humanity.

Green called himself a Christian and identified his moral ideal with the Ideal of Christianity. He thus became the bridge on the march of religion in England between the critical and the conservative elements, between those who would make clear at any cost their points of difference by using fresh terms and new organizations, and those who stand on the old ways and trust for the future to the gradual transformation of inherited forms of faith and worship.

We noted the climax of anti-theological criticism reached in 1877 in the *Fortnightly*. It is interesting to put beside it the sermon preached in Balliol in the same year by Green, and published in his works under the title of ' Faith '. It gives us the gist of his teaching, the lines of the eirenicon which he laid down between the old faith and the new knowledge. He was speaking to a group of the ablest and most thoughtful young men in Oxford with their minds full of the constant and powerful criticism of Lewes and Huxley. He speaks of ' the conflict between religion and science which is nowadays on the tongues of all and in the hearts of many '. He tells them that

' the human spirit is one and indivisible, and the desire to know what nature is and means, is as inseparable from it as the consciousness of God and the longing for reconciliation with him. The scientific impulse on the one side and the faith that worketh by love on the other, exhibit the same spirit in different relations. . . . A proposition which asserts divine causation for any phenomenon is not exactly false, but turns out on strict analysis to be unmeaning. . . . But the very existence of science is a witness to the reality of the spiritual, though this, just because it is the source of knowledge, cannot be one of its objects. . . . God is not to be sought in nature, nor in any beginning or end of nature, but in man himself. . . . Reason is self-consciousness. It is only as taken into our self-consciousness and so presented to us as an object, that anything is known to us. . . . Thus everything we know is known to us as a constituent of one world. Hence arises the conception of what we call the uniformity of nature, which, though only recently formulated, is really involved in all knowledge whatever. Nature remains to us an endless series in which the knowing of anything implies of itself something further to be known. A rational self-consciousness supervenes upon sense and the data of sense, and makes this material into knowledge. But there is always a margin beyond what it can know and thus it cannot know the absolute. This rational self-consciousness is the element of identity between us and a perfect being, who is, in full realization, what we are only in principle and possibility. . . . This is the principle in man by virtue of which he projects himself into the future or into some other world as a more perfect being than he actually is. This best is his God.'

Green died in 1882, only forty-six years old, and his influence grew steadily in Oxford and in England for some time after that date. It was somewhat similar to that of his contemporary Seeley at Cambridge, but cut deeper, as the work of a more penetrating and philosophic mind. Not original in its foundations, his work was truly original in bringing together various aspects of earlier thought, and eminently English in its union of a moving sincerity, a yearning for the reconciliation of the sound elements in conflicting views, and a passionate devotion to the ideal of general welfare and progress.

Oxford, once oddly called ' the home of lost causes and impossible loyalties ', produced also the prophet of the next movement which has profoundly influenced religion in England. Arnold Toynbee was a pupil of Green's, and carried into wide spheres of activity one side of his teaching. The impulse which in Green was primarily philosophic, became in Toynbee predominantly social. He turned to the analysis of economic and social problems, and become convinced that the solution of social evils must come ultimately through personal goodwill and intimate study. His conviction struck fire in men, and through the labours of Canon Barnett and many others was the moving spirit in schemes of social settlements among the poor throughout the world. The practical bias thus given to the general teaching of Green has become ever since more and more prominent in England. It largely supplanted the eager questioning about fundamentals which had exercised the more active minds in the 'sixties and 'seventies. Young men, who twenty years before would have been absorbed in the bearings of Darwinism on religion, now spent themselves in efforts to understand and ameliorate social suffering. Green's teaching contains the fullest warrant for their action.

If we carried our analysis to a later period still, we should find that, by the beginning of the twentieth century, the dispersive tendencies of thought had become accentuated. The active tendency, the idea that we learn mainly, if not entirely, by doing, had by that time formed a school of its own which took the name of ' pragmatism '. And over against this had arisen a school of critical thinkers more minute and thoroughgoing in their criticism than any who had preceded them. These men subjected the idealism of Green to a searching examination in detail, asking what are the elements of that self-consciousness from which he would build up both the world without and the world within. It is a process comparable on the psychological side to the atomic analysis in physics, and, as in that, we cannot yet foresee the issue. But, looking at the matter broadly, there can be no doubt that the active tendency was the salient characteristic of the later decades of the nineteenth century, and this activity was shown not only in manifold conquests of nature and discoveries in the world but also in a new temper in religion which saw its goal in works of philanthropy and efforts at expansion more clearly than at any previous epoch in the Christian era. So great, indeed, was this rush to action that it might be maintained with some show of reason that it contained within it the seeds of the catastrophe of 1914. Men became absorbed in action to the neglect of the fundamental questions, 'Why are we doing all this?' and 'Whither are we rushing?' Such feverish activity, in fact, though it may form habits and build up institutions, may act as a positive hindrance to abstract thought, an anodyne to evils that all the time are undermining the whole fabric of the social being.

So far as specially religious activities are concerned, the increasingly practical spirit of the age was shown in the tone of teaching and preaching, in the growing devotion of religious people to good works, especially of an organized kind, and in a quite unexampled extension of Christian missions by all the churches in the world. On each of these points a word is needed before we advance to our summary conclusion on the whole matter.

Some recent writers on religion have declared that the greatest of all religious revolutions was the change from the primitive religions of nature to the ethical religions which begin to hold sway in the early settled communities, such as Egypt, and of which Christianity is the purest type. In this view the progress of religion consists essentially in bringing its conceptions more and more nearly into harmony with the highest moral ideas of mankind. If this be so—and it is certainly one very important aspect of the truth—then the increasing stress laid by all Christian teachers in the later nineteenth century on the moral bearings of their message is a striking confirmation of progress, in religion as in other departments of human life. We may be emboldened to believe more readily in the truth of the great saying that ' man becomes more and more religious ', when we notice how, in our own and recent times, both the public and the preachers are turning to the good will, the good life, the desire to help one's neighbours, as evidence of religion, apart from creed or formal practices. The most respected voices in progressive England taught us this forty years ago, and a large part of the nation has tried to practise the lesson. Preachers dealt more and more exclusively with conduct, and their influence went to strengthen the impression left by philosophers like Green, writers like Carlyle, reformers like Toynbee, coiners of telling phrases like his who wrote of religion as ' morality touched with emotion ', and of ' a something not ourselves which makes for righteousness '.

Closely related to this was the extension of philanthropic organization in the latter part of the century. Put Sydney Smith on one hand and any active and devoted clergyman of a hundred years later on the other : how vast the difference in ideal ! Yet no man was more alive than the great Canon of St. Paul's to the manifold evils of his time. The modern parish and diocese is a network of societies and agencies for improving the moral and social condition of its members. This, far more than doctrine or preaching, is now the accepted test of its efficiency, and, like the great extension of foreign missions, it dates very largely from the 'eighties. The gospel of work, preached outside the churches by men like Ruskin and Carlyle, found a ready echo within. Toynbee Hall, founded in 1884, was but a shining example of that organized effort for social improvement by moral agencies, in which all civilized countries and all the churches have taken part. The Anglo-Saxon world— Great Britain and the United States—have been conspicuous in this work.

The spirit which inspired it is of course of the essence of primitive Christianity, and we are now tracing the way in which the ancient spirit reappears transformed, with modern language and modern methods. The parallel with missions abroad is striking, both as to time and as to manner of development. Here again we have a part, one of the most vital parts, of primitive Christianity. It was the field on which one of the greatest founders of the Christian Church did his most glorious work, the field on which Columba, Aidan, and Boniface, with all their followers from the British Isles, went out to labour and often to die in the sixth, seventh, and eighth centuries of our era. The impulse never died out in the Christian world, but in those parts of the West which broke away from Rome it slackened during the sixteenth and seventeenth centuries. That was the age of the Jesuit missions, most skilful of all in adapting their methods to the minds they worked upon. Then came in the eighteenth century, and especially at the end of it, a great general revival, contemporary with the movement for the freeing of the slaves and the new impulse of humanity. Within a decade from 1792 were founded six of the most important societies for Christian propaganda which still exist in Great Britain. From that time onward throughout the century the stream has never ceased, but it gained strength in the 'seventies and 'eighties at the same time that social reform at home became a stronger element in religious work. In 1872 David Livingstone died at Ilala, after thirty years given to the exploration of Africa and the service of its inhabitants.

It was the last continent to be explored which gave the world the most perfect type of Western missionary. He combined in a high degree the moral, religious, and scientific qualities which make up that type. Great explorer, great student of nature, ' Great Doctor ', he earned the last title all through the continent by caring for the bodies as well as the souls of the natives. Moral training was the first note in his teaching, love the first note in his religion. His work and character gave the death-blow to the slave-trade and set at its highest point the ideal of the strong and cultivated man in dealing with the weaker and less advanced members of the human family. A host of missionaries to Central Africa followed his death in 1872. Many of them, both there and in China, lost their lives. In 1885 the murder of Bishop Hannington in Uganda set the stream running again strongly in Livingstone's wake.

By the end of the century it has been reckoned that there were to the credit of Christian missions throughout the world something over five million Catholic converts and about the same number of Protestant—a curious commentary on the bisection of the Christian world carried out at the Reformation. We are not concerned here to criticize their methods or to compare one result with another. The next chapter will indicate some of the services of missionaries in exploring the world. They have been a powerful factor in the Expansion of the West. But it is right to add at once that, whatever may have been their shortcomings, they have represented on the whole the humane and civilizing side of Western influence.

They have been a force on the side of pity, and, thanks to the missionaries, the exploitation, which weighs so heavily on the Western conscience, has been less inhuman than it might have been.

It is time now to draw together the threads of this discussion and to try and see its main features as a whole, but without venturing into the most recent times of all. The effect of the war we leave deliberately aside, for it is impossible to forecast it, impossible to descry the currents of thought which may be turning beneath the sighs of suffering and the clamour of the fight. Our inquiry here, though difficult, is on safer ground. We are asking if the various symptoms of religious change, noticeable towards the end of the last century, seem to fit together into one plan of progressive movement. If so, they may have more chance of permanence ; they may survive the cataclysm and all the confused thought and pessimism which it has helped to engender.

The answer we would offer may, perhaps, have been anticipated from the questions we have raised, and it is one of tempered and critical optimism. There may be traced in the later decades of the last century a movement in religion which does thus hold together, and form a growing unity and a growing expansion. Two sides of this movement may be distinguished, on both of which there is a consistency which gives good hope of reality and permanence. There is a consistency in the lines of religious growth as we may trace it from the earliest times, and there is an internal consistency, a principle of growth within which seems to hold the various manifestations together. On each of these aspects a few words may sum up our conclusion.

We have noticed frequently that some feature which becomes prominent in this period is but the fuller development of a germ of thought or life belonging to an earlier age. So it was with the increased emphasis on the ethical side of religion. This led us back to the greatest revolution of all, when moral religions began to take the place of the primitive religions of nature. So it was with social reform. The zeal of recent years is but the fuller manifestation of the spirit which inspired the early Church and bade its members ' Feed my lambs ', for ' Ye are all members one of another '. So with the missionary spirit. So, one might say, even with rationalist criticism itself. It has been the mark of every step towards a higher and purer religious life to discard superstitions and approximate to reason. Nothing is more fortifying than thus to find anticipations of our own efforts and early believers in our own creed. We can stand with more confidence in the present if we feel beneath us the foundations of the past. This is as true of religion as we have seen it to be of science, and as we know it to be of our national liberties.

The present is the evolution of the past; this is, of course, true of any age. It is no special feature of the nineteenth century. But the nineteenth century first realized it, saw for the first time the living past in the present, and in the sphere of religion, the sphere of self-consciousness at its highest point, this realization has its deepest meaning and its greatest value.

We find then in this new age, when the historical spirit has become dominant, a new outlook in religion also. The religious mind now becomes conscious that it has within it the work of all the pioneers who have built up its ideals in the past. The early poet still speaks to it, the man who first adored the mystery which hides behind the simplest phenomena of nature, the flowing of the stream, the shining of the star, the shooting of the corn. It still contains the social bond of primitive religion whose God protected the tribe and held its members together with a tie more close than blood. The Greek who first exalted the divine and found it in the noblest human type, the early

Christian loving his brethren in the faith and struggling to build a new heaven upon earth—all are still alive, and in the developed self-consciousness of the modern age give added force to action and added depth to thought. The consciousness of all this is, of course, only present in the minds of a small and fully educated class. It is the insight of learning, the religion, it has been said, of a man of letters. But unconsciously the forces of the past operate in the minds of all.

It will be seen that we have travelled back to Green's self-consciousness by another route, and we are now prepared to rest in that as the centre of the modern movement in religion. But we need to interpret it broadly, with all the light of history in its genesis and all the richness of the world in its content. And we need, too, to recognize a real divergence in the interpretation put on the data of self-consciousness by different thinkers. To one school it is the voice within us of a Universal Spirit, ' more deeply interfused ' than man can be in all the phenomena of the universe. To another it is the Human Spirit itself, not to be identified with the external world, but welling up from an unknown infinity behind us and with infinite capacities before. But in taking self-consciousness in either sense as the final note in our review of religious growth, we are in full accord with the whole trend of modern philosophy since Descartes. From Descartes onwards the philosophers have sought to explain and reconcile the phenomena of the world from our consciousness outwards, not as in the ancient world from external facts inwards, nor as in the scholastics from a revealed canon given to us from above. The external and the divine are not denied, are facts of experience to be reckoned with, but we approach them now from another standpoint which has become clearer and wider since Descartes's time, following his lead. He cut away the errors of self-illusion and authority,

and made men ask the simple questions what are the clear unshakable beliefs to which every man would cling as part of his
very being. Since then the growth of an evolutionary doctrine
has widened this view, and makes the question apply not
only to the individual but to the race which has built up these
ideas in the ages of its collective being. But the psychological
starting-point which Descartes indicated still remains, and it
has continually enlarged its scope. In poetry, in fiction, in
politics, as well as in philosophy and religion, the psychological
basis and the psychological explanation are now as prominent
as the historical, are in fact the other side of the same question.
Now the effect on religion, which is closely allied to philosophy,
has been the greatest. Every complete treatment of any religious question in recent times, say from Schleiermacher to
William James, is partly historical and partly psychological, and
the psychological has grown steadily in importance. 'What
does it mean to the individual soul ? ' 'How has it come to be
what it is ? ', these psychological and historical questions have
put into the background questions of the meaning and truth
of dogmas, even for a time questions as to the social value of
religion.

It will be remembered that T. H. Green, at a critical moment
in the progress of religious thought in England, turned to a
developing self-consciousness as the key to the movement. He
no doubt derived this view from Hegel, but he thought it out
again in a way of his own. If we follow him in regarding it as
the typical view in this period, we must be careful to keep to
the broad middle path on which it connects with other lines
of modern thought, and avoid identifying it with the extreme
and mistaken forms into which at all ages it has descended. It
is significant that the same recent period has seen a revival of
mysticism which is the doctrine of the supremacy of self-

consciousness carried to the furthest point in depth, without extension and without the proper balance of the objective world. This was obviously not Green's view, nor is it the view of self-consciousness which represents the dominant tendency of the last fifty years. For this last fifty years is also the period in which our knowledge and consciousness of the external world has become the most extensive and precise. Our developing consciousness therefore must be regarded, and has by the best thinkers been regarded, as correlative to external facts as well as deeper within, a mirror of the world as well as a mirror of man. And this, too, is a patent mark of the new spirit in religion. We are now accustomed to a view in which all good things, the beauty of nature and the joy of living, as well as knowledge itself, are all included in that manifestation of the Highest to which our being tends. The barriers of asceticism, partly mediaeval, partly puritan, have been broken down, and our ideal of the Best does not now seem to grow only as one side of our nature by some stern law imposed from without, but embraces all congruent things, and will, as the self develops, embrace still more.

But the main condition of the self, of which we are now conscious, still remains to be explained. It is this. The individual self does not stand alone; by itself it is even the worst of guides to the ideal. Self-centred in one sense we must be, but not self-contained, and of all the achievements of recent religious thought we should perhaps put first the wider, the more social self. The same century has seen the attainment of the highest point in both conceptions, superficially opposed, inherently but two aspects of the same thing, a completely developing self-consciousness or personality, and a humanity from which that self derives its depth and fullness and with which it is constantly striving to make itself more equal.

The perception of the developing self, developing in history as well as in the individual soul, the projection of the Ideal before us, sometimes in the fitful light of our own personality, sometimes in the radiance of another and a greater, the gradual filling out of this ideal by all the achievements of a slowly perfecting humanity, the pursuit of this ideal by one's self becoming wiser and greater-minded, but always in fellowship with others, in family, in country, or in the world, with whom and for whom we have to live—these are the characteristics of the new religious growth. Just in so far as these things are actually in process, under whatever formulae of faith they may be expressed or concealed, so far Western man is becoming more religious.

NEW KNOWLEDGE ON OLD FOUNDATIONS

WE noted in the last chapter how the wide sweep of synthesis which carried men away with it about the middle of the century was broken into shortly after by a more searching criticism. Green's doctrine, based on Hegel, of a divine self-consciousness finding its highest known manifestation in our own spirit, gave way for a time to another point of view, or rather various points of view, which sought rather to ascertain what was involved in each separate act of conscious life. By this process more was attributed to the external not-ourselves, less to the evolving and creating spirit. One might draw an analogy between the generous idealism of the earlier school of imaginative art and the 'realism' of later writers and artists who aim at picturing life just as it is, and give us minute, faithful, and interesting work, but without the inspiration to action of the earlier masters.

In science there was a somewhat similar movement. The comprehensive vision of Darwin and his contemporaries was followed by a minute examination of what a variation really is, and under what conditions it took place in the organic world. Analysis again supervened on synthesis. The previous generalizations were not explicitly denied, but left alone, while spade-work went on round the foundations of the building with a vigour and a persistence alarming to those who still desired the old house to live in. In physical science, with which we shall mainly deal in this chapter, while the new facts and the extended methods have proved at least equally surprising, the net result seems more continuous with the old positions. This reason, as well as the extreme interest of the new discoveries, are good grounds for giving some special attention to them. This evolution is the most perfect example we possess of ordered progress. The old mechanics, founded in the seventeenth century, had justified themselves by a thousand fruitful applications in practice, and, as their generalizations were laid in accurate observations and quantitative laws, the later expansions and corrections were possible without destroying the original structure. We glanced at some of these discoveries in Chapter V as influencing industrial production. Here we shall consider the subject as a branch in the tree of knowledge, and carry its growth farther down to the end of our period.

The physics of the seventeenth and eighteenth century, of which Galileo and Newton were the master-builders, were primarily concerned with the mechanics of mass. It was the heavenly bodies, the greatest known masses, which first revealed the laws of mechanics to minds sufficiently gifted to perceive them. The nineteenth century added to these the mechanics of the particle, and has carried its analysis farther and farther on the road to the infinitely small. But a glance back to antiquity sheds a flood of light on this development, as on most aspects of human thought. The ancient mind had begun to play on the threshold of the subject. Democritus was the pioneer among the Greeks, and Epicurus combined some theory of atomic action with his general philosophy. But Lucretius is the immortal monument of ancient daring and insight on this sphere, and when we read in his terse and pregnant lines how one should learn to look for the effects of invisible forces in the world around us, in the wind which is as powerful as the stream, in the small bodies which are in constant and violent motion in every mass of matter, we can almost believe that electrons are being described in Latin verse.

' These " first bodies " which form a denser mass, when brought together, held fast by their own close-tangled shapes, form enduring bases of stone and unyielding bodies of iron and the like. But those which spring far off and rebound, leaving great spaces between, these furnish us with thin air and the bright rays of the sun.' What hindered the foundation, then and there, of a true science of chemistry and physics, anticipating the evolution of two thousand years later ? Two obstacles, the positive hindrance of a rival and more powerful philosophy, based on a theory of life rather than of matter, and the negative drawback of a want of accurate observation and experiment, with results expressed in mathematical form. The positive hindrance was Aristotle, whose more philosophic mind and biological bent dominated science for a thousand years. And on the mathematical side, men had yet to reach the simplest laws of motion, the mechanics of mass, before they could devote a fruitful gaze to the molecule. They had not even the mathematical notation in which the necessary equations could be expressed.

These conditions were realized by the end of the eighteenth century. The calculus had been invented a hundred years before. The fundamental laws of motion had been formulated and inquiries were in full swing as to the nature of that thinnest form of matter to which the name of ' gas ' had been attached by Van Helmont early in the seventeenth century. The wind, which Lucretius had taken as a typical example of an invisible force, was found to be susceptible to many other forms of sensible measurement—to contain, in fact, many secrets both of matter and of life. The discovery of oxygen in the eighteenth century was the first definite step in chemistry, and chemistry became scientific in the exact sense when Lavoisier, by the careful use of the balance in his work, had demonstrated the constancy of material weight.

The total weights of substances after a chemical process were found to be identical with what they had been before. The way was now open for Dalton and an atomic theory of a scientific kind.

Dalton, the Quaker schoolmaster of Cumberland and Manchester, deserves to have his name attached to the theory, for he first put the floating notions of elements and atoms on the solid basis of numerical laws. These, though they have been modified and expanded in a thousand details since his time, have held good as a whole, and the atomic theory has become, in consequence of its quantitative basis, a guiding thought in nineteenth-century science. The history of ' elements ' from ancient times down to Dalton and the nineteenth century would form by itself a chapter full of instruction in the evolution of thought. The vague ideas, the groping after hidden truth, the want of exact methods, go on from the unique element of the Ionian philosopher, the ' water ' of Thales, the ' air ' of Anaximenes, the hot, dry, cold, and wet of Aristotle, down to the eighteenth century. Then the foundation of a scientific chemistry put order into confused theories. Lavoisier had already established that, since the total of the weights is constant, then, if by any chemical process a substance which we thought elementary had lost weight, we should know that it had been combined with some other substance and was not a pure element. Dalton then showed that the atoms or particles of any one element are all alike, but that they differ from the particles of any other element both in size and weight, and that in combinations of different elements the particles come together according to some invariable numerical ratio. He was helped to his conclusion by applying the golden rule of using always the simplest hypothesis which would cover the facts. Thus in the five different compounds of oxygen and nitrogen called ' oxides ', a fixed weight of nitrogen is engaged in each case, and the weights of oxygen are as $1:2:3:4:5$. That is to say, the complex molecules of the oxides are formed by the combination between two atoms of nitrogen and first one atom of oxygen, then two, then three, then four, then five. This is the atomic theory in a simple case, and it was the first introduction of a quantitative law for the combination of elements.

As chemistry sets out to discover what an element or homogeneous substance is, and how these homogeneous substances behave towards one another when they are brought into contact, we have by the first decade of the nineteenth century, when Dalton made his discoveries, the first sketch of the science firmly set out. Note that it is in mathematical form, and is thus a link with the older and sister science of physics. The whole subsequent course of inquiry has tended to draw the two closer and closer together.

Since Dalton's time the number of recognized elements has increased from twenty-six to eighty-eight,[1] and their recognized combinations both natural and synthetic, i. e. made by man, have grown proportionately. Dalton's simple laws, discovered at a time when very few of these compounds were known to chemists, still hold their own in the complexity which has succeeded; and this complexity itself has revealed new and marvellous laws of mathematical symmetry and links with all other facts in the material universe.

The first direct sequel of Dalton's work was the fixing of the relative atomic weights of all the known elements and the discovery of fresh ones in the process. This went on steadily throughout the century, and as the number of the elements increased it was noticed that their weights formed an approximately regular series, capable of being divided into sets of eight or octaves by the somewhat greater gaps in the scale at those points.

[1] Moseley, who fell in the Great War at the age of twenty-eight, predicted the discovery of four more.

The law, like nearly all discoveries in science, was due to several, sometimes unconsciously, co-operating minds, but it is rightly associated with the name of a great Russian chemist, Mendeleeff, who carried it out most systematically and made most use of it for further discoveries. The seventy-eight elements are, therefore, arranged in these octaves, and the weights of all the rest are expressed as multiples of hydrogen, the lightest of the gases, which is taken as the unit. It was later found that, by slightly correcting the unity weight of hydrogen, so as to give oxygen the value 16, most of the other elements could then be expressed as whole, or very nearly whole, numbers. This is now the practice in any table of atomic weights, and they proceed from hydrogen to the metal uranium, the heaviest known (= 240). In arranging this series of octaves it was found that certain places in the scale remained unfilled. Mendeleeff became so confident in the truth of his Periodic Law that he predicted the discovery of the missing elements and in some cases gave names to them in advance. He has been often justified and may be justified again. He also found that other qualities of the elements were in some way connected with, or dependent upon, their atomic weights. The corresponding members of each octave, taken according to their order of weight, form together what are called cognate groups. Thus the first elements, i. e. the relatively lightest, from each octave form one such group together, the next lightest another group, and so on, and it is within these groups that the common properties can be found. Thus, to take one sub-group—the sub-group, or half of each group, being still more clearly cognate than the whole—we find that if fluorine, the lightest in that group, does a certain thing, chlorine, the corresponding element in the octave higher, will do it more, and so on with the rest. This sort of regularity applies to all the properties of the given element—its melting-point, its power of combination with other substances, its atomic volume, &c. All the properties of an element are, in short, a periodic function of its atomic weight, and may be set out in a mathematical curve. Later on, down to the days of radio-activity, confirmations have continued to arrive; but before we arrive at that point in our story we have to retrace our steps a little to pick up another clue. This is our knowledge of electricity, the force which was ultimately to prove the most potent in the universe of matter, the common form into which, as it now seems, all the rest may be resolved.

At the time when Dalton was analysing marsh-gas at Manchester, Volta was constructing at Pavia his piles of copper and zinc disks, and Oersted was beginning his experiments on electric currents at Copenhagen. These were the means which in later hands were to lead to breaking up the 'indivisible' atom and discovering a solar system in every particle. Michael Faraday's is the name which stands out most clearly at this stage of discovery, as Dalton's in the formulation of the laws of atoms. Both were men of modest origin, and owed their success to a genius working persistently in early life in a quiet sphere. Both, like Tyndall, Mill, Spencer, and many more, who have profoundly influenced the national life, grew up outside the course of ordinary academic education. Faraday, like Dalton, was by origin a north-countryman, his father having migrated from Yorkshire to London. The elder Faraday worked as a blacksmith at Newington, where Michael was born in 1791, and he apprenticed his son to a bookbinder. Popular lectures on science gave the boy his early stimulus, especially the lectures of Sir Humphry Davy at the Royal Institution which had just been founded by Count Rumford, an American citizen of cosmopolitan education. Here Davy did his work in chemical analysis, and succeeded in isolating the two new elements, potassium and sodium, about the time when Faraday joined him as an assistant, in 1813. He had had the good sense to recognize Faraday's talent from notes of some of his lectures which the young man had sent him as a proof of his industry and interest. The alliance thus formed determined Faraday's career. The Royal Institution became his home for life. He began his work in the chemical field, following the lines of Dalton and Davy. But his decisive discoveries came a little later, when he was put in touch with the experiments which Oersted had been carrying out in Denmark and Ampère in France. This was in 1821. The foreign scientists had established the fact that an electric current drives out a magnetic one at right angles and vice versa, but they had not succeeded in making this action continuous. This was the capital achievement of Faraday, due to a keen practical intelligence working with true appreciation of scientific fact. Faraday produced the rotation of the wire round the magnet, and the correlative result, an electric current inducing a continuous flow in the magnet. The dynamo was thus invented, which has enabled electricity to be produced in unlimited quantities for commercial uses, and in the realm of theory it forged another link in the unity of matter. Magnetism and electricity were shown to be different forms of the same force, and before long Faraday went on to detect connecting ties with other natural forces, especially with light itself, the speediest of all forms of motion. He summarized the point of view which he had reached, when he tells us some twenty years later that ' a few years ago magnetism was to us an occult power, affecting only a few bodies. Now it is found to influence all bodies and to possess the most intimate relations with electricity, heat, chemical action, light, crystallization, and through it with the forces concerned in cohesion. And we may in the present state of things well feel urged to continue in our labours, encouraged by the hope of bringing it into a bond of union with gravity itself.' We shall see later how, by discoveries which even he did not dream of, much of his vision has since his time-been realized. But before that we must note the formulation of these electro-magnetic results in mathematical shape. This was made possible by the calculus of the seventeenth century. The equations which followed from this were found equal to expressing in exact terms all the new relations which Faraday and the physicists revealed. It was near the end of the eighteenth century when Lagrange published his *Mécanique Analytique*, one of the greatest treatises applying mathematical forms to physical facts. In that work the author declared his intention of 'reducing all the science of mechanics to such general formulae as any one could work out by algebra without any diagrams or mechanical constructions'. It is a branch of science in which, at that time, the French far outdistanced us, and indeed the whole world, owing partly to our superstitious following of the letter of Newton. Fourier's work on heat, published in 1822, was another example of the same French genius. It was inspired by a similar spirit to that of Lagrange and had similar results, notably on Lord Kelvin. See now how this profound work on the lines of a wide but well-grounded synthesis bore its rich harvest in later years ! Early in the 'sixties Clerk Maxwell was studying at Cambridge the results of Faraday's researches and the methods by which he had arrived at them. He was carried away by admiration for the insight and the intuitive mathematical genius displayed, but was eager to connect the results with the whole previous course of mechanical science and to express them in the accepted mathematical form. ' I perceived ', he tells, ' that his method was also mathematical, though not exhibited in the conventional formal mathematical symbols. That is, Faraday in his mind's eye saw lines of force traversing all space where the mathematicians saw centres of force attracting at a distance. Faraday sought the seat of the phenomena in real actions going on in the medium ; they were satisfied that they had found it in a power of action at a distance impressed on electric fluids.' Working thus to bring Faraday's work and thought into accord with mathematical mechanics, Maxwell turned back to Lagrange's equations and was able from them to develop others expressing the new results in electro-magnetism. The new facts which Faraday had discovered could now be accounted for on a theory of stresses and motions in a supposed material substratum, the all-pervading ether, and the same point of view, the same equations, were found to be applicable to light as well. Hertz, twenty years later, working on Maxwell's lines, showed how electro-magnetic waves could be set up which differed only from the waves of light by virtue of their much greater length, and thus wireless telegraphy was invented.

In this achievement of Clerk Maxwell, summed up in his treatise on Electricity and Magnetism, we see the work of mathematical unification carried to the farthest point which it has yet reached. It is important to notice that the result is attained by constantly enlarging and correcting certain general forms which man has found to cover the phenomena of his experience and to enable him to predict their recurrence. These forms are independent of the ultimate nature of the 'material substratum' that may lie beneath them. Men still dispute as to the final explanation of gravitation. Is it also to be referred to stresses in the ether ? Meanwhile, the laws of Newton hold good. And so the later discoveries to which we have now to turn, our knowledge of radio-activity and the mysterious substances which exhibit it, may alter, indeed have already profoundly altered, our view of the nature of the facts with which we have to deal, without affecting the validity of the laws in which the mathematicians have described their workings. In the evolution of the mathematical synthesis of physical phenomena three great stages may be distinguished and remembered. The first was in the seventeenth century, when Galileo's discovery of the behaviour of a falling body led to the Newtonian system. The second arose from the study of the steam-engine and other heat-evolving machines at the beginning of the nineteenth century : this gave us the principle of the conservation of energy. The third is bound up with Maxwell's and Hertz's equations in the last quarter of the century, which included electricity, magnetism, and light, as well as heat, in one comprehensive view.

The rays which have so largely occupied men's minds in recent years take us back, as well as electric phenomena, to Faraday's labours, and most of their interesting terminology was introduced by him. He had discovered in the course of his experiments, when analysing various liquids and gases by electric currents, that there were many new forms of electrical action, new shapes in which electricity appeared to clothe itself. He disengaged the particles of electrified matter which flowed from one of the two poles towards the other, and noticed that those flowing in one direction, the negative, formed a class distinct from those flowing in the opposite direction, the positive. Dr. Whewell, the famous Master of Trinity, had followed his experiments with the closest interest, and Faraday consulted him as to the best nomenclature for these particles as well as for other electrical facts. The Master, who was a scholar as well as our first historian of science, suggested a series of Greek words, many of which have now become part of universal scientific speech. The electrified particles became the ' ions ' or wanderers, the negative travelling by the downward way ' cathode ', the positive by the upward ' anode '. And thus the Greeks, the founders of science, who first imagined an atomic conception of matter, lived again in the latest form in which the theory was advancing to fresh conquests.

It was found that the ions, whether to be regarded as electrified particles or actually particles of electricity, might be produced in numerous ways. Mere heat, if carried to a certain point, would produce them as well as an electric discharge passing through a space where certain gases had been diffused. The 'Crookes tube', in which cathode rays pass through a highly exhausted atmospheric medium, has been the most familiar instrument in recent times. The ions were then subjected to the closest examination of all their properties. The negative particles or cathode ions have been found to possess the more exciting qualities, and to them has been given the title of 'corpuscles', a title which recalls in many ways the *corpora prima* of Lucretius. These negative ions, or corpuscles, now called electrons, have turned out to be far the quickest of the travellers. It is they alone who can be compared for speed with light. Light passes at the rate of 186,000 miles a second : the new corpuscles travel at velocities varying up to a half or more of the speed of light. Their weight is a thousandth part of the lightest atom ever known before.

The latest form of the atomic theory was soon to present itself, based throughout on electricity. The atom of the old physicists, the atom which Dalton began to weigh and to compare in different elements, may be resolved, some think, into electricity manifested in diverse forms. The positive particles, or atoms of electricity, form the nucleus, round which the negative 'electrons' may be conceived to rotate. These electrons are now conceived to be absorbed by all bodies in direct proportion to their density, and they communicate heat, light, and motion to all the bodies which they strike.

Helmholtz, who in 1847 had summed up and announced to the world the facts which established the doctrine of the conservation of energy, had foreseen the development which would take place in electrical theory. ' The chemical law', he said, ' leads up to the conception of the material atom, and the electrolytic law suggests the idea of an electric atom. Electricity, whether positive or negative, is composed of elementary parts which behave like atoms of electricity.' The results of two other lines of inquiry, unknown when Helmholtz spoke, or when Faraday was making his experiments, must now be reviewed in our brief space. They are man's boldest approaches to the secret structure of the material universe, and both lead to fresh unification and visions of unity. The first is spectral analysis ; the second is radio-activity.

Sir Isaac Newton had discovered that white light is composed of different coloured rays in the spectrum, and he also had started the theory, disputed by Huyghens, that it was made up of minute particles darting out from the sun and other light-giving bodies. It is interesting and comforting to reflect that the two centuries and a half that have passed since have reconciled in a more comprehensive synthesis the two views, Newton's particles and Huyghens's waves. In this, as in other parts of physical science, six generations have widened the structure on the old foundations of truth. Two friends, a Frenchman and an Englishman, Fresnel and Young, made perhaps the greatest contribution in the interval. They lived about the Revolution time, and analysed much farther the wave-motions which form light ; they showed how in a natural ray these waves not only move up and down like waves in a pond, but also from side to side, and how when polarized, i. e. reflected in a certain direction, this complex vibration is destroyed and the waves of each ray move only in one direction. It was by experiments on light thus polarized that Faraday gained the first inkling of the close connexion between light and electricity.

But the further discoveries due to the spectroscope are the work entirely of the nineteenth century. In the first two years of the century new rays were revealed at both ends of the spectrum, heat-rays beyond the red, chemical rays, which give us photo-graphy, in and beyond the violet. And, in the year before Waterloo, Fraunhofer, an apprentice to a glass manufacturer in Bavaria, first saw the black lines in the spectrum which go by his name and which have led to all the discoveries of astro-physics. Newton had admitted the sunlight to his prism through a round hole in a shutter. Seen in this way the colours of the spectrum overlap one another. Fraunhofer happened to use a narrow slit instead of a hole, and saw black lines dividing the colours. He proceeded to make his slit narrower still and used a prism of very pure glass ; he then saw 576 of these black lines. As none of these lines appear when the light of a candle or a lamp goes through the prism, Fraunhofer concluded that in some way sunlight was defective and some of its coloured rays were missing. He measured the lines with the greatest care, and found that in every ray of sunlight they come in exactly the same places. They were still the same when he looked at the light of the moon and the planets. But when he turned to the stars he found a difference. There were still dark lines, but they did not fall in the same places. He argued, therefore, that there must be some real difference between the light of the sun and the light of the stars, and this was the first step in the study of the heavenly bodies by means of the spectrum. Nearly fifty years passed before the puzzle was solved, but meanwhile many experiments were being tried on the light of other burning substances, which all fitted in with the complete explana-tion when at last it came. It was found that the light from a white-hot solid, a poker for instance or a piece of incandescent carbon, will give a continuous spectrum resembling the sun's, but in which no dark lines are visible. But burning gases only produce a few bright lines, and these are different for the gas or vapour of every substance. And the test is so true and delicate that the smallest portion, e. g. the gas from the eighteen-millionth of a grain of sodium, will give the yellow line which belongs to it. Nor does the mixture of different gases in the burning interfere with their light. Each gas still gives out its appropriate lines. The spectrum was thus clearly shown to be a potent instrument of analysis, and by its means several new metals were added to the list of elements : but still the black lines in the solar and the stellar spectra were unexplained. At last, in 1861, two German chemists, Bunsen and Kirchhoff, working at Heidelberg, in arranging a new spectroscope to gain more accurate results, discovered that the bright yellow line of the sodium spectrum fell exactly in the same place as a certain black line in the solar spectrum. Next it was found that if full sunshine was passed through the sodium flame, the black started out more strongly than ever. To account for these facts, the hypothesis was framed that every burning gas set in front of white light from a burning solid or liquid absorbs and so negatives just those rays which it gives out itself in burning. Kirchhoff confirmed this theory by putting white light from a burning solid, lime light, behind the sodium flame and noting that the tell-tale black line appeared at once in the spectrum. Around the solid or liquid body of the sun or the stars there must therefore be an atmosphere of various gases, absorbing particular rays. The fifty years since Kirchhoff have increased enormously the fineness of our instruments and the fullness of our results. The spectroscope has added to our knowledge, both of the heavens and of the earth, as much as any other instrument which modern science has evolved. It combines in a hundred forms with the telescope, the microscope, and the camera to make supreme engines of material research. It has brought again into the closest association with terrestrial life the celestial bodies with which man, in his earliest impulse of thinking, connected his fate. The earlier mechanics of Galileo and Newton had brought the stars into partnership with ourselves in the first laws of motion and the first conceptions of mass. The latest results in astrophysics have renewed the association in a still more intimate way. They have shown us a like constitution of matter pervading the whole universe within our ken. All the well-known elements of earthly chemistry are found in their gaseous state in the sun and stars. And strange new laws seem to make their appearance, and differences between themselves and us, and between one star and another, which stir our imagination to the depths. In the planets, as they cool, an atmosphere has been detected like our own, and among the stars there is a progression from those of the greatest heat and apparently the most simple structure on to those which comprise more and more of the elements we know and are more like our own sun in their structure. The hottest of the stars are composed very largely of hydrogen, hydrogen moreover in another form, which suggests an evolution of the elements themselves. As the temperature of a star decreases, one after another of the elements seems to make its appearance, and the metals always appear first in their primitive or dissociated form. But certainty is barred to us for the present by our ignorance of the meaning of many of the facts which the spectrum reveals. Of the interior masses of the sun and stars the spectroscope cannot give us the same insight as it does of the gaseous envelopes. We try to peer within, and we are beginning to set up a comparison between what these envelopes contain and that new constitution of matter which radio-activity has discovered on earth. This is the companion line of inquiry which converges on astrophysics in the speculation of living men.

France and Poland have collaborated in a striking way in the study of radio-activity—Becquerel and Niewenglowski, Pierre Curie and the Polish lady his wife. The Becquerels—grandfather, father, and son—all professors of physics in Paris, all doing abundant, distinguished, and original work, form one of the most notable cases of inherited genius. Henri Becquerel, the son, the discoverer of radio-activity, succeeded his father as Professor of Physics at the Musée d'Histoire Naturelle, where they worked together in the old house of Cuvier in the Jardin des Plantes. In 1895 Röntgen, while experimenting with a Crookes tube, had discovered that certain rays from it, which he called X-rays, though enclosed in a black cardboard box, had the power of passing through various substances opaque to ordinary light and of affecting a photographic plate. He put forward the theory that the phenomena were due to longitudinal vibrations in the ether instead of the transverse of ordinary light. The discovery set men thinking whether the power of emitting such rays might not belong to phosphorescent bodies generally, and Niewenglowski obtained some penetrating rays of light emitted from calcium sulphide previously exposed to the sun. These rays would go through a sheet of metal and develop a photographic plate. Becquerel was on the same track, but he tried his experiments with various substances, and among them with the metal uranium, the heaviest of the known elements. He experimented first after exposing the substance to light; afterwards he found that the rays were emitted spontaneously even when it had been completely sheltered from any previous exposure to light. Becquerel had therefore discovered a new property of matter, the emission of an unknown type of rays or even the manufacture of them; for the fragment of uranium showed no sign of diminution. Any substance containing uranium gave out the rays. The Curies had been following Becquerel's work with close attention, and after Becquerel's results with uranium they resolved to examine the ray-emitting power of pitchblende, the substance from which uranium is derived. In various specimens of this mineral compound Mme. Curie found a radio-activity four times greater than in uranium itself.

She and her husband set to work by the most laborious processes to reduce the pitchblende and isolate the substance which had this greater power. In 1898 they announced that ' it is possible by the methods of ordinary chemical analysis to extract from pitchblende substances of which the radio-activity is in the neighbourhood of 100,000 times greater than that of metallic uranium '.

These words announced the discovery of three new radio-active elements, radium, polonium, and actinium, and others have been added since. All are of exceedingly high ray-emitting power, in the case of radium itself 1,300,000 times the power of the uranium which had first disclosed its secret to Becquerel. None of these substances have been completely isolated. They are always tested in some combination, but they are known as elements through the individuality of their spectra, which, as we saw just now, are always distinguishable, with whatever admixture of other gases the element may be burnt. And now occurred one of the most striking of the many confirmations of Mendeleeff's Periodic Law. In the second group of Mendeleeff's table, which contains barium, there was a vacant space for a substance heavier than all the others in that group. This space was exactly filled by radium as soon as Mme. Curie had determined its atomic weight, and the truth of Mendeleeff's Law was confirmed by the fact that radium behaves in all its chemical properties so much like barium that it is very difficult to distinguish them. But on the side of radio-activity the new elements put immeasurable force and power of expansion into Becquerel's original discovery. He could now test the properties of his rays in substances emitting them a myriad times more abundantly. His subsequent researches and those of the many later workers in the field have now composed a body of knowledge of the most varied and astounding kind, much of it still incomplete and hypothetical, most of it pointing towards a new and revolutionary idea of the history of matter, yet none of it incompatible with the law which experimental methods ordered by mathematical reasoning had already established in our minds.

The rays from all these bodies were found to have common properties. They penetrate matter with an ease inversely proportional to its weight. Aluminium being light is easily penetrated ; lead being heavy is opaque. They resemble Röntgen's X-rays in their power of modifying a photographic plate. They cause many substances to shine in the dark. They make the air a conductor of electricity, and in this respect are identical with both the corpuscles and the positive ions. They have many chemical effects, and work on living bodies in various and powerful ways. By means of magnetism they have been further analysed into three classes : some which have little penetrating power and are only slightly bent by the strongest magnetism—these are the α-rays ; others very penetrating and easily deflected—these are the β-rays ; and a third class, less understood than the rest, but perhaps the same as X-rays, cannot be deflected by the strongest magnetic power and have an extreme power of penetration. These have been seen to affect a photographic plate through a foot of solid iron.

The two classes α and β, alpha-rays and beta-rays, are the best known, and seem to correspond to the positive ions and the corpuscles respectively. Sir William Crookes has invented a little instrument which shows the bombardment of a zinc sulphide target by the alpha-rays from a morsel of radium. The effect is like the starry heavens on a clear night. And yet, though this might be continuous day and night for years, no appreciable loss would take place in the weight or the bulk of the radium till centuries had elapsed. Such is the glimpse which we have now obtained of the depths of the infinitesimal world. The beta-rays, which are identified with the negative ions or corpuscles of electrolysis, have been more thoroughly studied than any of the others, and their wonders appear the greatest and the most pervasive. From a tiny pinch of matter which looks for all the world like common salt, a rain of projectiles proceeds which, if unimpeded, would go round the earth five times in a second. These rays come nearest in speed to light, and in mass their particles are a thousand times smaller than the atom of hydrogen. More potent than light, they can pass through bodies considered opaque, and yet they possess powers kindred to light in causing phosphorescence in bodies they strike. Thus we see in the properties of radium, particularly in the β-rays, which are identified with corpuscles and are the 'electrons' of the electric theory of matter, a series of links which bring all the forms of matter together. But there is another quality which has led some men of science farther still. A sort of gas is given off by radium which has been called the 'emanation', and possesses some of the properties of the radium itself. This emanation decays away like the radium itself, giving off a-particles and changing into another substance also radio-active. And the final product of the disintegration is lead. A new process of disintegration in the atom is thus revealed, which seems at present to be independent of all known chemical laws. And beyond the emanation comes another substance deposited on surrounding bodies by the emanation itself. This emanation was first called 'Emanation X' to denote its still unknown nature. But more and more symptoms point to the fact that it is to be connected with a group of elements classified together in the Periodic Law which are alike in not entering into any chemical combination, and in this respect differ from all other elements. It has, in fact, been identified with one of them, helium, which was discovered in large quantities in the atmosphere of the sun, and has been since then recognized by Sir William Ramsay as a constituent of certain minerals on the earth. The helium

2170   S

atom is the next to hydrogen in lightness, and it has been shown by Rutherford and Soddy that it consists of the alpha-particles given off by the emanation from the radium, the alpha-particles being about twice the mass of the hydrogen atoms, much heavier than the beta-particles from the same source.

No wonder that a whole school of chemists has arisen who hold that we may see in these facts the proof of a transmutation of matter constantly going on. Those who believe in this can find support for their theory in other facts and other probabilities both about terrestrial and celestial matter. We must remember that we are in this region allowing our imagination to lead us on. We have here no such certainties as mathematics could afford for the laws of motion up to the last quarter of the last century. The advocates of an evolution of matter avowedly connect it with the evolution of life, to which, as we saw, the methods of exact quantitative science are only now beginning to be applied. Yet the eager mind presses on, and if in no other sphere of human life were there any evidence of an age of hope, we may fall back on science, for here the thinker, while scrupulously loyal and reverent to his masters in the past, is always encouraging himself by visions of the triumphs to come.

What then may we think of those depths of the stars which the spectroscope has not yet connected with facts on the earth? The spectra of stars as well as of nebulae contain many lines which indicate substances not known to us, at least in that form, on earth. They have been identified in many cases with primitive forms of the elements we know; and more still remain to decipher. We seem bound to turn to the conception of a universe of an infinite variety of matter, incessantly changing, but changing by some intelligible law which our minds may fathom and express in ordered form, if we apply to the facts the same methods which have brought success in the past. And when we notice that from star to star, according to its heat, the elements appear broadly in the order of their weight, the first sketch of such a law seems to arise. Those heaviest of elements, uranium, radium, and the rest, from which radio-activity and the emanations appear, have not yet been discovered in the solar or stellar spectra. But helium is there in large quantities in many groups, disappearing only in the cooler stars, and we cannot forbear to connect with this transition of the forms of matter, observable in the heavens, those transitions which radio-activity has revealed on earth. If such a series of evolving elements were arranged, the lightest and most attenuated would occupy one end of the scale : Mendeleeff had claimed a place in his scale for elements even lighter than hydrogen, of which the ether should have first place. And from these we should proceed on lines of ordered evolution to those heaviest of all substances, such as radium, in which unlimited energy appears to be stored by age-long transformation from more attenuated forms. It is a speculation merely, but a speculation which gains colour from a multitude of facts, the fact among others that radio-activity is not confined to those substances which specially exhibit it. Fresh rain and snow are radio-active, and many metals to a slight extent. Those substances in particular which come from mineral springs or water that has lately passed through the earth emit the rays. All forms of matter may, it seems, possess the power, and it is the special quality of the heavy atom.

It is a speculation, too, but one that comes nearer to proof, that all matter is merely electricity in diverse forms. It has been calculated by Sir J. J. Thomson that the whole of the mass of the moving particles given out by radium is due to the electrical charge which it contains, meaning by mass simply the quantity of matter. We may then think of all atoms as made up of electrical particles or electrons in motion. Magnetism is a force developed at right angles to the direction of the motion of these particles, and light would be a disturbance in the ether caused by a change in the motion.

Much of this we know needs more elucidation. It has not the clearness or the definition of the earlier mechanics. But it illustrates continuously, as they did, the growing tendency of the human mind to see things whole. At every point in the history of thought, it is true, fresh distinctions are being made, fresh sciences are being constituted. The mere classification of the sciences is now a stupendous task which perplexes a committee of scientists for years on end. And yet at the same time the sciences themselves are constantly coming closer together, so that we can no longer see the sharp line dividing physics from chemistry which appeared visible in the early years of the nineteenth century. We see now that we are dealing in both with the same order of facts, and the main question appears to be how far we shall be able to carry into the whole field the same methods of exact measurement which have been found successful in that part, or aspect, of the subject which is more commonly called physics. Astronomy, which began as the study of a set of remote bodies acting upon us, and among themselves, in some ordered fashion in which we only took a part as being a similar great body ourselves, is now more and more completely merged in one comprehensive science of inorganic matter.

Between this, indeed, and the science of life a gulf still remains, but, headed by Pasteur, a host of chemists have been in recent years invading the realm of organic things and gaining a wealth of new knowledge in it. Pasteur, whose name both as a discoverer and a benefactor of mankind stands among the greatest, initiated in the 'fifties and 'sixties the scientific study of the most minute organisms. He disproved the theory of their spontaneous generation, and showed how fermentation and various diseases in plants and animals were due to the presence of tiny organisms coming from without, but thriving, if unchecked, in the body they attacked. And the study of the cause led also in many cases to the discovery of the cure. Pasteur led the way to Lister and to a mass of remedial work. These applications of science belong to a later stage in our story. We note them here as another example of the science of minute things and of the way in which one science links up with another. Some chemists, indeed, who have still later been exploring the properties of substances in solution, hold out the hope of being able to pass directly from the sphere of inorganic to organic matter. But here, if we would treat as science only the positively known, the barrier remains which Pasteur fortified. And another barrier lies between the sciences of the lower animal life as a whole and the sciences of human nature which involve a conscious ideal and describe the process of humanity in its achievement.

But there is one analogy so striking, between the progress of physical science as we have traced it in this chapter and the general evolution of mankind, that we cannot pass without dwelling on it for a moment. Just as the physical sciences have developed by gaining continually greater fullness and distinction in detail while becoming more and more a unity, so with human nature, whether we consider the individual man or the whole society to which he belongs. The individual has grown, not withered, in the ages, and he has grown precisely in proportion to the extent in which he has taken other men, and the world of nature also, into his soul. This was the paradox, if paradox it be, which confronted us in the last chapter. From one point of view religious growth is the development of personality : from the other it is the sinking of the personality in a greater whole. But the two aspects are not really opposed. They are inseparable, being in the race, as in the normal man, but two aspects of the same truth.

It can be then no idle fancy to suppose that as man's power of thought is his supreme and characteristic quality, his whole nature must gradually and in the issue be dominated by it. If in his abstract thought he is constantly attaining, as we have seen, more perfect harmony in the midst of expansion and growing distinctions and multiplicity of detail, so there should be in the conduct of his life some corresponding rhythm. The remaining chapters of this book deal with the practical side— the actions of the West, and especially of our own nation, in the same period in which we have observed this unexampled increase of physical knowledge. The practical sphere has also become in the same age wide and multifarious beyond all precedent. We shall look carefully to discover if, in the maze of objects, the conflict of passions, the obstacles to concentrated action, there are traces to be found of a reflection of the unity of thought in any unity of purpose.

THE EXPANSION OF THE WEST

EACH aspect of our subject seems, when we have once entered fully upon it, to be the most absorbing, to have the most links with the whole. It was so with liberty and nationalism. The whole world seemed to turn on securing greater freedom for individuals and the right of existence for nations. It was so with Socialism and education, and in the highest degree with the evolution of religion and the growth of science. We shall have the same feeling in the present chapter. Simultaneously with the profound changes in thought and the new discoveries which we have sketched in the last two chapters, another process was coming to its conclusion, which, to a visitor from Mars, would undoubtedly appear as the most remarkable social transformation ever witnessed on the globe.

That nucleus of progressive people who, since the advent of the Greeks long before our era, had agitated and advanced and knit themselves together round the Mediterranean, had, since the Renaissance and the adventurous voyages of the fifteenth and sixteenth centuries, spread their influence wider and wider over land and sea. A vast new continent had been added to their ken, and had become in its northern part the home of the most numerous and vigorous of Western nations. Throughout the East the Western man had passed, and in many places had set up an abiding home and centre of his civilization. In the nineteenth century he had pressed farther south. Every habitable island had been visited and most of them occupied in force. A new southern continent had been completely pegged out by Great Britain, and the giant peninsula of Africa, whose northern shores formed one side of the Mediterranean enclosure, was at last shedding her veil of mystery and falling into Western hands. Africa indeed, with its exploration, its partition between the European states, the schemes for its exploitation and its better government, brought to a climax this process of Western expansion in the last two decades of the nineteenth century.

This process, which has tended to make the whole world one, may be traced back to the beginnings of history. Science and its applications have made it speedier and more profound. It goes back to one of the earliest racial movements on the globe, the concentration of tribes round the Mediterranean basin and their subsequent radiation from it. It becomes prominent with the rise of the other symptoms of modern life—the growth of trade, the spread of science, the activity of the revolutionary age. It comes to its culmination in the present age and is intimately bound up with the greatest of wars. And it throws down to Western man the greatest of challenges. Having done this thing, having overrun the world by the power of your science, your engines of peace and your weapons of war, are you now able to control your work for the good of the whole, and make a smiling and stable home of these hasty dwellings which you threw up in an eager fit of emulous activity?

We have briefly to sketch the steps by which the leading nations of the West, and especially ourselves, have come to occupy this position of trust for the rest of mankind, and in particular the more recent steps towards the end of the last century. We shall then point out—for this is a book of hope—the lines on which at their best the Western settlers have been proceeding to make their occupation, with all its superior resources of power and knowledge, a boon to the lands which they have occupied. Without ignoring the evils we may quite fairly dwell on the signs of good.

At the end of the Napoleonic wars—the point at which our detailed study begins—England stood out as pre-eminently the naval and colonizing power in the world. She took little spoil for herself in the treaty which concluded that long conflict ; but any effective rivalry had disappeared. France was then beaten, as Spain, Portugal, and the Dutch, her earlier rivals, had been beaten before. England held without dispute the northern part of North America, the southern corner of Africa, the whole of Australia, the dominant position in India, beside a large number of islands and stations throughout the world. The organization of her domains, the development of the self-government which had always distinguished them—these things were still to come. But the main features of the new world-order could already be discerned. France having lost her share of North America and India in the Seven Years' War, and being foiled in her grand designs of Napoleon's time, set to work to build up a new empire in other lands. Two regions—beside the island of Madagascar—were in the nineteenth century brought under her sway. The first was the northern part of Africa, which lay facing her southern coast and had for many years afflicted both herself and other European Powers through the depredations of pirates. It was the Barbary coast of long and ill renown. Here in the reign of Louis Philippe she conquered and began to civilize Algeria and the adjacent lands. From this starting-point and her old station of Senegal she proceeded to acquire dominion over the greater part of north-west Africa. Her other sphere was in the East. There, from an old settlement in Annam, she went on to Cochin-China and Tonkin.

The other two great extensions of Western power in the century were effected by Russia and the United States. The

Russian was the greatest next to our own, but the least Western. She gradually spread out eastward and south-eastward, covering the whole of Siberia and pressing thence on northern China, crossing the Caucasus and impinging there on Turkey, invading Turkestan and seeming to threaten there our hold on India. The expansion of the United States, somewhat similar in extent, was exactly opposite in direction. They gradually crossed the continent during the century, settling on their march multitudes of adventurous and exiled men from all the countries of the Old World. The gold of California, discovered about the middle of the century, hastened the expansion, and by the end of the 'sixties the first trans-continental railway had linked up the two oceans and made a highway through the States.

The world-colonizing efforts of Italy and Germany, latest in attaining their nationhood, were subsequent to all this. Germany, as we shall see, acquired her empire almost at one rush, at the critical moment which is the turning-point of this chapter.

The world was thus fairly completely portioned out between the chief claimants for colonies before the acutest period of dissension begins. Many things had contributed to the allotment we have described, the geographical position and vigour of the homeland being the predominant factors. To our visitor from another planet the extension of Western power, the linking-up of all the globe by physical means, railways, steamships, and telegraphs, and by the increasing currency of European laws and ways of life, would have appeared the salient fact. It was indeed stupendous, the longest stride towards unification which the world had seen. And yet in the same period another and less obvious movement was going on which was destined to become as decisive for the fortunes of mankind as the process of unification itself. This was the spread of self-government in the British part of this Western empire. In this England was unique. In adventure, in scrambling for the spoil, she had played during the sixteenth and seventeenth centuries much the same part as her rivals in the game, as Spaniards or Portuguese, Frenchmen or Dutch. Towards the end of the eighteenth century, when her position of superiority was assured, she had slackened in the pursuit. Most of her gains in the nineteenth century had come to her rather without the seeking. But from the beginning, and markedly after the loss of the American colonies at the end of the eighteenth century, she had pursued a different course of political dealings with her dependencies from any other of the competing Powers.

Self-government was from the first the mark of English colonies alone. Virginia was the earliest, and here, in 1619, on instructions from home, the governor of the trading company which had founded the colony ten years before called together an assembly of representatives from every township ' to consult on the needs of the colony '. It was the first extra-European Parliament. The New England colonies, which followed shortly after, carried the same principle still farther, until in the War of Independence they attained what seemed to them at that time the only logical goal of self-government. There was nothing of this among our competitors. France owed more than we did in early days to the efforts of her missionaries, who were the direct emissaries of her Most Christian King, in Canada, in Syria, in Indo-China. It was through the heroism of the Jesuit and other orders sent out by France that she held the line of the St. Lawrence and the Great Lakes in the seventeenth and early eighteenth century. It was to protect her missionaries in Annam that France went to war in 1858 and won her Eastern provinces. But neither East nor West did she attempt to set up self-governing colonies, not having the model at home ; and when in the nineteenth century a new spirit prevailed in France and other countries, it took the form for Algeria of actual incorporation with national assemblies in Paris. Deputies from Algiers sit in the Chamber. To the Spaniards and the Dutch, our earlier rivals, their foreign possessions appeared still more exclusively as estates.

The nineteenth century completed for Great Britain the circle of her self-governing daughters of kindred blood, and has raised the question of self-government in other parts of the empire where the inhabitants before our occupation were not accustomed to it. The three great white commonwealths, Canada, Australia, South Africa, gained unity among themselves and self-government in that order. Canada received, in the throes of the American revolt, a foretaste of the perfect liberty which was to follow in the nineteenth century. The Quebec Act of 1774 assured to the French their religion and their civil law, and to us their loyalty. It was the first step in the policy of bold tolerance which the South African Union has exemplified still further in our own time, and which is fast making the British Empire, so far as it is white, an empire only in name, in reality a free alliance of self-governing peoples.

It would be foolish as well as untrue to claim the self-governing unity of the British commonwealth as a pure triumph of British wisdom. There are blots enough on the picture, and at every turn necessity or accident has played some part. Just as the American revolt provoked the Quebec Act, so the Canadian rebellion of 1837 led to Lord Durham's Commission and the grant of constitutions in 1840. The two Canadas were formed, each with a complete system of responsible government on the English plan. In 1867 all the provinces united in a Dominion of Canada covering half the continent. Lord Durham had taken with him on his Canadian mission a brilliant, energetic, though unscrupulous man, whose name deserves to be commemorated in the briefest record of English colonization, Edward Gibbon Wakefield. He combined, as Robert Owen and many others of our countrymen have done, a humanitarian with an industrial bent. It is an honourable feature in a nation of shopkeepers. Having to spend three years in Newgate for an early escapade, he began writing works on social reform, especially the condition of rural England. Vigorous, incisive, picturesque—something like Cobbett in his writings—he surpassed him in his practical remedies. He became the leading writer on the art of colonization, on plans for settling emigrants on the land, and for making the scheme pay both in a financial and a human sense. He attacked the reckless way in which land had been given away in Australia and the serious limitation of immigrants which ensued ; and he became in turn the chief promoter of the South Australian Company and of the New Zealand Association. He spent the last ten years of his life in New Zealand after it had received a constitution in 1853, and died there in 1862.

Australia had received her constitutions in 1852, the year before New Zealand. At each step the British commonwealth has marched more boldly and gained strength by strength. In the case of Australia the colonies were allowed to elect single-chamber assemblies in order to decide on the constitution they preferred. They all adopted the English system with two chambers and responsible ministries. In 1900 federation came and the Australian Commonwealth.

Africa remained, and leads us to the two critical decades at the end of the century. And the still greater question remained, the treatment by the stronger and self-governing people of the multitudes of coloured men with whom, in all parts of the world, the white settler was coming into closer and closer contact.

The last two decades of the nineteenth century are marked by a decided change in the English temper towards expansion, which coincides with a rush of the other Powers to acquire an empire likewise. We noticed that during the greater part of the century Great Britain had added to her possessions abroad rather reluctantly and, as it were, by inevitable accidents. This was conspicuously the case with India. It is no doubt possible to condemn certain actions of the Company or the Government which succeeded it: the annexation of Sind in 1844 by Lord Ellenborough was one of these. But on the whole, each extension of British sway was practically necessitated by the special conditions of the case. A military and depredating tribe, such as the Gurkhas, adjoined the more settled territories under British rule. It became necessary to check or suppress them in order to preserve the good order of the Ganges lands. This was a typical case, and occurred just after Waterloo. Wars with the Pindaris and the Mahrattas in Central India followed, and in the 'twenties our first intervention in Burma took place. All these wars were caused by neighbouring lawlessness. The Afghan wars which began in the 'thirties had the additional motive of safeguarding India against the expected encroachment of Russia, who was advancing all the time from the north-west. Oudh was annexed by Dalhousie in 1856 to save it from extreme misrule. The annexation acted, however, as an additional stimulus to the mutiny of 1857, which was a revolt of the native mind against this gradual extension of British rule and the introduction of Western methods. The mutiny meant the end of the old East India Company, and India as a whole became at last a dependency of the British Crown. The story, as Macaulay first pointed out, was one of the most astonishing and romantic in history, and yet it has always remained generally unknown and uninteresting to Englishmen at home. There could be no clearer proof that the acquisition of this—the most

important part of our empire in the stricter sense of the term—
was not deliberately planned by the national will. Drake and
the crusade against Spain in the sixteenth century are a part of
the national Epos, like Alfred and the Danes. The occupation
of India is not. Only the two incidents of the Black Hole of
Calcutta and the siege of Lucknow—stories of suffering—are
enshrined in the national consciousness.

In the last two decades of the nineteenth century a change,
as we have said, took place in the national policy, and it was
principally connected with events in the north and the south
of Africa. Gladstone, opposed to the change, was a leading
figure in both. We saw in the eighth chapter how, though
sympathizing with France in the cruel and unwise termination
of the Franco-Prussian war, he yet adhered to a policy of strict
non-intervention. He had no conception of England taking a
place in a settled scheme of world-policy, well thought out
beforehand and modified in detail to suit the changing occasions
of the moment, and seeking allies and shaping her conduct
accordingly. In this he was typical of his countrymen. To be
just and friendly to other nations, observing one's pacts with
them, and for the rest leaving them as much alone as possible;
to preserve one's own possessions in safety—with of course
a reasonable regard for profit and prosperity; to check the
oppression of the weaker people with whom one came in
contact, so far as the Government had cognizance of it—these,
one may say, on a broad view, were the cardinal principles of
our actions abroad, and in these many leading men of both great
parties, Lord Salisbury as well as Mr. Gladstone, were at one.

But Africa, north and south, put this policy to the test and
sharply modified it. It is curious to note how the storms in both
centres, north and south, developed at about the same time.
In 1880 the Boers of the Transvaal, which had been annexed by
us in 1877, revolted. In 1881 they defeated our troops at Laing's

Nek and Majuba Hill, and Mr. Gladstone shortly afterwards granted them self-government with a general reservation of British suzerainty.   In the following year a revolt in Egypt broke out under Arabi Pasha, a colonel in the Egyptian army, against the influence of France and England, who were jointly controlling the Khedive, to whom large sums had been lent by French and English bond-holders. We will take the issue of the Egyptian business first, as it matured more quickly.   Gambetta, the strong man of France who would have advocated a forward policy, had fallen in January 1882, and the French, being in a mood of cautious non-intervention, left England to deal with the Egyptian revolt alone. Nothing could have been more repugnant to Gladstone's whole policy and temper.   None the less he went on while Bright left the Ministry.   The forts of Alexandria were bombarded, and a British army, landing in Egypt, occupied the Suez Canal, defeated Arabi's army and took him prisoner. It was a crucial step in the history of the British Empire, taken by statesmen most reluctant to move, and fully aware of the grave objections to which every aspect of the process was open— the support of bond-holders by armed force, our isolated action in the bombardment, the alienation from France, the assumption of responsibilities which could not be evaded and were bound to grow.   The occupation of Egypt, which we honestly wished to make as short as possible, has gone on ever since, with enormous advantage to the whole Egyptian population.   It became a regular Protectorate at the beginning of the Great War, France having before this been satisfied, first, by our recognition of her occupation of Tunis which took place in 1881 before Gambetta's fall, and, later, by our support of her action in Morocco just before the war.   When to this is added the conquest of Tripoli in 1912 by the Italians, we see the whole of Africa except Abyssinia and Liberia portioned out among the European powers before the Great War began.

But so far as feeling in England was concerned, the sequel in the Soudan of our action in Egypt had a greater effect than the action itself. A semi-religious revolt in the Soudan succeeded the suppression of Arabi's movement in Egypt, and Gordon, who had previously been Governor-General of the Soudan under the Khedive, was sent to withdraw the Egyptian garrisons. This was in January 1884. His actions there, his brave defence of Khartoum, the delay in relieving him, and his death almost exactly a year afterwards, form one of the best known and most debated episodes in English history. It is certain that these events, and what was commonly regarded as the surrender to the Boers after Majuba Hill, did more than anything else to upset the Gladstonian Government and to create the change in the public temper which we noticed above. Reaction and resentment against them coloured British activity in that age of 'imperialism', and hampered Gladstone's policy for the appeasement of Ireland.

The story of South Africa is even longer and more complicated. It was played out through a time of difficulties and mistakes, heroism and magnanimity, stubbornness and want of tact, in a great country full of great ideas. At last, under one of our happy stars, the Union of South Africa arose in 1909 to heal the feuds and civilize the whole country and take its share in the war of free peoples in 1914. The details, the due allotment of praise and blame, must be sought in larger books than this. But the main facts are plain.

After the successful constitution of the Canadian Dominion at the end of the 'sixties, public opinion turned with hope to similar action in the four states of South Africa. In 1874 a Conservative Government came into power with Disraeli at its head. It was the beginning of that rise of imperialist sentiment which became strong later on in reaction against Gladstone. Lord Carnarvon, as Colonial Secretary in Disraeli's

Government, took up with energy the idea of a South African confederation on the Canadian model, and Froude, the historian, went out on a mission to inquire into and promote the plan. Sir Bartle Frere followed in 1877 to put the policy into effect, but the difficulties of the case were too great for the hasty methods and the vacillating home-policy with which they were attacked. Whereas in Canada the rival European race, the French, were practically confined to one province, and had been rendered loyal a hundred years before by wise concessions, in South Africa our rivals, the Boers, pervaded the whole country except Natal. They were farmers and sturdy fighters, descendants of the Dutch colonists who had first occupied the Cape in the middle of the seventeenth century. The fortunes of war had given us the Cape finally in 1814, but the British remained a minority even of the white population, and surrounding both Boer and Briton was a large and vigorous coloured race whose lands the white man coveted, whose disorders provoked his interference, and about whose treatment the typical Briton and the typical Boer had differed from the time of Livingstone onwards. Here were grounds enough for constant friction, and to these were added the discovery of diamonds at Kimberley in the 'seventies and of gold in the Transvaal in the 'eighties. Hence freedom in unity, which had come so easily to Canada, was not to be achieved in South Africa till after thirty years of incessant struggle and one of our longest and most repugnant wars.

The Boers set themselves to defeat the earlier and ill-advised schemes of 1874. In 1881, when a Gladstonian had succeeded the Disraelian Government, the Transvaal revolted to secure an independence which had been refused to them for the asking. They gained it practically, with a vague reservation of suzerainty, after defeating our troops in two small engagements. The gold in the Transvaal brought up the question again twelve years later on a larger scale and with fiercer animosity. The gold-fields had introduced a vigorous European community bent on making wealth and enjoying life. They were the social antipodes of the Boer farmers who surrounded them, and they were excluded from all political rights. Another new fact made the situation still more acute. Since the grant of independence by Mr. Gladstone, both Dutch republics—the Transvaal and her sister state on the Orange River—had been hemmed in by fresh British territory to the north and west. Bechuanaland closed their western frontiers, and the organizing genius of Rhodes had built up a new domain to the north, and was in course of building a giant railway which was ultimately to be an all-British line from the Cape to Cairo. Hence the Boers saw themselves being swallowed up, and contested every point, first in the negotiations and then on the veldt, with the desperate heroism of brave men at bay.

The British Government which went to war with the Transvaal for the Uitlanders' rights, and finally subdued the two republics in 1902, was composed of men and supported by men who had defeated Mr. Gladstone's plans of Home Rule for Ireland in 1886 when it was first introduced, and again in 1893 when it passed the Commons but was rejected by the Lords. The Government which finally granted South Africa union and self-government in 1909 was composed of men who had supported Home Rule for Ireland and passed a Home Rule Bill through both Houses of Parliament just before the war. The Great War came, and both sides in the long debate seemed to be at last united. Both realized that the safety and progress of humanity demanded the co-operation of free and strongly organized national units, that the promotion of this ideal had been England's historic mission in the world even when she was least conscious of it, and that her worst lapse was in the case which lay nearest to her own doors.

But before this awakening arrived, there were many painful and difficult steps to take which are yet in most cases far from finished. The most obvious and perhaps the simplest was the completion of that world-distribution among the Western Powers of which this chapter is a sketch. Africa—for we have not yet done with Africa—was the meeting-place of all the competitors from Europe. We have seen a part of the process, France, Italy, and England entrenched in the north and south with a small slice reserved for Spain on the Morocco coast. Now we must speak of Germany.

It is a remarkable fact that all the German colonies date from those last two decades of the nineteenth century in which the competition among the other Powers became intense and universal and the whole land-surface of the globe seemed in process of being surveyed and divided up among them. But the reasons are as patent as the fact. The Great Elector of Brandenburg had founded, it is true, a few settlements on the west coast of Africa towards the end of the seventeenth century. But there were no German sea-dogs to carry the flag afield, no strong State at home to feed them with men and cover them with its name. Two centuries were to pass before the German State was made, and meanwhile one of its master-builders, Frederick the Great, had laid down as a cardinal principle of policy that ' All distant possessions are a burden to the State. A village on the frontier is worth a principality two hundred and fifty miles away.' The desire for over-sea possessions did not appear again in German history until after the Empire was founded in 1871, and when it did arise it was the result of three distinct impulses in the national life. The first came from the large increase in population which followed the consolidation. Between 1870 and the end of the century the population of the new empire increased from over forty to nearly sixty millions, half as much again. There was a stream of emigration which has slackened in recent years, and as these emigrants went to countries, principally the United States, which were not under the German flag, there was naturally a comparison with other lands, especially England, whose nationals formed settlements abroad which were off-shoots of the motherland. The second and more direct cause of the foundation of colonies was the trading instinct. Trading stations were sought by Germany, and began to be acquired early in the 'eighties, wherever valuable properties could be obtained and commerce carried on with the surrounding natives. This was the origin of the first colonies both in the Pacific and in South-west Africa. Then, in the 'scramble for Africa' and the antici-pated scramble for China, a third factor, the competitive passion, came strongly into play. Was the greatest military Power in Europe, the most prosperous and progressive, the most rapidly increasing nation, to be the only one which had no colonies—the badge of success, the stepping-stones to a world-empire?

1882, the year of Arabi's rebellion in Egypt, may be taken as the beginning of German colonization. In that year the German Colonial Society was founded to promote the move-ment. Bismarck was still in power, and, though he declared himself even in the year of his death to be ' still no colony man ', he acted with his accustomed decision as soon as he found that the country demanded action. Two such actions were taken in 1884. Some German trading stations in New Guinea and other Pacific Islands were placed under the German flag, and the coastland of South-west Africa north of the Orange River to Cape Frio was annexed. From this point onward the partition of Africa among all the Powers proceeded rapidly. The Cameroons and East Africa were taken by Germany, France pressed forward from the basin of the Senegal, the Congo Free State was recognized under the protectorate of Leopold of Belgium, Italy began to annex land in the north-east on the Red Sea, and England cleared up her difficulties with Portugal on the south-east, France in the centre, and Germany wherever she found her. Part of the price of the latter settlement was paid in 1890 when Lord Salisbury handed over Heligoland at the mouth of the Elbe to the German Empire. It was the great year of agreements about Africa, the year in which the Powers at the Brussels Conference bound themselves to united action for the benefit of the natives, the year, too, in which the new Kaiser William II dropped his old pilot, Bismarck.

During the same period in which the partition of Africa was being carried out, Germany was taking steps to gain a hold in another region where, as events have shown, she had more chance of maintaining it. Possessions in Africa or the Pacific were at the mercy of the British fleet. While, as in the South African and the present war, we maintained our command at sea, no help from Germany could reach the object of our attack ; but going eastward she could travel by land. Nothing but the narrow Bosphorus breaks the continuous land-line from Berlin to the Persian Gulf. Hence very soon a Berlin–Bagdad railway became to the German expansionist the proper answer to Rhodes's all-red railway from Cairo to the Cape. The Kaiser's old pilot, though not in theory a colony man, had made the first move in this direction also. Already in 1883, ten years before the Armenian massacres, Bismarck gave notice to the Powers that his policy would be no further intervention in Turkey for the assistance of the Christian subjects of the Porte. In the same year Prussian officers began to be employed by the Sultan to train the Turkish troops. Steadily, from this time onwards, the German hold was strengthened. Turkey was supported by German influence in her dealings with the other Powers, and in return concessions, especially railway concessions, were made to Germans which would ultimately fit into the grand continuous scheme. Previous British applicants were sometimes expropriated from their possessions in favour of the German, and in 1899 the concession of the whole line—Berlin to Bagdad—was at last announced. It followed, aptly enough, the visit of the Kaiser in 1898 to Palestine, when a solemn service on the Mount of Olives proclaimed him at once a pious Christian and the friend of the Mohammedan world. The British opposition and various counter-stipulations which it was thought necessary to make were finally settled in 1914, just before the war broke out.

There remained only one large tract of the earth's surface not yet assigned in any sense to any of the Western Powers. This was China, greatest and most mysterious of nations, with an area larger than the whole of Europe and a population probably between a fifth and a quarter of the human race. And it is perhaps the most significant fact in the whole course of her inscrutable history that still, after the widest expansion of the West, she remains unassigned. One of the first events, indeed, in the Great War was the ejection of a considerable body of Europeans, the Germans in Shantung, from their settlement, and the substitution of the Japanese in their place. But though China has remained substantially intact, yet the last decades of the nineteenth century brought it into closer relations than before with other Powers. For a moment it seemed possible that China too might be partitioned. This was averted by the vastness of the task, by the jealousies of the competing States, above all by the presence, in the Japanese, of a neighbouring and more sympathetic people who had of their own initiative absorbed the Western methods and were able and ready to turn their newly-acquired weapons against the West that taught them. But though the West could not take forcible possession, yet early in the new century the wave of change overran at last even the Chinese barrier, and the spirit of it began to work in the most conservative medium on the planet. Our summary of these events must be short and sad.

The dealings of the West with China in the nineteenth century, compared with their earlier relations in the Middle Ages and the Renaissance, are one of the least hopeful aspects of the period. It would, indeed, be hard to base a theory of progress on the contrast of those early envoys—William of Rubruquis or Marco Polo—visiting with friendly admiration the empire of the Great Khan, discussing religious questions at conferences on the steppes, with the British gunboats of 1840, forcing tons of opium on the reluctant Chinese at the cannon's mouth. It is as hard to see progress here as in the cotton-mills of 1800, where joyless infants were giving their puny strength to feed the new machines, or in 1914 on the battlefields of France and Flanders, where the best of our young manhood have laid down their lives that the world might live. Again, the friars of the thirteenth century, the Jesuit missionary, Matteo Ricci, of 1600, were clearly doing a work of far higher order, and in a far nobler spirit, than the traders of the nineteenth century, who finally secured, after repeated wars and long-drawn negotiations, the opening of five Treaty Ports and access to the interior of China. The second of the wars (in 1857), when the French and English fought together against the Chinese, also gave the Western Powers the right of permanent residence for their ambassadors in Pekin. It is an interesting commentary on the different working of persuasion and of force, that while Ricci became Li-ma-teu, honoured both in his life and in his burial-place by the Chinese, the Legations which were forced on China by war had again to be defended and rescued by a large allied army in the Boxer War of 1900.

England took the first step in using force to open Chinese doors to Western trade. France and Russia, pressing on her from the south and north, gained the largest territorial advantage. The French, who had an interest in Annam, based long ago on their protection of the missionaries, proceeded in the 'seventies to assert a protectorate over both Annam and Tonkin. Later on they branched out into railways in the province of Yunnan. The Russians in the same way began to establish themselves in Manchuria, and in the 'nineties carried their Siberian railway across Chinese territory to Vladivostok.

But the war of China with Japan in 1894 was the turning-point. A war between two kindred Eastern nations, it had the effect at once of exalting the Japanese spirit, giving her the lead in China and the Chinese waters, and throwing down a challenge to Russia and the West. It was the coming-of-age of a new Power, born of Eastern traditions and Western science.

China and Japan had fallen out over Korea. Her victory might have given Japan at once the Port Arthur peninsula and the suzerainty over Korea, had not three of the European Powers intervened to prevent her. These were France and Russia with large advancement in their eye, and Germany waiting for her chance. Great Britain stood aloof, and from that time dates the close friendship of England and Japan which became an alliance in 1902. From the same time dates the common action of England and America in Eastern questions. Ultimately this union of three Powers to ward off the aggressions of others and to preserve the freedom of the East became the decisive factor. England and Japan were unassailable at sea, and the United States were soon to give evidence of a larger admixture of disinterested international zeal than could be claimed for any other of the participating Powers.

Soon after the temporary set-back which the intervening Powers had administered to Japan, Germany's chance arrived. On the strength of the murder of two missionaries she seized Kiao-chau, and thus made herself mistress of a central point on the Chinese coast commanding the province of Shantung.

Russia followed by occupying Port Arthur, from which she had just excluded Japan, and we felt bound to defend our own interests by leasing Wei-hai-Wei as a naval base. This was in 1897, and soon afterwards the resentment of the Chinese broke out in the Boxer Rising—fanatical, anti-foreign, and hopeless, but fomented by the Chinese Court. All the other Powers, including America and Japan, now combined to march on Pekin and relieve the Foreign Legations. Pekin was occupied and largely destroyed. But Japan and America distinguished themselves by their good order and moderation. Four years later Japan had her revenge on Russia in the great war in which she finally acquired Port Arthur, Korea, and a dominating position in China from which she is not likely to be displaced. And a little later still the United States took a nobler revenge on China herself by returning to the re-constituted government the indemnity imposed on her for the Boxer Rising.

It is a gloomy story, though the clouds lift somewhat towards the close. The China of the new age, with its Parliament and its President and its Western education, does not come within the scope of this sketch. We must stop at the point where the Powers of Europe, partly defeated by their own ambitions, partly rallying to a better ideal of their relations to the East, have called a halt.

The New World, the first scene of European expansion, has, by virtue of that very fact, remained outside the area of the recent competition. When in the sixteenth century the stream of adventurers began to follow Columbus across the Atlantic, two cardinal facts were soon established which have governed the development of the Americas ever since. In the northern portion of the great land-mass a nucleus of settlers made their home, partly from England and partly from France. They went not merely as traders, not to exploit the country and bring back wealth to be consumed at home, least of all did they go as administrators of settled realms such as we found in the East, but they went to live and thrive and spread themselves in a new land sparsely inhabited and with untapped resources of every kind. Soon, as we have seen, the Anglo-Saxon element gained the upper hand. The French were not alienated nor driven out, but their political expansion was checked and the colonization of the northern part of the continent proceeded on the whole on English lines. Farther south the occupation of the continent followed, broadly speaking, the boundaries which Columbus and the Pope had suggested, the Portuguese taking the eastern sphere and the Spaniards the western. This, as modified a little later, gave Brazil to Portugal, and Mexico and the western part of South America to Spain. But Spain and Portugal, the daring pioneers in the first age of discovery, had no staying-power. They were on the decline at home ; and, at the beginning of our period, their authority was renounced by the settlements they had made. The Monroe doctrine of 1823 only formulated as a principle of policy what was already established as a system of facts.

The United States had been strengthened by their severance from England in the War of Independence, strengthened above all in their republicanism and their determination to resist any encroachment by a reactionary Power.

Ever since the invasion of Spain by the French in 1808, the Spanish colonies had been throwing off their allegiance. The war in Europe meant for them the chance of independence ; and in Bolivar they found their hero of romance, their unconquerable leader, who reappeared after every defeat and ended as the liberator of three great States in South America— Colombia (which he joined with Venezuela), Bolivia, and Peru. The United States followed the movement, which went on spreading to all the other colonies both of Spain and of Brazil, with sympathy and encouragement. In 1817 she sent commissioners to open up commercial relations with those who had made good their revolt. When, therefore, in 1822 the Holy Alliance at the Verona Congress proposed to suppress the revolt of the Spanish colonies in America, the step at once evoked the recognition by the United States of their independence. The following year President Monroe made, in his message to Congress, the pronouncement which has always passed by his name but was actually drafted by John Quincy Adams. It summed up the general situation and the feeling of the States, and accorded fully with the policy of Canning. The spirit of the preliminary clause has governed their foreign actions for nearly a hundred years. ' In the wars of the European Powers ', it stated, ' in matters relating to themselves we have never taken any part, nor does it comport with our policy so to do. It is only when our rights are invaded or seriously menaced that we resent injuries or make preparations for our defence.' It will be noticed how carefully President Wilson adhered to the traditional policy of his country before he took the decisive step which must inevitably modify it in future. But the more operative clauses are those that follow : ' With the existing colonies or dependencies of any European Power we have not interfered and shall not interfere. But with the Governments who have declared their independence and maintained it, and whose independence we have on great consideration and on just principles acknowledged, we could not view any interposition for the purpose of oppressing them or controlling in any other manner their destiny by any European Power in any other light than as the manifestation of an unfriendly disposition towards the United States.' Most general and decisive of all was the clause prompted by the rival claims of Great Britain and Russia to territories in the north-west which were at that moment under discussion. ' The occasion has been judged proper for asserting as a principle in which the rights and interests of the

United States are involved, that the American continents, by the free and independent condition which they have assumed and maintain, are henceforth not to be considered as subjects for future colonization by any European Powers.'

The United States thus stood forth as the champion of the whole New World, a champion prepared to fight for its freedom against the Old World from which it sprang. The daughters' houses would only receive their old relations as visitors and on their own terms. Expansion, therefore, in the Americas has during the last century followed its own lines quite independently of European rivalries. Only one breach of the Monroe doctrine has occurred, when during the Civil War the French supported for a time Maximilian, Napoleon III's candidate for the crown of Mexico. As soon as the war was over, the United States demanded the recall of the French troops. The hegemony has never been tainted with tyranny, the leading state abstaining from imposing her own will upon her weaker fellow-nations, refusing even to attend a Pan-American Congress until 1889. Only with Mexico has the peace been broken between the leading Power and her colleagues. Touching Mexico on the south, the United States touched the old Spanish empire on the continent, and in her onward march she absorbed, first, Florida, then Texas and the lands west of Texas, till on the Pacific sea-board she found the sphere of a new and active development. It was this trend westward which gave her Hawaii and part of the Samoan Islands towards the end of the century; led to her special interest in China which we have noticed; and, when war broke out with Spain in 1898 over Cuba, induced her to retain the Philippine Islands as a dependency, while Cuba itself was given independence. The westward sweep brought also new and somewhat jealous relations with Japan, which a common interest in the Great War, as before in the Chinese rising, seems likely to appease.

The growth of great cities, the clearing of the bush, the spanning of northern and southern continents by railways, the rush of men, the piling up of wealth, these things we shall not attempt even to sketch. But there is one aspect of American expansion which fits in so aptly with our general argument that it is right in a hopeful view to lay some stress upon it. It is this. America, first scene of European expansion, last of the Great Powers to expand again in the recent movement, seems in more than one sense to be a link between the continents and between the old and new in human settlements. By her transcontinental railways and her Panama Canal she now unites Great Britain, which was the extreme west of the ancient world, with the extreme east of China and Japan. But the knitting up in spirit far transcends this physical union. It is one aspect—perhaps the most important—of the goal to which our study of the century has been directed. We saw in an earlier chapter how towards the end of the eighteenth century the idea of a common humanity became current in the world, a being of all races and lands, deriving traditions, instincts, powers, from common roots in the past, and destined in the future to closer and closer co-operation for the common good. Such ideas were reiterated, expanded, and explained by hundreds of thinkers in the nineteenth century. But it is a far cry from a doctrine, however true, held however fervently and intelligently by small groups of men, and the application of the same truth to the government of nations and the healing of mankind. The truth to be operative must be expressed in public actions and embodied in institutions and forms of law. The New World, standing outside most of the agreements of the other Powers, guarding for the most part a careful isolation, was a wheel wanting from the chariot which must carry the fortunes of the world. Who can doubt for a moment that if on July 29, 1914, the German war-party had known that not England only, but the United States in all their strength, would oppose the violation of Belgium, there would have been no war ?

Hence the gradual emergence of America from her Western seclusion was not only a good thing for the world, but a necessity, if anything like world-order is to be maintained or world-progress achieved. But the special quality of the American intervention is here rather in question than her needed presence in any league of nations which is to be. Wherever the United States have added their strength to an international movement, it has been more strictly in the interests of humanity and of peace than the action of any other Power. For the spirit of the common action is at least as important as the action itself. There was little humanity in the scramble for Africa, though the Brussels Conference of 1889 declared that the purpose of the Powers should be ' to put an end to the crimes and devastations engendered by the traffic in African slaves, to protect effectively the aboriginal populations of Africa, and to ensure for that vast continent the benefits of peace and civilization '. They paid this homage to duty and to human rights, and within ten or fifteen years the Congo population had been decimated by oppression. Official records of inhuman crimes in the German colonies are known to all men : similar offences, though not often so great, have been committed at some time by white men of all nations in contact with the black. There was little humanity among the Powers, united though they were, as they stood round the prostrate form of China after her defeat by Japan, or in the Concert of Europe in 1895, which looked on without action while tens of thousands of Armenians to whom reforms had just been accorded were massacred before they could enjoy them.

Can we trace any improvement in the spirit of the leading Powers in their treatment of the world they have overrun ?

The answer may, we think, be given in the affirmative, but it is a qualified one and still rests rather on promise of improvement than on actual performance. To substantiate our answer we should need to survey the colonial activities of all the Powers separately in recent years, for little has been done collectively since the Brussels Conference of which we spoke. We should note in our own empire general rest and contentment for the last twenty-five years, the only exceptions outside the British Isles being the Boer War and spasmodic sedition in India. We should note the continued extension of self-government to all parts of it and marked prosperity in most, notably in Egypt, as the direct result of our rule. We should study the provisions of Sir Frederick Lugard's code for North Nigeria, and rejoice at the general acclamation of loyalty there and elsewhere when the war broke out. And we might think with pride mixed with sorrow of the Herero who wrote home from British South Africa, ' Let me tell you that the land of the English is probably a good land, since there is no ill-treatment ; white and black stand on the same level ; there is much work and much money, and your overseer does not beat you, or if he does he breaks the law and is punished '.

Turning to the United States we should be struck by the generosity and thoroughness with which their comparatively small colonial domain has been administered. Sums raised from it by way of tariff have always been returned for the good of the colony, and large sums spent for education and humanitarian work. The medical work done by the International Health Board would alone qualify the Americans as the pioneers of humanity in expansion. They have begun a campaign against yellow fever on the South American and African coasts as they have already stamped it out in Panama and Cuba. And, latest and most interesting experiment of all, a hospital ship started last Christmas to cruise about round Mindinao in the Philippines and the three hundred islands of the Sulu Archipelago, taking nurses, doctors, operating-rooms, and floating wards to regions never before visited by a Western medical man. At home, in the latter part of the nineteenth century, a new and humane policy was adopted towards the Red Indians, who since 1871 are carefully tended in large reservations. And surely lynching has died out in recent years?

France's best present to the optimist would be her government of Tunis. Here she has kept a strong but not obtrusive control and improved the country greatly in all measurable ways. Roads, railways, schools, have spread apace, and trade has more than quadrupled in the last twenty years. Tunis for the French corresponds to Egypt for the English. In Algeria they have had some of the same difficulties, surmounted by the same chequered success, as we have had in India. From their old settlements of Senegal on the west, the Ivory Coast on the south, and Algiers on the north, they have opened up in the last forty years a great empire in the west of Africa, linking it up with roads, irrigating it by wells, civilizing it in the old Roman fashion with the added assistance of modern science. The aerial post initiated in 1917 between Algiers and Timbuctoo must be the first example in the world of regular communication through the air. It is another link with the revolutionary age, for in 1783, the year of Jouffroy's first steam-boat at Lyon, in the presence of Louis XVI and his queen, the first balloon invented by the Montgolfier brothers ascended at Versailles.

XII

SOCIAL PROGRESS

WE traced in the last chapter some of the concluding stages of a secular movement in world-history, the spread over the globe of Western nations and Western ideas. At the opening of the twentieth century it appeared nearly complete, with every great tract of the planet traversed by Western explorers, a flag of the New World hoisted at the North Pole, a flag of the Old World at the South, and colonies and spheres of influence won by the invaders in every quarter, except the great land-mass of the Far East and the island-empire that protects it. We saw these settlements acquiring freedom and individual development, becoming in various ways independent of their mother-states, and we suggested that the culmination of the process was to be found when the United States, themselves an offshoot from the European centre, began a colonizing move-ment of their own, joined forces for international purposes with the older Powers, and helped to infuse a higher degree of humanity and idealism into the common stock. But at the best the plan of Western expansion and world-control remains a sketch, and its further completion depends mainly on the extent to which ideals of a higher and a fuller life for all obtain the upper hand at home, among the populations which have thus assumed responsibilities for the civilization of others. ' How ', the Bible asks, ' shall a man love God whom he has not seen, if he love not his brother whom he has seen ? ' How, we may add, shall a slum-child in London or Manchester, the future citizen of a civilizing race, promote the humane treatment and the higher life of the negro or the coolie, if he has no higher life of his own ? Very often, indeed, the unspoilt member of some other race which we have set out to rule—the Red Indian on the Great Lakes, the Arab in the desert, the Kaffir in the bush —has a far freer and fuller life than many members, perhaps even the average, of the dominant race which can control him by its superior organization and science.

But, for the moment at any rate, the West has a predominance over the other portions of the globe, and we have to trace the steps, if any, by which the Western nations have prepared themselves for their greatest task by civilizing their own people. Force they have, irresistible force, when used collectively, the force of applied science and organized numbers. But in order that this force should be used for the best advantage of all mankind, it is necessary that the ideas of the leading nations should be humane as well as powerful, enlightened as well as organized. They have to recognize, if they are to be a blessing and not a curse to the world, that a higher life for all, and not mere power or mere acquisition, whether of land or wealth or rule, must be their aim. And this higher life must be aimed at, and to some extent enjoyed, within the bosom of the governing nations before they can extend it to the races whom they influence. They must recognize, too, that the higher life of one man or one community will differ widely from that of another, that no one can advance to a higher stage of his own being, except on lines which the nature and previous history of that being will dictate ; and this implies wide sympathy and knowledge, as well as a profound love of freedom in the minds of those who must, whether they will or no, put their hands to the task.

Now there is one point in our survey which must strike every student of the period, whether he shares the hopeful view which we suggest or not. It is this. The movement towards the elevation of the home population, though later in date than the movement of expansion, and not so rapid, has yet advanced simultaneously with it in later years. There was no democratic movement indeed, no idea of social reform, when the Spanish adventurers first crossed the Atlantic at the beginning of the seventeenth century. But when, after the outburst of science, the industrial revolution gained full sway at the end of the eighteenth century, at once both colonial expansion and social reform became prominent factors in modern life; and at the close of the nineteenth century, when, as we have just seen, the expansionist movement was at its height, social reform had become the leading interest in domestic politics among all the nations of the West. We made the expansion of the West our leading topic for the last decade of the last century, as it was then that the acutest jealousies arose first between France and England and later between Germany and the other Powers, and it was then that the United States entered the arena, completing and somewhat civilizing the area of competition. We take social reform as the leading topic in the succeeding decade because in that period a new government came into power in England of which the first motto was appeasement abroad and social legislation at home. The same statesmen who granted self-government to South Africa gave old-age pensions to the poor and passed a budget largely increasing the burdens on the rich for the sake of the less well-to-do.

But this movement, culminating at the beginning of the present century and running its course vigorously even during the war, must be traced back, like our other streams, to early fountains in the age of revolution. The life of one great man, born in 1819 and dying in 1900 on the threshold of the new century, typifies very aptly the growth of the English mind and English public policy in the matter. John Ruskin is, for us children of the nineteenth century, the figure which best represents the spirit of social reform as it struggled to life after the depression of the Napoleonic wars, found expression in the middle of the century, and became dominant at its close. Ruskin himself called Carlyle his teacher, and this no doubt describes the influence of a powerful upon a more receptive mind. Yet in its breadth and tenderness, its joy in all forms of life and beauty, the younger was, if not the greater, certainly the more persuasive and liberal nature. Of all his English contemporaries, the nearest to Ruskin is William Morris, who had the same joy in beauty, the same intense yearning for a Utopia of happy and loving people. But Ruskin is nearer the heart of the social movement, because he more than Morris criticized, and on the whole criticized soundly, the dogmas of political economy which were supposed to bar the way to social action of a remedial kind, and at the same time, unlike Morris, he avoided committing himself to one political solution and one organized party for carrying it out. His attitude of sympathy, now with some Socialist measure, now with a paternal despotism, now with a craft-guild, and now with individual initiative, was, though vacillating, much nearer to the general mind than a partisan solution could ever be. It is interesting to remember that Sydney Smith, one of the pioneers of reform in the *Edinburgh Review*, the famous orator of Dame Partington and the Atlantic, was still alive to welcome the publication of *Modern Painters*. It appeared in 1843, two years before Sydney Smith's death, and he greeted it as a work of transcendent talent, presenting most original views in powerful language. 'It would work a complete revolution in the world of taste.' Here was Ruskin's beginning as a new force in art. His social gospel and his views on political economy come in his mid-career. It was in 1860, in the *Cornhill Magazine*, that the four essays were first published which we now know as *Unto this Last*. Nothing illustrates better the gulf which separates those days from the present, or even from the time of Ruskin's death, than the fact that the editor, Thackeray, was

compelled by an outburst of public indignation to suspend the
publication of what we should now regard as rather commonplace views.   Another famous editor had to yield to the same
storm ; for two years later Froude began a new series in *Fraser's
Magazine*, and again, after the fourth number, they were suspended.   It was the same generation and almost the same year
in which Darwin threw our Victorian fathers into a panic by
another commonplace.

What were the living truths which take us back even now to
these little volumes ?   What was the gross offence which led
the subscribers to the *Cornhill* and to *Fraser's* to demand their
suspension ?   It was an unsparing attack on society organized
according to the accepted ‘ laws of political economy ’.   In
such a society the persons who become rich are, generally
speaking, the ‘ industrious, resolute, proud, covetous, prompt,
methodical, sensible, unimaginative, insensitive, and ignorant ’.
Those who remain poor are of the opposite characters.   It was
a little essay on the psychology of money-getting and money-
keeping.   It described the spiritual tendencies of the ideal
implied in the orthodox economics, a world governed by the
unrestricted action of the laws of supply and demand.   But it
was imaginary merely, for no society has been, or ever could be,
thus governed, as Ruskin himself was most insistent in asserting.
What he desired was that the higher ideal, the more comprehensive truth, should be raised from its obscurity and made the
recognized canon of all social and economic action, both public
and private.   The abstract and partial truths which the econo-
mists had formulated should be put in their place and the master-
truths should reign supreme.   What is the master-truth in this
matter ?   The same essay gives it in simple and unquestionable
words which take us back to the greatest of the revolutionary
poets.   ‘ There is no wealth but Life—Life, including all its
powers of love, of joy, and of admiration.   That country is the

richest which nourishes the greatest number of noble and happy human beings.' It was the doctrine of Wordsworth, with not so much of hope perhaps, but with more practical suggestion, applied to the industrial world and the poor half-truths on which it had been nourished.

What we have to sketch in this chapter is but a commentary on this text, and the text itself has never been put more pointedly or enforced with happier or more striking illustrations than by Ruskin himself. The essays from which we have quoted come exactly half-way in his life, at the age of forty, when he turned from being primarily a prophet of art to being primarily a prophet of social reform. But there is no real break in his teaching. The same ideal of the service of man lies at the bottom of his appreciation both of art and of industry. Both were to be tested by their effect on life. The art which he put first, that of the Gothic cathedral and the early Christian painters, rested on a happy, affectionate, and reverent frame of mind in the artist. The work which he put lowest, that of a machine-worker in a modern factory turning out ugly and shoddy goods, involved degraded conditions, hatred, contempt, or complete indifference in the worker. When he had grasped this contrast he went on to see that the former condition of happiness in beautiful work could only be achieved again when the general conditions of production had been transformed. ' This disgusting nineteenth century must, I can't say breathe, but steam its last.' We are living now when the last puff of the nineteenth century—in years but not in spirit—has for some time passed away. How far has Ruskin's ideal, which, in its broad outlines, must be the ideal of every person of sufficient intelligence and goodwill, approached its realization?

The judgement is a difficult one, not, in the opinion of the present writer, because the balance is on the whole doubtful, but because of the infinite complexity of the details on which it is based. If we consulted a manual of socialistic legislation, there could be no doubt at all. Every year since Herbert Spencer extolled the 'Man versus the State', there has been more and more legislation contrary to his principles. The State has gone on steadily increasing its control in the interest of the general good, and we shall note the principal steps in their place. But we must admit at once that the mere fact of the State, or any smaller governmental unit, increasing its control is not a good in itself. It may or may not be. Does it, we want to know, increase the good life of the community, that is, the number of noble and happy beings which it contains? Statistics, of course, give one some light, though we need constantly to check them and to test their meaning. We can see the declining death-rate and the rising income-tax set out in a curve. But no one yet has plotted the curve of nobility or even of happiness ; and, though Ruskin is often fanciful enough, it is no idle fancy that both goodness and happiness are things of the soul. Accurate measurement, then, of the things we most prize is not to be had, and we must rest content with external indications and general impressions. State action we may safely treat as an indication of the general determination to get a certain thing done, but we cannot overlook its attendant evils and its frequent failure to attain the end. Better than either indication of an advance would be the direct evidence, if we could get it, of an honest man and an honest observer who questioned himself and questioned others in all ranks of life. How far am I, and how far are you, enjoying my life and work and loving my fellow men ? How far am I, and how far are they, increasing in knowledge and in the power to accomplish what we desire ? How far, too, are we all advanced in the power of appreciating, and increasing, the store of beauty in the world ?

The short answer which we have to make may well fall into the same divisions as these possible grounds of judgement.

We will first note the change in public policy which came over the country after the middle of the last century, the increasing trend towards Socialist legislation. Next will come the collective efforts of the whole population, especially of the working classes, voluntarily to improve their own conditions. Statistics of health and income naturally follow this, and give us the occasion to refer specially to the part played by medical science in improving the conditions of life. And the final question will then arise, on which nothing but personal impressions are available: Are our people in themselves, i. e. spiritually, nearer to the ideal of happy union and nobility of character at the end of the period than at the beginning ?

Obviously all that could be said within our narrow compass will only amount at the best to a summary of headings for further thought and inquiry. No complete answer is possible, least of all in a score of pages.

We have already noticed, in the fourth chapter, the beginnings of a new period of social thought and legislation. The Reform movement of 1830, which gave us the first Reform Bill and coincides with the advent of Louis Philippe in France, was liberal in the stricter sense and not socialistic. It sprang from the spirit that animated Bentham, of removing legal and constitutional abuses and giving every man a fair and, as far as might be, an equal chance of looking after himself. No doubt there was a strong humanitarian element behind the agitation, and Sydney Smith has an interesting argument showing, truly enough, that the effect of placing political power in the hands of a larger number of people must be to increase the attention paid to their interests in a hundred ways. But there was certainly at that time no idea of the State doing for people what it was supposed they could do better for themselves, no idea of interfering with freedom of contract, with the free operation of the laws of supply and demand. We saw that Francis Place

was what we should now call an ' individualist ', and that the
People's Charter was far removed from a Socialist manifesto.
But a social and even a Socialist movement was rising at the
same time, and it gained its first fruits through the action of
another set of men. The factories gave the opportunity, and
the men who promoted legislation to control them were mostly
Tories—Southey the ex-revolutionary poet, Sadler the Conservative business man, Shaftesbury the philanthropist peer.

The point is an important one for two reasons. It shows, in
the first place, that the social legislation of the last half-century
arose directly from industrial conditions, and these had been
transformed by science. The organization of industry through
science led to the organization of labour and its control, partly
by the State, partly by the workers themselves. And this
division and compromise between the controlling parties has
persisted to our own time. In the second place the early
history of factory legislation makes it clear that social reform
was from the first a national business. The Ten Hours Act was
no party measure, and found its warmest friends among those
who had opposed Free Trade, and its strongest foes among
Peelites like Gladstone and Radical mill-owners like Bright.

Gladstone's change of attitude between 1847 and 1864 is
characteristic and significant. In 1847 he opposed the Ten
Hours Bill, the only member, Shaftesbury tells us, ' who endeavoured to delay the Bill which delivered women and children
from mines and pits ; and never did he say a word on behalf of
the factory children until, when defending slavery in the
West Indies, he taunted Buxton with indifference to the slavery
in England '. By 1864 he had been converted, though he
remained to the end reluctant to extend the intervention of
the State in social and industrial affairs. His advance from the
position of 1847 to, say, his action concerning contracts between
Irish landlord and tenant in 1870 and 1881 was typical of a

change in the national mind. Partly, the State was stirred to action by the general speeding-up of the national life. It could not afford to do its business worse, or at any rate much worse, than the many private persons who had combined. Partly it was compelled to certain measures to defend the public. The old stage-coach had bowled gaily along the common highroad practically free, fit emblem of the age. But the railway which was superseding the coach in these years of transition was a very different story, and the best example of the change. It was the direct offspring of science and organized industry of the modern type. It could only be laid down by taking private property compulsorily on a large scale. It involved grave risks to multitudes of persons. Hence, from the first the railway has been fathered by the State, hedged round by regulations of every kind, and in an increasing number of cases has become the property of the State outright.

Great businesses, of which the railway is only one case, became with science and organization the rule of the world. The logical Socialist sees in them the inevitable forerunners of a universal machine, directed by the State, in which all property and every instrument of production will belong to the community thus organized as one body, and in which every individual will take his orders from a duly-constituted authority. But human life is not thus logical, and there are signs that men in all countries are awakening again to the manifold chances of doing well and serving the common weal in a state of greater freedom. In the 'sixties and 'seventies the need of regulation was still great, and government, especially in England, had to climb a long ascent of organization and regulation, individual checks and public ownership and control.

The extension of the franchise to include the working classes both in town and country was a reform demanded by all reformers, individualist and Socialist alike. This was done by the two Acts of 1867 and 1884, the first passed by the Derby-Disraeli government but largely modelled by the Liberals; the second, passed by Mr. Gladstone almost simultaneously with the fall of Khartum. Yet, in spite of the large increase in the agricultural vote, the Liberals were actually weaker in the new Parliament which followed in 1885. Besides this a strong party of Irish Home Rulers emerged which gave Ireland the casting vote in the English House of Commons and converted Mr. Gladstone to the establishment of an Irish Parliament. The question which thus first arose as a side-issue became for many years the burning topic in English politics, while social reform, which was at the root of the democratic advance, went on quickly gaining fresh adherents among Home Rulers and anti-Home Rulers alike.

The 'Unauthorized Programme' which was urged on Mr. Gladstone in 1885 by the Radicals, with Chamberlain at their head, was the symptom and the watchword of the new spirit. It demanded free education, cottage farms and yeomanry holdings, better houses for the poor, a graduated income-tax, public acquisition of land, and an extension of local self-government. We look back now with amazement at the moderation of the demands. But for our present purpose we are interested to compare them with the People's Charter of fifty years before. Both manifestoes were considered monstrous at the time. Both filled the upper and the middle classes with fury and panic. Both are now commonplace, and if not fully carried out are fully promised with the assent of all parties. But whereas the Charter of 1838 was entirely political, the Programme of 1885 was almost entirely social. The political power which had now been won was to be used to gain advantages for the poorer at the expense of the wealthier members of the community. This is by no means to condemn the later purpose, but it certainly suggests a danger in the course of obtaining it. The Programme aims solely at things to be got and given ; it does not touch on sacrifices to be made or restrictions to be endured by all the citizens. The drawbacks of the method in practice could be illustrated by almost every item. Take the first, free education. This was granted by a Conservative government in 1891. But the necessary sacrifice by the working classes of their children's time for education was never insisted on, and always successfully obstructed when proposed. At last the great upheaval of the war completed many sweeping changes in franchise, in agriculture, in housing, in wages, and in education, which the slow processes of fifty years—since Household Franchise—had been attacking in detail.

But the extension of State action which has taken place in that time is not mainly a matter of giving to the poor at the expense of the rich. It consists much more largely of acts of protection, restrictions on the freedom of contract in the interest either of a weaker party or of the whole community, the intervention of the State between conflicting parties to avoid a strike or to determine a rate of wages, lastly the extension of collective trading either by the State as a whole or by municipalities and smaller units of administration. Each of these matters now constitutes a vast sphere of activity, employing thousands of minds : each is the subject of a library of specialist literature. We can mention only one or two typical cases to illustrate the whole.

Factory legislation was the first field of Western Socialism. It still forms the bulk of socialistic laws. Dependent persons have to be protected from the effects of their own carelessness or weakness, or from the greed or negligence of their employers. To put the matter in a more positive way, as Robert Owen and Mr. Sidney Webb would put it, a 'national minimum' needs to be established for all workers in matters affecting their health or efficiency. A full century of factory laws, developing this tacit assumption, takes us from the first timid effort of 1802 protecting the children and giving them a modicum of education, down to the Trade Boards Act of 1909 which deals with wages. The Act of 1850, coming nearly midway and clinching the Ten Hours Act, became an important turning-point. The normal day for women and children became necessarily that of the men also who worked with them. Other factories and workshops were gradually brought under the same protection which had been first afforded to the textile workers.

Later on protection of other kinds was given. Dangerous machinery was to be fenced. Proper ventilation and other sanitary arrangements were to be made, and due intervals allowed for meals, and so on. The last subject for the State to deal with was one of the most fundamental and most difficult to touch, the payment of adequate wages. This was reached in the first decade of the new century, when in the Trade Boards Act provision was made for setting up in certain ' sweated ' industries joint committees with Government assessors. It should be noted that in this extension of State activity we were following the initiative of two of our own colonies, New Zealand and Victoria, which were the first countries in the world to try the experiment. The recent minimum for agricultural labourers is a further extension.

But the activity of the State in social and industrial matters was by no means limited to the passing of laws. Gradually in recent years it has assumed more and more the position of general arbitrator, supreme pacifier, preventer of disputes. Some time before the war, agents of the Government were being constantly invoked to heal a coal strike or avert a lock-out of transport workers. All this was a new thing and not necessarily a bad one. In cases of sufficient gravity it is clearly the duty of the State to prevent serious loss to the body politic. But it might seem the stronger course, more consonant with the traditions of a self-governing people, for those concerned voluntarily to come to terms in their own interests and the interest of the public. Given sufficient intelligence and public spirit, they can themselves see the right solution. The State, if frequently invoked, especially in matters where it is not able without legislation to enforce its will, is liable to become too cheap. It is wasteful to use a steam-hammer to crack a nut, and no sane man would resort to it if his own nut-crackers were sound enough.

But we are alluding to the alternative method of dealing with disputes not so much for the sake of an argument, which is alien to the purpose of our book, as to introduce the other side of the organizing age. Many people who argue from the spread of State-control, State-businesses, and the like, to the speedy advent of the Socialist State, quite overlook the fact that the same century which has witnessed this development has also witnessed an unexampled growth of the free organization of citizens for almost every purpose. The Trade Unions are the most cognate to the immediate question, but they are only one form of thousands in which the social spirit has embodied itself in order to defend and elevate the individual. The triumph of the Unions came in 1875 at the hands of a Conservative government, after the Liberals had begun the legalizing process in 1871. The legal protection of Trade Union funds, the permission of combination, of striking, even of ' picketing ', subject to the general criminal law—these things, which were secured in those two years, were the completion of a work begun and carried to partial success by the reformers of the 'twenties. The final success was gained through skilful and persistent pressure on the two great political parties by the organized workmen, assisted by a group of middle-class men, mostly the same Positivists who had spoken a word for France in 1870. It will be noticed that this change in the law followed rapidly on the Reform Act of 1867, which gave the town-workmen a vote. In fact the Act of 1867 made the Trade Unions a living force much as the Act of 1884, which enfranchised the agricultural labourer, made Home Rule. The first two Labour members appeared in Parliament in 1874, just before the Trade Unions were freed.

But though Government action was necessary to remove restrictions which the law had itself imposed, it is most important to remember that the Unions have always been in England the free combinations of free men. As such, their educative influence, as well as their effect on industrial conditions, have been immeasurable. They have done more to make the British working-class what it is than all the factory legislation and State-education put together. Other countries have had these or better. England has had for the building-up of her workers a set of institutions which they have themselves framed, which spring from the self-governing aptitude of the race. It is for this reason that the Unions have during the last fifty years led the industrial advance. To them is mainly due the steady rise in wages and reduction in hours. What the State has done has been on the whole supplementary to what the workmen in their unions could do for themselves. And so when a great occasion has arisen, as in the war, they have sometimes been able to express the whole mind and true judgement of the people better even than Parliament itself.

The possibility of carrying the self-government of industry still further by means of Guilds or Syndicates of the workpeople themselves, owning wholly or in part the instruments of their production, has been discussed from many points of view in quite recent times. These plans belong rather to the realm of reconstruction than to any history of the past. But they all indicate two things. One that the capacity of both workpeople and employers to organize forms of industry for themselves is

far from exhausted. The other, that in any such organization
a powerful place must still be retained for the State as a whole,
reconciling differences in the last resort and subordinating
sectional interests to the general welfare.

Looking to the past, the Co-operative and Friendly Societies
would stand next in importance to the Trade Unions as forms
of voluntary organization for the advantage of the workers.
In both of these, with slightly differing aims and methods,
you find the free and deliberate purpose of individuals, mostly
people of the poorer classes, to assist themselves at the same
time that they assist others in like condition. They all proceed
upon the principle that we can only live and thrive with the
help and through the well-being of our fellows. Confidence
and goodwill, the sinews of the social body, must be strong in
all if they are to prosper. The Friendly Societies, indeed, can
trace back their origin to the ancient guild, but they were
transformed by the industrial revolution, and they have survived
and flourished through many vicissitudes until the Insurance
Act of 1911 incorporated them in a national system. The
Co-operative Societies are a still more striking and illustrative
case. For, as we know them, they owed their inception directly
to Robert Owen when he was labouring at New Lanark to
humanize the new industrial order. He established, for the
workpeople in his own works, shops on the co-operative plan,
where they could buy good provisions at a fair price and divide
the profits between them. This is the simple principle of
co-operative distribution, and Owen went on to advocate it
for production and as a national system. It fell at that time
with his own failure, but reappeared in the famous Rochdale
experiment of 1844 to which Co-operation, both in England
and in the United States, is accustomed to look back as its
immediate fountain-head. The little shop in Toad Lane,
Rochdale, with its 28 members and its capital of £28, had

become in 1906 an organization in Great Britain alone of 14,000 stores, 2,250,000 members, over £33,000,000 capital, and sales of over £63,000,000 a year.

The movement has its counterpart in all other Western nations: in France it has largely taken the form of co-operative buying for agricultural purposes; in Germany it has been the foundation of a system of co-operative banks which make advances to their members on the common credit. Thus both in France and Germany, and especially in the latter, the co-operative idea has been more fruitful on the productive side, while with us it has tended till now to be limited to distribution, where the difficulties are less and the profits readier. But there are strong and numerous efforts being made to press the principle to other uses which are obviously possible, given confidence and goodwill in the members and skill in the management. It should be noted as a special feature in English and American co-operation, and germane to our present topic, that no help has ever been sought from the State.

One other branch of social progress through voluntary collective action must be touched on, before we pass to the other indications of an advance. This is education. We traced in Chapter IX the spread of schools for all and the extension of their scope. We saw that if education was to be universal some compulsion was necessary, and that the State had in practice stretched out its hand farther and farther until it has certain relations with all the universities as well as the direct responsibility for the elementary instruction of every citizen. This was both right and inevitable, nor does it by any means necessarily involve the dragooning of opinion or the suppression of initiative. But if we are asking for the actual spiritual influences which count for most in the national life, if we are looking below the surface-facts of school attendance or examinations of any grade, we shall at once be faced by another complete set of

organizations—many sets in fact—which have only the slightest
connexion, if any, with the State, but of which the influence
would appear to outweigh what we are accustomed to call
'education'. We will mention four which are of fairly recent
origin and appeal mainly to those who have only passed through
elementary schools and have not had the deeper intellectual
impress of a learned society or a long academic training:
The Adult Schools, the Boy Scouts, the Women's Institute,
the Girls' Friendly Society. A fifth might be mentioned
which is growing rapidly throughout the world and is prominent at Universities, the Student Christian movement.
Here are societies, typical of hundreds, which depend entirely
on the free-will of those who belong to them, which often,
like Churches, become the dominating factor in the lives of
their members, help them through life, form their minds,
and inspire their conduct. Now such bodies are very
characteristic of recent times; they are largely religious in
spirit, and their religion has certain common features which
illustrate our argument. They are without exception humanitarian in a definite and formative sense. They all train their
members to believe, and to act in the belief, that the good of
others is our own good also, that we develop our powers by
such action, and that this in fact is the nature and genesis of all
true progress in the world. We know how in the various
societies this spirit is developed in connexion with different signs
and symbols of traditional origin. Some, like the Boy Scouts,
go back to the ancient crafts of primitive man, others take a more
definitely religious form. But that social service, and spiritual
growth through such service, is the true root, is clear enough.
It should be equally clear to the student of history that this
expansion of the essential and immemorial principle of all
morality is on a wider scale and affects more sides of life than
anything we have seen before.

People sometimes compare the transitions of our day with the troubles of the Roman Empire in the early centuries A. D., and there are certain parallels. But if we consider on the one hand the prevalence of secret societies and superstitious rites in those days, and on the other hand the open spread in our own time of the principles and practice of service, who but the most determined pessimist can doubt ? What was then the tender plant, pushing its way through heavy soil, is now a mighty tree that shelters us all; and if there are rents by tempest in its branches, it is yet plainly upstanding, stronger with the sap of two thousand years, able to replace the wreckage of the storm.

Society has thus everywhere become, at least within its national boundaries, far more united at the end than it was at the beginning of our period; and this closer texture is the result, the expression, of a growth of the social spirit in a thousand forms. This fact of triumphant association is indeed so indubitable and so impressive that we might be inclined to rest in it alone as sufficient evidence of the progress of humanity. One of the most stimulating thinkers of America, Dr. Josiah Royce, whose loss we have had to lament during the war, was thus impressed, and wrote a little book to explain the profound importance of the principle of insurance and to advocate its extension to international problems. Just as each national community was built up on insurance, each of us in some society or other, or through the State, guaranteeing the health and maintenance of others, and provision for their survivors after death, so he would have had an international fund to provide for cases of desolation, whether by natural calamities or by acts of war.

But it is clear that to answer the question of Progress as a whole we must go farther. However united, however confident in their fellows and self-sacrificing men may be, the ultimate question is larger. What are these men like in their other human qualities, they who thus hold together and keep one another alive ? What is our approach to Ruskin's society of noble human beings, happy in themselves, with joy in life and beauty, and a zest and power for further growth? Statistics, i. e. numerical summaries of general facts, and personal impressions, must be our help to any judgement. And if we arrange our results under the time-honoured headings of health, wealth, and wisdom, we must be careful to interpret each in the widest sense.

On physical health the doctors have given us in recent years a vastly growing mass of help. The care of health, the State's concern in and control of it, the immeasurable expansion of our knowledge and public interest, these by themselves would form a useful compendium of the progress of the century and no bad indication of progress in other matters. It is interesting to note how the capital steps in the 'health movement' have kept pace with the general movement. The first step, the taking of a census, was authorized by Parliament in the first year of the nineteenth century. It had been opposed and defeated in the middle of the eighteenth as being 'subversive of the last remains of English liberty and likely to result in some public misfortune or epidemical distemper'. The next step, the public registration of births and deaths, followed shortly after the first Reform Act. A registrar-general was appointed by the Act of 1836 who superseded the clergy in their functions of registration. Then, in the year of the Chartist demonstration and the revolutions abroad, the Public Health Act of 1848 was passed, which created a supreme authority, which under the reforming ministry of 1871 became the Local Government Board.

A striking personal figure serves as a link between the early reformers and the later expert treatment of health by the State. Sir Edwin Chadwick, who was born in 1800, was secretary and heir to Jeremy Bentham, and, dying in 1890, had seen nearly all the great steps taken of which he had been a leading advocate throughout his life. His *Report on the Sanitary Condition of the Labouring Classes* in 1842 led directly to the establishment of the first Public Health Board in 1848. His was the most encyclopaedic mind and the keenest spirit devoted to public health that the century produced.

In matters of health and wealth we may use statistics to good purpose, and the health statistics confirm the hopes of the reformers. In 1908 the death-rate was the lowest on record, being just over 14 for every thousand of the population. In the first decade of the returns under the Act of 1836 it had been something over 23. That is to say, that over 300,000 lives in our population of 35,000,000 in England and Wales were being saved annually through the improvement in the conditions of life and the curing or prevention of disease. In particular cases the improvement is far greater. The big towns are naturally the most unhealthy, and it is in them that the improvement is greatest. In the first year of life, which, as the most dangerous, has received latterly the closest attention, a reduction in the death-rate of Great Britain has taken place (1916) to 92 in a thousand from well over 100 in previous years.

But this bald fact of keeping so many thousands more alive is but a small part of the truth. The lives they live have been rendered by medical science and by the spread of games and the outdoor life both happier and safer. Many diseases, leprosy, cholera, typhus, small-pox, have practically disappeared. Others, such as typhoid and scarlet-fever, are far less prevalent or fatal. Others again—cancer, syphilis, tuberculosis, are being studied and guarded against with a care and a possibility of prevention quite unknown before our time in the world. Pasteur, as we saw in Chapter X, by exploring bacterial growth, opened a new road to health, and Lister, following his track, has initiated a new era in antiseptic surgery. If we add to these the names of Morton and Simpson, who introduced anaesthetics, we have probably a set of men who have done most to relieve physical pain in the last half-century. No one could mention these without adding the unique and heroic figure of Florence Nightingale, who, in a life of intense and concentrated energy, transformed the whole practice of nursing.

No branch of our subject is therefore better fitted to inspire hope than progress in medicine, no men are personally more hopeful than those who profess and practise it. They are sure that we shall some day conquer cancer, nay, that colds in the head will become a thing of the past. The fact merits some attention. How is it that hope springs so much more abundantly in the soil of medical than of moral or political science ? No moralist seems to expect a day when impurity or covetousness will have quite disappeared, and the optimists who anticipate an absolute and final abolition of war are few and fullblooded. Why this difference ? Here we must tread cautiously, and make but a brief excursion into the dim country where we discern the figures of free-will and sin, moral retribution and salvation by faith or by works. But some answer must be attempted, because it involves a whole school of thinkers who played a large part in the period under review.

Medical science is more hopeful and more successful because it has attained a higher degree of prevision, and this is based on a more complete knowledge of the facts and a stronger determination to use the knowledge for amelioration. No one can doubt that, at least up to a point, prevision is possible in social as well as in sanitary matters. The brain is a leading factor in both, and we cannot rationally bisect its action and say, in questions of bodily health such and such results will follow such and such conditions, but in moral and social questions there can be no prediction. It was, for instance, quite possible for any one to foretell that by allowing the workpeople in the early factory days to herd together in badly-constructed and insanitary houses, without any thought of social amenity or health, the unfortunate dwellers were bound to deteriorate not only in physique but in all their qualities of happy and efficient beings. Robert Owen, as we saw, was a pioneer in the theory that by altering the environment you could modify to any extent the being of those who lived under it. Greater minds took larger views of a kindred nature, and later in the century the doctrine became prevalent that man might study all the laws of his evolution as he had studied those of plants and animals, explain his past, and predict his future. To this the wiser thinkers of the school, like Auguste Comte, added the proviso that it was within man's power by the determination of his will to modify his fate, subject to the necessities imposed by physical laws. Here was an extension of the utmost moment of Bacon's dictum referring to external nature. He had said, ' Study the laws of nature in order to command by obeying her.' The new school added, ' Study also man's nature and history in order to modify that by due observance of its laws.'

The impulse which this new doctrine gave to social reform in the later years of the nineteenth century was immense. We trace it in a multitude of thinkers, in libraries of statutes, in a host of social experiments and institutions. John Stuart Mill, who was largely a disciple of Comte's, gave the most hopeful, though an obviously exaggerated, expression to it when he predicted the ultimate conquest of all the great sources of human suffering. Here is an optimism comparable to that of the medical man, in fact not distinguishable from his. And if we asked Mill why in the matter of war or poverty or vice we had fallen so far short of the success attained in dealing with disease, his answer would have been, in the first place, that we had not taken sufficient account of the adverse circumstances, i. e. that our realized knowledge was insufficient, and that, in the second place, we had not seriously set our minds to the task. In other words, that political and social science and art are not yet so far advanced as the science and art of medicine. But medicine remains the great exemplar, for it is the most perfect type of accurate and systematic knowledge applied to the good of man, applied now in an increasing measure to 'keep the nation in health' rather than cure diseases which might have been prevented.

In quite recent years, especially in the first decade of this new century, many steps have been taken, connected with health, which take us some degrees farther on the way to Ruskin's ideal, things which have in them also the germ of beauty, of a fuller life as well as a longer and more vigorous one. The Town Planning Act was carried by the same ministry which came into power in 1906, passed the Insurance Act, and gave old age pensions to the poor. Town planning is part of the movement which has given us garden cities both in Great Britain and abroad. The linking of beauty with health, of happiness with industry, are the important points, and it is well that in aiming at these the beginning has been made with dwelling-places. Architecture was the mother of the other arts, and in our new social renascence the housing of the people takes a leading place. Around better houses, pleasing as well as healthy, will grow the love of other beautiful things and a spirit of active happiness which must find its sphere in extending the welfare of others as well as its own. And already we are encouraged by the example of many such settlements with thousands of improved houses. But it is easier far to draw these hopeful auguries from statistics of wages and savings, from the building and the planning of model houses, from the inception of profit-sharing and industrial councils and the like, than to reason safely and optimistically on the spiritual facts. For some will point to the obvious falling-off in great works of imaginative genius, and others will deplore the no less patent spread of inferior literature and vulgar taste.

What then of our third heading, the verdict on wisdom? Some points indeed are clear and good. Mere illiteracy has almost disappeared. The statistics of crime have strikingly improved. The 483 in every 100,000 who were in prison at the beginning of the present century sank to 88 for last year. The war accelerated rapidly a previously existing movement. On the whole we may infer a large average gain, without, at the one end of the scale, conspicuous genius, or at the other the masses of degradation which disfigured our country a hundred years ago. There is an undoubted process of levelling up, and we may wait with confidence for new eminences to appear and wider vistas to open up. For such a view there is much to be said, but for any want of hope there is surely nothing. But before we could answer fully we should need a definition of wisdom. If we may include in it the rapid intuition of the rightness and true bearing of a great issue, like the defence of Belgium, then our whole people may be said to have possessed it and to have advanced notably in wisdom since the mistakes and apathy of 1864 and 1870. If it is a part of wisdom to persevere staunchly in a decision once taken and to show heroic fortitude and unfaltering discipline, cheerfully, even light-heartedly, for over four years, on the field, in prison, and on the sea, then the record is bright indeed. Or when we look at the habitual good humour and tolerance in bearing hardships at home, the taking of a quiet and unselfish place in a crowd, the help to one another, the sympathy with distress, then our people, and the poorer rather than the richer among them, have clearly a large share of wisdom, and it has grown since the spread of elementary education and the better ordering of our cities.

But if we go deeper and ask for evidence not only of fortitude and width of sympathy and good temper, but of increasing knowledge, of joy in beauty, of the power to give a reason for the hope that is in us, of foresight and intelligent preparation to meet the future, or of the highest achievement, the realization of the present as the meeting-place of past and future, then we should find less cause for satisfaction. It would be a small number of whom we could predicate wisdom in that sense, and the advance in such wisdom would be small in any class, especially among those, doubtless the majority, who abandon the reading of serious books when they leave school, whether at fourteen or sixteen or eighteen.

The present writer has no doubt that even in this, the more difficult side of education for a predominantly active people like ourselves, there has been advance since the School Board began its labours in 1871. But, as we saw in Chapter IX, the work of compulsory schools was made rather wide than deep. This is a quality which must inhere to compulsion applied to things of the mind. For a hopeful view we shall remind ourselves that education will be deepened in a hundred streams beside the formal channel to which we are too apt to confine the term. The nation willed its greatest act of education when on the 4th of August, 1914, it unanimously decided to enter on the greatest of wars. It was the beginning of a process unforeseen at the time, which was destined to carry us far beyond the conclusion of a victorious peace into a region where we must all learn more intimately than any nation has ever learnt before the matters that concern the interests of the whole world. We become, perforce, one of the mainstays of all humanity, and to fill that place our knowledge must be not only world-wide but profound. For the common things of mankind go back to the love of freedom, the association with fellow-men, the development of varied national types in differing lands and climates, the kinship of all in the growth of science and the expansion of the human spirit. Progress on these lines, of which the earliest steps are not wanting, will be the next and weightiest task if

the Gods approve
The depth and not the tumult of the soul.

XIII

INTERNATIONAL PROGRESS

THE last chapter, dealing primarily with social progress at home, brought us ultimately to the largest issue, the need of a deeper recognition of the common good and achievements of all mankind, the need of co-operation throughout the world. We have no intention of sketching on these lines a detailed programme for the future ; it arises only as implied in a true view of the past. No one could, in fact, forecast a closer international union in the future unless he had seen it growing, steadily for ages, and more rapidly in recent years ; that is the only aspect of the question which comes within our scope. But it may be commended in passing to the eager spirits in every country who are determined to take some steps to avert another war. If we are chiefly moved by the horrors of the present, and only feel, ' This is so terrible that it must not occur again ; it must be prevented somehow,' we are not adding perceptibly to the chances of its prevention. Many things are terrible, the loss of friends by death one of the worst : yet this, and much more, we know, has to be borne while human life endures. But if we can show that forces are at work in the direction which we desire and that these forces have been growing in strength as they proceed, then we may face the future with some hope. The task may be a hard one, it may demand not only a strong will but many sacrifices, but we shall be working with the course of things, and a better fate, assisted by our efforts, may prevail.

No better measure could be given of the recent change in the public mind on international questions than to compare the view taken by the earliest English writer on the constitution with that of any contemporary thinker, not to mention the promoters of a League of Nations. Sir John Fortescue, who wrote and suffered during the Wars of the Roses, gave us the first, and, within its limits, a very sound account of the principles of English polity. He is summing up in the fourth chapter of his *Governance of England* the admitted objects of all government as he conceived it. ' A king's office standeth ', he says, ' in two things : one to defend his realm against their enemies outward by the sword ; another that he defend his people against wrong-doers inward by justice, as it appeareth by the said first Book of Kings.'

A delightful and primitive statement, showing clearly how the mediaeval policy, as divorced from the Roman and the Catholic incorporation, looked back for its inspiration to the kings of Judah and Israel, and was entirely innocent of constructive ideas. It was, in fact, purely defensive, and in view of the feudal wars and disorder which were afflicting the West, the most wholesome and necessary ideal which could then be pursued. The world had indeed in that fifteenth century to be born anew, and it started from the fundamental necessities of order and defence before it could proceed to the complex task of building—from the mass of fresh material which the Renaissance was to provide—a new City of Man.

But let us put beside Sir John Fortescue's doctrine the thesis recently developed by an able writer [1] that since modern conditions have tended more and more to make the whole world one, it has become a primary duty of government to develop and regulate the relations of states to one another. Instead of probable assailants they are actual and inevitable partners in a common work. They may break bounds and run amuck ; against this occasional danger we must take our precautions. But the normal condition is quite otherwise. The modern

[1] Mr. C. Delisle Burns in *The Morality of Nations*.

state, by the nature of its activities, is bound inextricably to every other state, and the question consists not in the continuance or the severing of these, for they are essential, but how we shall regulate and foster them. Shall the partnership be an amicable one or are the partners to be continually dragging one another into the law courts ?

The steps which have led to this knitting-up of the world are not primarily political. They are rather the free activities of traders who have carried their goods across the steppes of Asia, of explorers who have rounded the Cape and crossed the Atlantic, of inventors who have pierced mountains and laid cables on the beds of the ocean, above all of scientific men who have united the intellect of all nations in the common task of promoting truth. Statesmen have as a rule followed these efforts and not initiated them. The story of their results would be the history of civilization since Marco Polo. Some aspects of it have been alluded to in previous chapters. The point which immediately concerns us is the incomparable acceleration of the process in the last hundred years. Even the war, though it has arrested this development in certain directions, has actually assisted it in others. The greater part of the world-community still survives and is far more closely united by the war than it was before.

The truth of the matter has been largely obscured by the traditional prominence hitherto assigned to political relations in the strict sense of the term. If you take up any collection of the great treaties of the nineteenth century, you will find that it consists almost entirely of provisions as to the government of certain territories which were in dispute before the treaty was signed. Nearly all such treaties are, in fact, the concluding acts of wars which have been waged for the right of governing certain territories. It is the question of political sovereignty which is most at stake. But if we altered our point of view to a

closer accordance with modern facts, many other agreements between nations would take their place in the foremost rank of real
importance. Take, for instance, our two principal allies at this
moment in the war, France and the United States. We have
happily had no war with either for more than a hundred years,
not with France since Waterloo, not with the United States
since 1814, when the fight turned on questions of commerce
which arose from Napoleon's decrees. In any collection of
leading treaties therefore nothing will be recorded as having
passed between the three protagonists on the Allied side,
although their firm union is now unquestionably the most
important fact, political as well as social, in the world. This is
not because there is nothing to record, but because the treaties
and agreements which have been made do not fall under the
heading which history is accustomed to consider as important.
Two or three examples of the other type will illustrate the
difference.

Between France and ourselves in the last sixty years the
following agreements have been made which have all tended
in the direction of fuller intercourse and counteracted war. In
1860, after the triumph of free trade in England and the object-
lesson of two International Exhibitions, an Anglo-French com--
mercial treaty was passed which reduced the customs duties in
both countries to the lowest point, and was followed by similar
treaties between other Powers. It was due to one of Cobden's
most strenuous efforts, and inspired as much by friendship as
by desire for trade. The last twenty years of the century were,
indeed, full of jealousy and friction, often acute. We touched on
the causes in Chapter XI, but by 1904 an understanding had
been reached with regard to Egypt which led the way to intimate
relations between England and France in all matters everywhere. In 1914 this was crowned by the signing of a general
arbitration treaty between the two countries. Between the

United States and ourselves we should select the Alabama arbitration of 1871, by the success of which the success of many later arbitrations was probably decided. The dispute turned on the damage done to Federal shipping by Confederate cruisers fitted out in British ports. The damages awarded by a composite tribunal at Geneva in 1872 were paid, though with some grumbling ; they were, in fact, so large that a balance was left in the hands of the United States Government for which no claimants could be found. Another question arose in 1899 and again in 1903 about disputes between Great Britain and Venezuela. The United States took their stand on the Monroe doctrine, and insisted, by threat of war, on arbitration. In each of these cases the award was given at the newly-formed Hague tribunal, and was in favour of our claims. The last and most important agreement between England and the United States was the general treaty of arbitration concluded just after the Great War began. It referred all possible matters of dispute, at least in the first instance, to arbitration, waiving the clauses as to vital interests and honour, which had been excluded in previous treaties. This was followed shortly afterwards by the similar treaty between ourselves and France to which we have just referred, and the three countries now stand in the closest union, both of action and of theory, which the world has ever seen between politically independent states.

These are a sample of the points on which stress would properly be laid if we were tracing the most important of all developments, the growth of humanity as a united being. And it will be noticed that, though arbitration occurs in them, and in some form must occur for the settlement of certain disputes between two independent parties, yet it by no means covers all the ground of inter-State relations. In bulk, if we surveyed the whole of the international agreements of the last hundred years, arbitration would be found to cover a very small part.

The mass of international agreements, like the mass of agreements between individuals in a separate state, consists of arrangements for mutual convenience in which it need not be expected that difference will arise, or at least difference which necessitates the intervention of a third party. All that is necessary is the tacit understanding, if you do not perform your part of the proposed bargain, I shall not perform mine.

The great extension of international relations, and of the agreements which they have occasioned, has taken place since the middle of the nineteenth century, i. e. since the time when the steamer, the railway, and the telegraph have been forming the material links round which have grown the moral and political. In these sixty or seventy years some thirty different agreements have been made between Western states touching matters of common interest, not political in the stricter sense. They have all arisen from the actual needs of private citizens, and the State has been called in as their representative to make a binding agreement. In no case have they led to war, and in very few have they been suggested by the results of war. The subjects include postage, telegraphs, navigation, railways, copyrights, insurance, sanitation, fisheries, prisons, the slave trade, and the liquor traffic. They form a network of relations, less close in the mesh but similar in kind to that which holds together the private citizens in every civilized state. It must suggest to the thoughtful critic who is not obsessed by the idea of the natural hostility of states, that a process is going on similar to that which transformed conditions of war between towns and castles and jealous individuals at home into normal relations of peaceful business. It has been said that the supreme goal of political activity should be the moralization of politics, and this is true enough. But we only strengthen the force of a philosophical ideal by showing how it is bound up with the necessities of our existence and will be realized slowly as man climbs his arduous ascent. States will learn, as decent citizens have already learnt, to treat one another well, not only, or even primarily, because they ought, but because they must.

There was a time, two hundred years or so before the writings of Fortescue, when it was thought that the ideal plan had been already discovered. If there were lapses, these might be deplored, just as we still deplore the occasional necessity of sending a criminal to jail. But of the right arrangements for securing a world happily at peace there could be no doubt, for God had revealed them clearly, both to our abstract reason and in the course of history. One of the greatest of poets has described them for us in words which will always live, reproving us for our errors and blindness, encouraging us to persevere. In his short, pregnant treatise on 'Monarchy' Dante asks what is man's end and purpose in living, what is it that distinguishes him from all other living things? He follows Aristotle in his answer. The height of human power, the quality of man that makes him man, is thought, the power of understanding things. Now this endowment is not an individual thing; no man can thus think by himself. It belongs to man as a species, and only by the multitude of other men can any one enjoy his faculty or increase it. The intellect is extended by action, by the ordinary dealings of life which come under the direction of politics, and by the work of the imagination which is the sphere of art. But all these things are subsidiary to abstract thought, which is the crown and essence of the human kind. Now just as the individual needs quietness and peace for that perfection of his work of thought which brings him nearest to the divine, so it must be with the human race. Peace is the best of all the goods ordained to bless us; and when the gospel of the new dispensation sounded to the shepherds from above, it was not riches, nor pleasure, nor long life, nor health, nor strength, nor beauty, that was sung, but 'Glory to God in the highest, and on earth peace to men of goodwill'. Then, turning to the practical side, Dante argued that, just as the individual needs one principle, his reasoning faculty, to co-ordinate and direct his life, so there must be one source of authority in every community. In the family it is the father. This is so well understood that it has become a proverbial curse to say, ' May you have an equal in your home'. So it is in the state. There must be one king, or otherwise ' every kingdom divided against itself will be laid waste'. So it must be with mankind as a whole. There must be one political head, who is the monarch or emperor, inheritor of that Roman sway which has been manifestly appointed by God to regulate the affairs of the whole world. Nor does the Holy Roman Emperor derive these powers from any other man, not even from the Pope. He holds them direct from God, even as the Pope holds his spiritual powers direct from God also.

Here was the mediaeval theory in its purest and completest form, full of Greek thought, Roman sovereignty, and Christian religion, free from the excess which led the popes constantly to assert a supreme authority and brought them into constant friction with the political sovereigns. This friction made Germany and Italy a desolation in the age of faith. The ideal itself was so ineffectual that it left France and England to the ravages of the Hundred Years' War, and England herself to the bloodshed and corruption of the fifteenth century. And when Sir John Fortescue writes after the accession of Edward IV, he never alludes to it, and describes the English polity as a simple machinery for warding off the elementary perils of a primitive state, attack from without and disorder from within.

But it was an ideal which contained so much truth and appealed so strongly to some of our deepest instincts that it has always floated before men's minds since then, leading some of them, like a will o' th' wisp, into Napoleonic and Germanic adventures of universal dominion, but inspiring others to an undying hope and a steadfast effort to secure the good in it and let the dangerous and temporary pass away. We need not criticize Dante's theory closely to understand its inadequacy to modern, or indeed to any actual, conditions of life. The simple fallacy meets us at the threshold, that because, in the individual, harmony and effective work are gained by the dom nance of one principle, therefore it must be one person who should rule, either in a family or a state or the world. This aspect of the matter need not detain us, for it is dead ; but the passionate belief in the essential unity of human nature and of human progress is not dead, and it gained from Aristotle's thought, interpreted by Dante, an intellectual force. We have seen in the nineteenth century a material approximation to the unity of the world, and we have in physical science a subject-matter for thought more perfectly unified than even the philosophy and theology of the schoolmen. But in clearness of apprehension that reason must be supreme, that reason is a social function belonging to the multitudes of mankind, that for the advance of reason there must be peace, nothing can surpass the vision of the *De Monarchia* or the *Paradiso*.

We must not forget, perhaps it is the most important point of all to remember, that the spiritual unity produced by the mediaeval system went deeper and lasted longer than the political. The Holy Roman Empire, summed up in Dante's *Monarch*, was never a reality outside an area, itself full of conflict, in Germany and Italy. But the Papacy, with the doctrine and the discipline for which it stood, was the weightiest fact in the world for a thousand years, and has yet by no means spent its force. It is a thought of profound significance for all later arrangements designed to secure the unity of mankind.

Those things are of most moment and have most promise of endurance which rest upon conviction and not upon force. The Papacy for many centuries was able to avert certain crises and to induce a certain order, even in the tormented ages which followed the break-up of the Roman Empire, and its doctrine, spreading to the barbarian tribes of the north and the Irish of the west, actually extended the world of Roman civilization. But when in the fifteenth and sixteenth centuries this Roman unity was formally destroyed, the question became urgent what forces or what organization, if any, could take its place in holding together the distracted and revolting minds, the jealous and competing states of the West. It was a problem infinitely more complex than Dante had imagined in his simple scheme. His end of intellectual unity cannot be impeached. His means must be transformed by the new thought and world-wide discoveries of mankind.

The political devices which were put forward by ingenious and well-meaning persons from the seventeenth to the beginning of the nineteenth century, need not stay us long : they are of interest chiefly as showing that the ideal of international unity and peace was still alive, at least in the breasts of those who made them. There was the ' Grand Design ' attributed to Henri IV, which would have made the Emperor of Austria, still Emperor of the Holy Roman Empire, chairman of a European federation. There was the *Essay toward the Present and Future Peace of Europe* by William Penn, and the *Project of Perpetual Peace* by the Abbé de Saint Pierre a century later, which had some influence on the makers of the Holy Alliance a century later again. These plans, like Dante's, all suffered from the fatal want of not facing the facts. They imagined, as he did, that by imposing upon a wayward world a theoretically admirable plan, you could by that very act reduce to order a multitude of eager, ambitious, active, often quarrelsome, men and nations. They omitted the essential preliminary which Rousseau pointed out, of changing the hearts of princes and of subjects. Some of the necessary preliminary work and how it has fared in the nineteenth century we shall deal with later. But on the political side by far the greatest advance was made, not by these abortive schemes, nor even by the grouping of the Powers which took place from time to time for special purposes, but by the growth of international law.

We have heard it stated during the war in various quarters that there is no such thing as international law ; and we know the grave fears that must beset all thoughtful minds as to the future power of insisting on the observance of its provisions. But its history gives one some ground for hope. For it actually arose in an age when the licence of warfare and the decadence of the controlling authority in Europe were at their worst. In 1625, when Grotius wrote the greatest of all books on the subject, the Thirty Years' War was at its height, and he states as his motive for undertaking the work, ' the licence of fighting which he saw in the whole Christian world, at which even barbarians might blush ; wars begun on trifling pretexts or none at all, and carried on without reverence for any divine or human law, as if that one declaration of war let loose every crime '. The savagery of that war turned his mind back to examples of the better spirit which had from time to time prevailed, showing mankind what should be their habitual practice. Italy, the nursery of ambitious cities and civilizing thought in the two centuries before, had provided, in spite of much cruelty, many humanizing rules. The constant intercourse and the frequent warfare of those Italian states had led them to evolve a system of inter-state comity, with passports and due treatment of accredited agents and respect for civilians and for the wounded in war, which is the commonplace of international law. A common practice on the sea arose in the same way from inter-course both round the Mediterranean and in the northern seas. On these and other cases Grotius could work, and he strengthened and interwove them into a larger code resting on the innate good instincts of human nature which restrain us from certain acts and prompt to clemency towards the weak and fallen, unless the mind is blinded by passion or perverted by an evil rule.

Here, then, in common usage and the common feeling for humanity and for right, the founder of international law dis-covered his corner-stones, not in the decisions of an international tribunal. But this is the better foundation and not the worse. If the validity of international law depended on the stability of some law-making authority, say Dante's *Monarch*, or the Papacy, or The Hague Tribunal, its chances of permanence would be small. In point of fact no system of laws which ever lasted, whether internal or international, was thus founded. All rest really on the consent, partial or complete, of those who enjoy them, and international law, as we know it, can be best understood as the early stage of a legal system. Thus the best writers on the subject have maintained that international law is real and valid, in spite of the absence of any recognized authority to enforce it, because the nations who have made it wish it so to be. The consent of the parties and their will to make it prevail : these are the fundamental sanctions. Given these, they will find out in due time the most effective way to secure obedience.

It may seem a paradox to take this high and confident line just after a terrific struggle caused by a breach of what were assumed to be the most unquestionable dictates of inter-national law. But history and calm reflection should go far to dissipate our doubts. It was in the throes of the most savage war which preceded this, that Grotius founded the first system of international law. We are refounding it after a still greater convulsion. That this is the true nature of the recent war is clear at every stage of its course. It began because the independent existence of one nation, the Serbian, was practically denied. We ourselves entered because the guaranteed neutrality of another, the Belgian, was violated. The United States completed the circle of the alliance because a third mandate of the code, long sacrosanct, was persistently broken, and civilian ships were attacked without warning or due cause. These were the turning-points, apart from the unnumbered breaches of conventions and humane understandings in other matters. It was primarily to re-establish these and secure their due observance in future that the whole world took up arms ; other improvements in the world-order will, it is hoped, be secured in the process. The force, therefore, which won the ultimate triumph, larger and more determined than had ever come together before, was essentially the guardian of international law.

It is, of course, no subject of congratulation that this vast employment of force has been necessary to maintain the right. But it is irrefragable evidence that international law has force behind it as well as the consent which gave it birth. And just as Grotius could glean from past history examples of a higher standard of conduct which he hoped to make universal in a future code, so we may refresh ourselves and fortify our purpose by recalling the advances made in the nineteenth century towards a goal even more far-reaching than his. We have alluded to some of them in passing ; we must now survey the whole field with a little more system.

The revolutionary age did not do much directly to further the cause of international law or international unity. The soldiers and the thinkers of the revolution were too apt to regard the laws and conventions under which other men lived as so many chains only made to be broken. Brotherhood was on their lips and a sword in their hands. But many words of wisdom were uttered then about the federation of the world as about most other questions of the future. Of all the writers of the age on that subject, Kant has had most influence on his successors, and he had a strong revolutionary element in his teaching. For much of his politics he had been to school under Rousseau, and he believed in, and advocated with perfect clearness and confidence, a world-community, of which, however, he does not specify the detailed forms. But he is right and emphatic on certain general principles which must govern any such union, and towards which we may trace some approach since his time. One is that each separate state which is to compose the union must be constitutional, what he calls republican ; another that the rule of law must be acknowledged as supreme in the public as duty is in the individual sphere ; another, on which he lays the greatest stress—putting it in the heaviest type, not used for any other statement—that regular and legal relations with other states are necessary if there is to be a satisfactory civic constitution at home. The political history of the century might indeed be treated as a commentary on these conditions. The first is one on which we have already traced a large advance throughout the century, and on which the Great War carried us farther still. This is the self-government of the constituent nations in the world-community. Next to that, as showing progress on the political side, comes the establishment of regular and lawful relations between the states. But for a complete picture of the change in the hundred years we need also some account of the vast expansion of the material links of the world-order ; and lastly of the growth of man's common mind, shown mainly in the mass and the influence of science, and also in the spread throughout the globe of common ways of life and thought.

Our review may give some grounds for thinking that, even in spite of the war, we have been living in a time of closer approximation between the nations than prevailed a hundred years ago. But we shall also see clearly that it is in Dante's realm of the pure intellect inspired by love that we come nearest to an atmosphere of unity and hope—hope for the salvation of the best that man has yet achieved, hope for the extension of his conquests and the healing of his soul.

The very title which imposed itself at once for this concluding chapter, all the language in fact which we habitually use when dealing with this subject, rests on the truth which Kant was the first to formulate in general and abstract terms in the last quarter of the eighteenth century. International unity, international progress, all regular international relations, imply the existence of strong, self-contained, and independent nations between which these further relations may grow up. The individual needs these steps on which to rise to the largest and most distant generalizations. Just as the child first finds his social being in the family circle, so every normal man will be more attached and take more pride and pleasure in the doings of ' his own people '—men generally of the same blood and tongue—than he does in those of the world at large. How hard it is to fit these attachments and aspirations into the framework of nation-states, the history of the last hundred years, unrolling itself in conflict and incalculable loss, is there to tell us. It is enough surely to convince the most imperialist and dominating spirit that the instinct of nationality is ineradicable; that, like the desire for freedom or for private property, we must build upon it and not attempt to crush it out. We are learning some of the problems well, in Ireland at our own doors, in Poland, in the Balkans, and among the Austrian subjects whom the war has set free. We have seen in Chapters II and VII something of the part that nationality has played in the last century. But we have now to add in this last and more comprehensive review another and more striking triumph of the principle. We saw how by 1871 Prussia had suppressed the Danes in Schleswig, had ignored the French attachment of Alsace and Lorraine, had assisted Russia in trampling down her Poles, and was engaged vigorously in trampling on her own. Now the Great War, in spite of the momentary occupation of Belgium and the martyrdom of Serbia, in spite of the temporary extension of German arms to the east, has already created more new national units and is in course of creating more. Palestine has been freed from the Turks, and the ancient claims of the Jews revived. The Arabs in the Sinai peninsula are practically free, and they are being encouraged to rally in Mesopotamia. Armenia and Persia, now freed both from Russian and Turkish usurpation, may hope for some national existence of their own. And it is important to observe that the Central Powers, even when in arms, were compelled by the vitality of the national principle in several cases to adopt the same solution. Finland was made definitely independent of Russia. Lithuania became a national unit, and is busy in defending herself against the encroachments of Poland, which in her turn is certain to regain a much larger being.

But the most casual glance at the varied shapes which nationality has assumed in the world will convince us that the abstract and ideal form in which Kant and many of the liberal political thinkers have presented the case requires infinite qualification and constant revision. We are dealing with the workings of the human spirit which is a changing and a growing thing; and we are dealing with the adaptation of this spirit to the material facts of its environment, which was not framed *a priori* to fit any perfect abstract theory. Two things only can we postulate universally about nationality; one, that it is a spiritual bond, a link between men, commonly of the same blood, who have grown together by common action and common suffering; the other, that it involves attachment to some definite portion of the earth's surface, a home-land to which its members turn with more affection and yearning than to any other place. Given these, there are innumerable types of political arrangement in which the national spirit may find rest. It does not always demand complete political independence, as we may see in the case of the Welsh, most ardent in national feeling, but without any desire for a separate republic or a crowned king of their own. Being a spiritual thing, nationality must have freedom to live and grow, and this growth will, in the normal case, where external conditions have not prevented it, lead to self-government. But freedom it will have at the cost of unceasing suffering and unrest. This freedom Great Britain has on the whole succeeded in securing for the nationalities embraced in its political orbit, and it is constantly extending it. If we turn from this to the international question, the bearings are obvious. Wherever, as in the east of Europe, there is an area of unsatisfied, unreconciled national units, there you have a focus of war. The oppressed peoples, wishing to change their condition, will be eager to provoke a disturbance, which, bringing in more powerful antagonists than themselves, will be likely to create some change in their own condition; and the oppressors, denying to subject-nationalities their natural demands—freedom of speech and life and self-control—will be the more apt to fail in the general obligations of fellowship with mankind, the observance of old loyal understandings, the making of new and more friendly agreements with other nations. Their skeleton at home makes them suspicious and secretive abroad. The war has burnt these lessons into our minds for ever, but it has at the same time shown the remedial forces fully at work. We have seen the national units rising on both sides in the conflict. We have also to note the strengthening of the international bonds which unite those who are engaged in it. Here again the contrast between the opposing alliances is extremely significant. The Central Powers were during the war closely united, but their union was a forced one and under the dominance of one undisputed chief. Defeat therefore leaves their future union in grave doubt. The Allies are a free association of a majority of the free nations of the world. With the exception of Russia, which was unfree when the war began and is politically undeveloped, all the original members of the alliance have held firmly together and gathered fresh recruits and fresh resources as they have gone on. It is a capital instance of the truth in Kant's analysis of the conditions of fruitful and permanent union between nations. You must have, he said, free governments internally to secure loyal international relations, and you must have law-abiding external relations if your internal politics are to be stable and progressive. The two things hang together and fortify one another, for both are rooted in the same principle—the treatment of other people as of equal account with yourself, and the free development of all, under an equal law. The greatest struggle in history has produced the greatest combination, a league of free nations in being. But, the timid or the sceptical may ask, must there not always be some special and over-mastering peril to produce so extraordinary an event? Must there always be some Germany to beat down before the rest of the world can be at peace?

Such prophecy is not within the scope of this volume; but any answer which could be given would necessarily turn again to history. Conditions created by wars and other special and calamitous events have often persisted afterwards and become a benefit. The world can never be the same hereafter, and a league of nations, called into being for a special work of defence and deliverance, should find abundant scope for its activities when the immediate necessity is over. We need not assume that men are always likely to be blind in that direction where their true interests lie.

Our general argument has brought us to the point where we can see, steadily advancing through the century and culminating in the war, a growth of new national units, sometimes attaining complete self-government, sometimes content with less than this, but always aiming at that measure of justice and of freedom which is essential to healthy human life. The area of the world prepared in this way for permanent and peaceful intercourse has been in the last hundred years enormously increased, and Great Britain, with her own league of free nations, has played a large part in the process. In fact our political system, constantly modified and variously understood, has been the nearest approach to an ideal for constitutionalists from Montesquieu onwards. France, in her third republic, after the third Napoleon was removed, is a conspicuous instance. Italy, under the guidance of Cavour, reached a like state. The smaller nations, when they broke their chains, organized themselves as far as possible on similar lines, and Germany herself made, in the revolution-year of 1848, a desperate effort at unification on constitutional lines. We saw in Chapter VII how a bad theory and a bad tradition ruined that attempt. In 1905 Russia, after her defeat by Japan, seemed likely to add her vast realms to the area of constitutional government. The first Duma met in 1906, and at its dissolution Sir Henry Campbell-Bannerman's famous cry, ' La Duma est morte, Vive la Duma ! ', rang across Europe as a reveillé from the oldest of parliaments to the latest born. There, as in Germany, the future is now veiled from our eyes, but for the rest Kant's judgement holds, that among the nations combined in law-abiding international bonds internal freedom also prevails.

What hope, we have next to ask, does the last century hold out for the general progress of legalized relations between the free nations which have thus been growing up ? On this the answer is unequivocal. The nineteenth century was an incomparable first, in the extension of international law and in the reference to arbitration of questions in dispute. The former development was the sequel to the growth of trade and science, and of industrial and medical art. As all these things are by nature international, they brought in their train a mass of inter-state conventions which as much exceed the similar agreements of earlier centuries as our statute law of the nineteenth century exceeds all the rest put together. The second development, that of arbitration, was the result of convenience and common sense, and is almost entirely a feature of the last century. The two earliest cases occurred just before the nineteenth century began. They are one of our many links with the revolutionary age. Just as England and the United States were the first nations in the first autumn of the present war to conclude a treaty for unrestricted arbitration, so in 1794 they were the first to appoint a ' mixed commission ' to define the boundaries between Canada and the States. The boundary thus fixed by amicable and business-like methods is the line which stretches three thousand miles across a continent, is not defended by a single fortress, and has never been threatened by a hostile assault. In fact the United States and ourselves decided formally to have no fortifications on this line and to withdraw all armed steamers from the Lakes. During the nineteenth century the use of arbitration to settle international disputes increased rapidly even before the regular machinery at The Hague was set up. From 1820 to 1840 there were eight cases ; from 1840 to 1860 thirty ; from 1860 to 1880 forty-two ; from 1880 to 1900 ninety. The establishment of The Hague tribunal coincides with the end of the century. The

Conference which led to the foundation of the tribunal was called on the initiative of the Tzar Nicholas II, whose enthusiasm recalls the early idealism of his ancestor Alexander I in the Holy Alliance. The proposal was at once strongly supported by England and the United States. The permanent tribunal was in fact the result of a special appeal to the Conference by Lord Pauncefote, who was at the time British ambassador in Washington. The primary object of the Conference, as set out in the Russian note, was something different, which proved unattainable at that time. It was to arrive at ' an understanding not to increase for a fixed period the present effectives of the armed military and naval forces, and at the same time not to increase the budgets pertaining thereto ; and a preliminary examination of the means by which even a reduction might be effected in future in the forces and budgets above mentioned '. The German military delegate objected, and this, the original purpose of the assembly, was put aside. Again in 1907, at the second Conference, the same thing happened. The actual results, beside the foundation of the tribunal, were the affirmation of many existing laws and customs of war by land and the attempt to extend them in various directions. Practically all have been violated in the present war, and when we read the proposed declarations against the ' launching of projectiles and explosives from balloons or by other similar methods ', or ' the use of projectiles the only object of which is the diffusion of asphyxiating or deleterious gases ', our heart may well sink within us. But it is a faint heart after all. Man will not remain content for ever to see a wise and perfectly attainable ambition unattained.

The tribunal which was constituted in 1899 was used with success in numerous cases, and reference to it seemed increasing when the crisis came. It will be remembered that the present war broke out owing to the refusal of Germany to submit the matter in dispute to arbitration, and in our own case from our resolve to enforce an international agreement by arms. The Allies were, therefore, both in their Eastern and their Western cause, a league of nations enforcing the findings of a world-tribunal. The greatest of wars was in effect the execution of a decision by the greatest of courts.

But we must pass on to the wider and deeper links. The Hague Conference and The Hague Tribunal, though the historian will note them carefully as landmarks in international progress, are rather to be classed with those earlier efforts, Penn's *Essay* and St. Pierre's *Project*, as symptoms rather than as great events.

We are not, it must be remembered, discussing any short cut to peace or any substitute for a League of Nations, but inquiring, purely in an historical spirit, what tendencies may be discovered in recent years towards an ideal which all admit to be desirable, though many doubt its near approach or even its possible attainment. The doubt and the denial come largely from the mistaken emphasis, in our education and in our habitual frame of mind, on the things that divide mankind—the contested frontier, the false point of honour, the greed of gain—rather than on the goods which unquestionably are due to unselfish co-operation, and unquestionably bring peace and satisfaction if we will only permit ourselves to contemplate and enjoy them. Human skill and perseverance in piercing the St. Gothard, human insight and synthesis in tracing the curves and learning the constituents of the most distant stars, human care and ingenuity in analysing disease and chasing the poisonous bacillus from the blood, the noble human emotion, in all its compass and gamut, which speaks in a symphony of Beethoven—these things are the true uniting forces; and, as a rule, in recording the achievements of the past, we put these in the smallest type or leave them out altogether. But they have been growing all the while, and the nineteenth century was their best flowering-time.

It is, of course, true—so obvious in these days that it is scarcely worth mention—that the railway may be a strategic weapon to bring troops through Belgium, that the airplane may be employed in dealing death to thousands, and the wireless convey instructions to contending fleets. These have been the portents of the war, and their warlike value happens to quicken invention and stimulate use. But, broadly speaking and looking to the future as well as to the past, the effect of the industrial inventions and scientific applications of the last century has been something quite different from war, not wholly good but certainly unifying. The analogy of a great state, thus somewhat superficially unified, may throw some light upon the larger problem. Russia had been linked up by a transcontinental railway, by telegraphs and telephones, as well as by a common system of law and administration. But the national soul was not fully awake. The disasters of war broke into this, and for the moment we see a chaos of conflicting chiefs, hostile parties, and petty nationalities. But does any one suppose that the previous unification, the material and mechanical links, will go for nothing ? Is it not certain, on the contrary, that the actual unity achieved, imperfect though it was, was a fact of permanent importance and that the ideal of a ' great Russia ' will remain to modify and bring together in some new form the congeries of smaller units which are arising from the wreck ?

It remains, however, profoundly true—the most important fact in our whole discussion—that the spiritual forces, of which we may trace the workings in the same period, are the supreme factors, both in building the individual soul and in giving a common soul to all humanity. This common spirit is best exhibited, and most powerfully enlarged, in the two channels of the growth of science and the application of science, especially in the art of medicine. We put these first not from any theory of their intrinsic worth. The inspiration of poetry or music is another, it may be a higher, thing than the unfolding of the mysteries of matter or the growth of the living cell. But in the history of science and its applications we have the most perfect example of a growing human product in which the diverse races of mankind have all taken a proportionate share as they advanced in civilization. There has been absolute similarity in the mental process and a growing solidity in the accomplished structure. In this region national differences are simply irrelevant, and personal jealousies merely a mark of personal inferiority. Now in this sphere, the international development of science and of medicine, using both terms in the widest sense, the nineteenth century, remarkable for so much, was most remarkable of all, for its advances were more than those of all the earlier centuries together. It is no fanciful analogy, but the closest approximation we can make to the truth, to say that this scientific structure, established and being taught at the close of the century in all Western countries, corresponded in its general relation to life, in the respect which it inspires in its students, in the number and international union of its teachers, with the mass of mediaeval theology and philosophy which was to Dante the sum of human knowledge. During the century we see this international character more and more strongly shown, from the time (1813) when Alexander von Humboldt induced the English and the Russian Governments to assist him in the first international experiment —an experiment in terrestrial magnetism—to the days just before the war, when world-conferences on all subjects of scientific interest were regularly held, and when the number of world-associations was so great that two bureaux had been set up—one at The Hague and another at Brussels—to co-ordinate their work. It is in this sphere, the sphere of pure intellect, that, as Dante showed, the unity of mankind is most fully realized. All seats of learning, whether universities or learned societies, or associations for spreading knowledge in wider circles, are in reality the organs of a true internationalism, and strengthen the human spirit by knowledge springing from a universal source and tending ultimately to the universal good.

But while we note the likeness on one side between the mediaeval ideal at its best with the modern ideal as it begins to shape, it is of equal moment to realize the differences. Modern knowledge, like modern life, is a constantly growing and infinitely varied thing. Freedom in its evolution, like individuality in character, are now prized by us next only to the supreme qualities of harmony in difference and peace in progress. In this the modern spirit stands in sharp contrast with the mediaeval from which it has been born. And there is another difference quite as vital between the spirit which breathes in the *Paradiso* and what we recognize as the best in the modern world. It is this. The old ideal was one of supreme blessedness in a state of contemplation, of rest in a vision of what the universe might be, if penetrated by Love and irradiated by Beauty. The modern spirit knows no such rest. It has the real world with all its 'Hearts of Darkness' to enlighten, and we see it at its best when in some national effort it determines to end ignorance and squalor at home, or in some international union resolves to redeem the horrors of an African tribe enslaved and decimated by Western greed. It is from such manifestations, too rare and often too feeble, but more frequent and stronger as the century went on, that we may augur the rising of a Heart of Light.

TIME CHART (pp. 342-5)

THE general plan is the same as that followed in the similar Time Chart to *The Living Past*. Equal spaces are assigned to equal times and only the most striking and significant names and events are included.

The development of France and England, which is treated as a leading thread in the book, is given the central position and analysed more fully. In this portion only the division into 'Thought' and 'Action'—or Culture and Politics—is attempted. To the left we pass into the New World, to the right through Italy and Germany to Russia and the Far East.

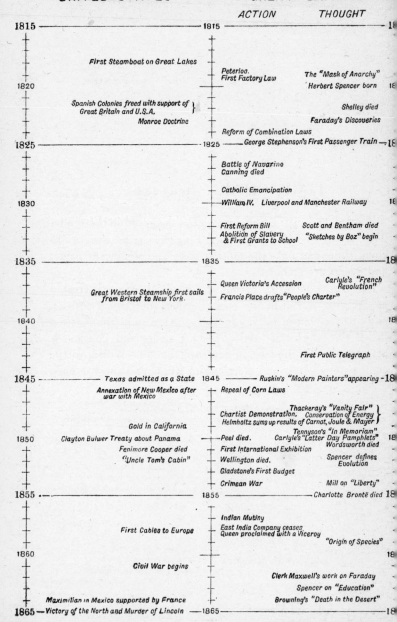

UNITED STATES

GREAT BRITAIN

ACTION   *THOUGHT*

1815 — — — — — — — — — — — 1815 — — — — — — — — — — — — 18

First Steamboat on Great Lakes

Peterloo.
First Factory Law   The *"Mask of Anarchy"*

1820   *Herbert Spencer born*   18

Spanish Colonies freed with support of }
Great Britain and U.S.A.   *Shelley died*

Monroe Doctrine   *Faraday's Discoveries*

Reform of Combination Laws

1825 — — — — — — — — — — 1825 — George Stephenson's First Passenger Train — 18

Battle of Navarino
Canning died

Catholic Emancipation

1830   — *William IV.   Liverpool and Manchester Railway*   18

First Reform Bill   *Scott and Bentham died*
Abolition of Slavery   *"Sketches by Boz" begin*
& First Grants to School

1835 — — — — — — — — — — 1835 — — — — — — — — — — — — 18

Queen Victoria's Accession   *Carlyle's "French
Revolution"*

Great Western Steamship first sails
from Bristol to New York.   *Francis Place drafts "People's Charter"*

1840   18

First Public Telegraph

1845 — — — *Texas admitted as a State* 1845 — — — *Ruskin's "Modern Painters" appearing* — 18

Annexation of New Mexico after — *Repeal of Corn Laws*
war with Mexico

Thackeray's "Vanity Fair" }
Chartist Demonstration.   Conservation of Energy
Helmholtz sums up results of Carnot, Joule & Mayer }

Gold in California   *Tennyson's "In Memoriam"*
1850 *Clayton Bulwer Treaty about Panama* — *Peel died.   Carlyle's "Latter Day Pamphlets"*   18
                              Wordsworth died
Fenimore Cooper died — *First International Exhibition*
"Uncle Tom's Cabin"   *Spencer defines
Evolution*
Wellington died.

Gladstone's First Budget

Crimean War   *Mill on "Liberty"*

1855 — — — — — — — — — — 1855 — — — — — *Charlotte Brontë died* 18

Indian Mutiny
East India Company ceases.
First Cables to Europe   *Queen proclaimed with a Viceroy*

"Origin of Species"

1860   18

Civil War begins

Clerk Maxwell's work on Faraday

Spencer on "Education"

Maximilian in Mexico supported by France   *Browning's "Death in the Desert"*

1865 — *Victory of the North and Murder of Lincoln* — 1865 — — — — — — — — 18

THOUGHT	ACTION	1815	ITALY, GERMANY, RUSSIA AND THE EAST	1815
	Congress of Vienna	1815	Holy Alliance	1815
		1820	Congress of Troppau	1820
Chevreul's Candles	Charles X succeeds Louis XVIII			
St.Simon died		1825		1825
			Beethoven died	
Victor Hugo's "Hernani"	Louis Philippe	1830	Revolution in Belgium. Mazzini in France. Freedom of Greece	1830
			Hegel died	
Cuvier died			Goethe died	
	Guizot's School Law			
		1835		1835
Comte's "Positive Philosophy" appearing				
			Schleiden and Schwann found Cell Theory	
			Neutrality of Belgium secured by Treaty	
		1840		1840
Comte's correspondence with Mill				
		1845		1845
	Second French Republic		Revolutions in Austria and Germany Frankfort Parliament Victor Emmanuel and Cavour in Piedmont	
Balzac died		1850		1850
	Napoleon III			
	The Crimean War · · · ·		· · · brings Piedmont into alliance	
		1855	Alexander II succeeds as Tsar	1855
	International Exhibition Treaty of Paris			
Comte died.	Occupation of Cochin China			
	War with Austria			
Work of Pasteur		1860	Garibaldi lands in Sicily	1860
	Commercial Treaty with England		Bismarck Chancellor to William I	
			Work of Bunsen and Kirchhoff	
Renan's Vie de Jésus			End of Serfdom in Russia	
			Marx founds International War with Denmark	
		1865		1865

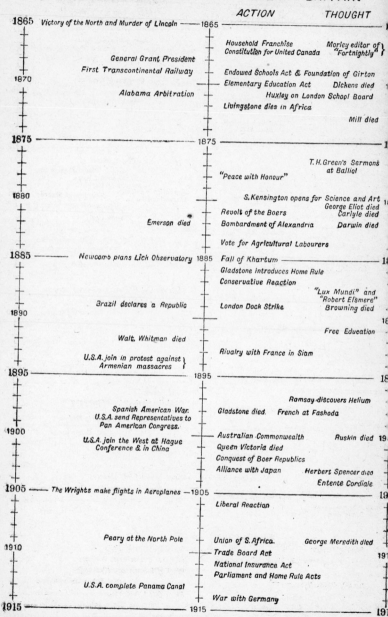

UNITED STATES

GREAT BRITAIN

ACTION   THOUGHT

1865 Victory of the North and Murder of Lincoln —— 1865		
	Household Franchise	Morley editor of
	Constitution for United Canada	"Fortnightly"
General Grant, President		
First Transcontinental Railway	Endowed Schools Act & Foundation of Girton	
1870	Elementary Education Act	Dickens died
Alabama Arbitration	Huxley on London School Board	
	Livingstone dies in Africa	
		Mill died
1875 —————————————— 1875		
		T. H. Green's Sermons
		at Balliol
	"Peace with Honour"	
1880	S. Kensington opens for Science and Art	
		George Eliot died
	Revolt of the Boers	Carlyle died
Emerson died	Bombardment of Alexandria	Darwin died
	Vote for Agricultural Labourers	
1885 Newcomb plans Lick Observatory 1885	Fall of Khartum —————————	
	Gladstone introduces Home Rule	
	Conservative Reaction	
		"Lux Mundi" and
		"Robert Elsmere"
Brazil declares a Republic	London Dock Strike	Browning died
1890		
		Free Education
Walt. Whitman died		
U.S.A. join in protest against }	Rivalry with France in Siam	
Armenian massacres }		
1895 —————————————— 1895		
		Ramsay discovers Helium
Spanish American War.	Gladstone died.	French at Fashoda
U.S.A. send Representatives to		
Pan American Congress.		
1900	Australian Commonwealth	Ruskin died
U.S.A. join the West at Hague	Queen Victoria died	
Conference & in China	Conquest of Boer Republics	
	Alliance with Japan	Herbert Spencer died
1905 —— The Wrights make flights in Aeroplanes —— 1905		Entente Cordiale
	Liberal Reaction	
Peary at the North Pole	Union of S. Africa	George Meredith died
1910	Trade Board Act	
	National Insurance Act	
	Parliament and Home Rule Acts	
U.S.A. complete Panama Canal		
1915 —————————————— 1915	War with Germany	

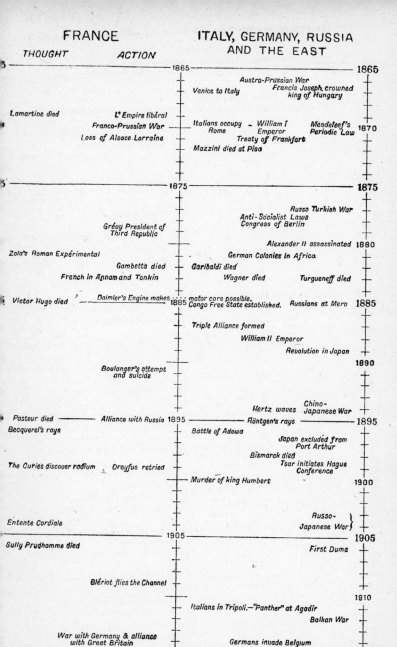

APPENDIX ON BOOKS

THIS is not to be regarded as a bibliography on the nineteenth century, but merely a list of a few, mostly familiar and easily accessible, books illustrating each of the preceding chapters. Preference is given to the least expensive, to those written in English, and to those mentioned in the text.

CHAPTER I. THE LEGACY OF THE REVOLUTION

Mrs. Gardiner. *French Revolution* (Longmans). A good short sketch of the events.

Carlyle. *French Revolution* (Everyman's Library). With Mazzini's criticisms in the fourth volume of his *Life and Writings*.

Wordsworth. *Prelude*.

Burke. *Reflections on the Revolution in France* (World's Classics).

Condorcet. *Tableau historique du progrès de l'esprit humain* (Steinheil).

Rousseau. *Contrat social* (Everyman's Library).

Rose, J. Holland. *Life of Napoleon* (Bell). Full and interesting.

Fisher, H. A. L. *Napoleon* (Home University Library). Short, masterly, and impartial.

The Life of Sydney Smith (Macmillan).

The Cambridge Modern History, vol. xii, ' The Latest Age '.

CHAPTER II. THE POLITICAL REVIVAL

William Cory. *Guide to Modern English History* (Kegan Paul). An extremely well-written and interesting account of the first thirty or forty years of the nineteenth century in England from the Whig point of view.

Seignobos. *Political History of Contemporary Europe* (trans. Heinemann). The best general survey of the whole field by an eminent and highly-trained historian.

McCunn. *Six Radical Thinkers* (Arnold).

Graham Wallas. *Francis Place* (Longmans). A recognized masterpiece, now in a cheap edition.

Bentham. *Theory of Legislation* (Clarendon Press).

Mill, J. S. *Autobiography* (Longmans), *Liberty and Representative Government* (World's Classics).

Driault and Monod. *L'Évolution du monde moderne. Histoire politique et sociale*, 1815–1909 (Félix Alcan). A very good short sketch, illustrated, and popular, giving due place to the different nations and the various sides of the evolution.

CHAPTER III. THE NEW SPIRIT IN LITERATURE

Taine. *English Literature* (Chatto & Windus). A standard book, full of suggestive comparisons between French and English writers.

Wordsworth (and others). *Lyrical Ballads* (Facsimile edition, Clarendon Press; *Poetical Works*, Oxford Standard Authors).

Scott. *Lockhart's Life* (Warne, Chandos Classics); and a good concordance to the novels.

Shelley. *Mask of Anarchy* (Oxford Standard Authors).

Victor Hugo. *La Légende des Siècles. Hernani* (Oxford Higher French Series).

An Anthology of French Poetry in the Nineteenth Century (Delagrave).

Balzac. *Eugénie Grandet* (O. H. F. S.), *Le Père Goriot* (Hutchinson), and *Le Cousin Pons* (Everyman's Library).

Lessing. *Nathan der Weise* (Clarendon Press). *Dramatic Notes* (Bell).

Goethe. *Götz von Berlichingen* (Ginn); and *Faust*, both parts (World's Classics).

Charlotte Brontë. *Jane Eyre* (World's Classics).

Thackeray. *Vanity Fair* (Oxford Thackeray).

Dickens. *Sketches by Boz, &c.* (Oxford Dickens).

CHAPTER IV. THE BIRTH OF SOCIALISM

Robert Owen. *Life written by himself* (Murray).

William Lovett. *Autobiography* (Trübner).

Beatrice and Sidney Webb. *History of Trade Unionism* (Longmans). The standard book.

Barbara and J. L. Hammond. *The Village Labourer* (Longmans); *The Town Labourer* (Longmans).

Pierre de la Gorce. *La Seconde République* and *Le Second Empire* (Paris).

Auguste Comte. *Early Opuscula* and 'Historical Philosophy' in vol. III of Miss Martineau's edition (Bell).

Karl Marx. *Capital: Revolution and Counter Revolution* (Swan Sonnenschein).

Toynbee, Arnold. *Industrial Revolution* (Longmans).

Carlyle. *Chartism* and *Latter Day Pamphlets* (Chapman & Hall).

Chapter V. Mechanical Science and Invention

Smiles. *Lives of the Engineers* and *Industrial Biography* (Murray).

Findlay. *Chemistry in the Service of Man* (Longmans).

Mach. *Popular Scientific Lectures* (Open Court Publishing Co.).

Helmholtz. *Popular Lectures—Conservation of Energy* (Longmans).

Wallace, A. R. *The Wonderful Century* (G. Allen).

Railways. An excellent article in the *Encyclopaedia Britannica* (11th ed.).

Gray. *Life of Kelvin* (Dent).

Chapter VI. Biology and Evolution

Lyell. *Principles of Geology* (Murray).

Darwin. *Origin of Species* (World's Classics); Centenary volume on *Darwin and Evolution* (Cambridge University Press).

Russell, E. S. *Form and Function* (Murray). A thorough study, highly stimulating, on historical lines.

von Baer. *History of Evolution* (Leipzig). One of the classics of science.

Francis Balfour. *Comparative Embryology* and *Manual of Embryology* (Macmillan). The shorter popular work on which he was engaged on his fatal journey to the Alps.

Herbert Spencer. *Biology* and *Essays* (for appreciation of von Baer) (Williams & Norgate).

Huxley. *Man's Place in Nature* (Everyman's Library).

Thomson, J. A. *Science in the Nineteenth Century* (Chambers). A short, well-balanced account, strong on the biological side.

Chapter VII. Nationality and Imperialism

Trevelyan, G. M. *Garibaldi* (Longmans). The three books, all of profound interest and careful study.

E. Martinengo Cesaresco. *The Liberation of Italy* (Seeley). A general study, mainly biographical, by a member of one of the liberating families.

George Meredith. *Vittoria* (Constable).

Bolton King. *Life of Mazzini* (Dent: Temple Biographies).

Headlam, J. W. *Bismarck* (Heroes of the Nations: Putnam's). Putting his work rather from Bismarck's own point of view.

Robertson, C. Grant. *Life of Bismarck* (Constable). Fuller and more critical.

Dawson, W. H. *The Evolution of Modern Germany* (Fisher Unwin).

Abraham Lincoln. *Speeches*; *Life*, by Lord Charnwood (Constable).

Lord Morley. *Life of Gladstone* (Macmillan).

Sir Herbert Maxwell. *Life of Lord Clarendon*, 4th Earl.

Chapter VIII. Schools for All

Birchenough. *History of Elementary Education in England* (University Tutorial Press).

Matthew Arnold. *Reports on Elementary Schools* (published by Stationery Office); *Reports on Foreign Schools* (Macmillan).

Cobbett. *Rural Rides* (Everyman's Library).

De Montmorency. *State Intervention in English Education* (Cambridge University Press); *The Progress of Education in England* (Knight, London).

De Guimps. *Life of Pestalozzi* (Swan Sonnenschein).

Dewey. *The School and the Child* (Blackie). Giving an American point of view.

Dyer. *Education and National Life* (Blackie).

Fitch. *Thomas and Matthew Arnold* (Heinemann).

Newman, J. H. *Idea of a University* (Longmans).

Education in the Nineteenth Century (Cambridge University Press), by various writers.

Chapter IX. Religious Growth

Green, T. H. *Works.* Especially the sermons on 'Faith' and 'The Witness of God' (Longmans).

Nettleship. *Life of Green*, with introduction by Mrs. Green (Longmans).

Caird. *Evolution of Religion* (Maclehose).

William James. *Varieties of Religious Experience* (Longmans).

Lord Morley. *Recollections* (Macmillan).

Comte. *The General View of Positivism*, trans. by Dr. Bridges (Routledge).

Loisy, Alfred. *La Religion*; and *A propos de l'histoire de Religion* (Nourry, Paris).

Newman, J. H. *Development of Christian Doctrine* (Longmans).

Cross, J. W. *Life and Letters of George Eliot* (Blackwood).

Tennyson. *In Memoriam.*

Tolstoi. *Life.*

Chapter X. New Knowledge on Old Foundations

Duncan, R. K. *The New Knowledge* (Hodder & Stoughton).

Faraday. *Researches.* (Everyman's Library).

Clerk Maxwell. *Treatise on Electricity and Magnetism*, 1873. Third edition, ed. J. J. Thomson, 1904 (Clarendon Press).

Dannemann. *Die Wissenschaften in ihrer Entwickelung und Zusammenhang* (Leipzig). The only passable general history of Science available at present. For a short elementary sketch reference may be made to

Fisher, Mrs. *Short History of Science* (Macmillan). Well-written and accurate, by one who was a friend of Lyell and Darwin, but not brought down to recent times.

Soddy, F. *Matter and Energy* (Home University Library).

Poincaré, H. *La Valeur de la Science*; *Science et Hypothèse*; *Dernières Pensées* (Flammarion). Three volumes in the excellent ' Bibliothèque de Philosophie Scientifique '.

Poincaré, L. *History of Modern Physics*. In the same series, also translated.

Chapter XI. The Expansion of the West

Ramsay Muir. *The Expansion of Europe* (Constable). A masterly survey of the whole development, written during the War, with a certain kindliness to Britain.

Blaikie, W. G. *Life of Livingstone*; and Livingstone's own Journals (Murray).

Milner, Lord. *England in Egypt* (Arnold).

Dilke, Sir Charles. *Greater Britain* (Macmillan).

International Policy, various writers (Reeves). Dealing especially with our relations to weaker races.

Captain Cook's *Voyages* (Everyman's Library).

Lucas, Sir C. P. *The British Empire* (Macmillan).

Chapter XII. Social Progress

Porter, *Progress of the Nation* (Methuen).

Hutchins and Harrison. *History of Factory Legislation* (King).

Beatrice and Sidney Webb. *Industrial Democracy* (Longmans).

Ruskin. *Unto this Last, &c.* (World's Classics).

Dicey. *Law and Opinion in England* (Macmillan).

Morris. *News from Nowhere* (Longmans).

Lytton Strachey. *Eminent Victorians* (Chatto & Windus). Especially for Florence Nightingale.

Lytton Strachey. *Queen Victoria* (Chatto & Windus).

Barnett. *Life of Canon Barnett*, by his wife (Murray).

Registrar-General's Reports on Birth, Mortality, and Criminal Statistics.

Mackenzie. *Health and Disease* (Home University Library).

Chapter XIII. International Progress

Dante. *De Monarchia* (Clarendon Press).

Fortescue, Sir John. *The Governance of England* (Clarendon Press).

Grotius. *International Law* (Cambridge University Press).

Penn. *Essay towards the Present and Future Peace of Europe* (reprinted) (Bellows : Gloucester, 1915).

Burns, C. Delisle. *The Morality of Nations* (University of London Press).

Kant. *Principles of Politics* (Hastie, published Clark). Contains the small but capital works on Universal History, Perpetual Peace, and the Principle of Progress.

Conrad, Joseph. *Heart of Darkness.*

For general reference

Gooch. *Annals of Politics and Culture* (Cambridge University Press), to the end of the nineteenth century. It needs to be brought up to date and might be somewhat revised in details.

Mr. Punch's Victorian Era. Political cartoons from 1841-87.

INDEX

MAINLY OF PROPER NAMES

Printed in England at the Oxford University Press

BY F. S. MARVIN

December 1920

THE LIVING PAST: a Sketch of Western Progress.
By F. S. MARVIN. Fourth edition, 1920. Crown 8vo ($7\frac{3}{4} \times 5\frac{1}{4}$), pp. xvi + 296. 5s. 6d. net.

CONTENTS:—Looking Backward; The Childhood of the Race; The Early Empires; The Greeks; The Romans; The Middle Ages; The Renascence; The Rise of Modern Science; The Industrial Revolution; The Revolution, Social and Political; Progress after Revolution; Looking Forward. Time Charts. Appendix on Books. Index.

'We most cordially welcome the second edition of Mr. Marvin's book, not only because of its permanent usefulness, but because it is calculated to provide an excellent antidote to that insidious poison of pessimism against which it behoves all of us to be on our guard. . . . We must express our admiration for the luminous manner in which he has developed his theme. The little book is of fascinating interest for those for whom it merely presents old facts from a new angle of view; it is a perfect godsend for those for whom it is primarily intended, namely young people beginning the serious study of history. . . . In Mr. Marvin's hands history gains a human interest for the young as well as for the mature mind, and the classics, brought into their due relation to the movement of human progress as a whole, acquire a new meaning and significance.'—
Times.

'An extraordinarily brilliant sketch. Historians nowadays tend to excessive specialization. Mr. Marvin supplies a wholesome and valuable corrective in this wonderful sketch of European history. . . . It is a notable achievement.'—
University Extension Bulletin.

THE CENTURY OF HOPE: a Sketch of Western
Progress from 1815 to the Great War. By F. S. MARVIN. Second edition, 1919. Crown 8vo ($7\frac{3}{4} \times 5\frac{1}{4}$), pp. viii + 358. 6s. net.

CONTENTS:—The Legacy of the Revolution; The Political Revival; The New Spirit in Literature; The Birth of Socialism; Mechanical Science and Invention; Biology and Evolution; Nationality and Imperialism; Schools for All; Religious Growth; New Knowledge on Old Foundations; The Expansion of the West; Social Progress; International Progress. Time Chart. Appendix on Books. Index.

'Mr. Marvin's previous book *The Living Past* has qualified him in an exceptional degree for this difficult study of contemporary, or almost contemporary history. He has extraordinarily wide knowledge, a judicial temper, a power of generalization, and perhaps more important than all, a clear and consistent conception of human history. . . . An unusually wise and fair-minded and stimulating book.'—*Times.*

'He has the gift of summarizing large topics clearly, and he is commendably impartial.'—*Spectator.*

'It is characterized by the same breadth and freshness of view which made *The Living Past* such an engaging study in compressed and co-ordinated history.'—*Scotsman.*

'He belongs to the small class of optimists who are also well informed. He sees in the nineteenth century the gradual triumph of the spirit of co-operation over that of competition; a truer realization of the justice of the claims of all to better conditions of life; and a series of conquests made by invention and scientific research.'—*Oxford Magazine.*

The Unity Series

THE UNITY OF WESTERN CIVILIZATION. Essays

collected by F. S. MARVIN. 1915. 8vo (9×6), pp. 3:6. 7s. 6d. net.

Grounds of Unity, F. S. MARVIN. Unity in Prehistoric Times, J. L. MYRES. Contribution of Greece and Rome, J. A. SMITH. Unity in the Middle Ages, E. BARKER. Unity in Law, W. M. GELDART. Unity in Science and Philosophy, L. T. HOBHOUSE. Education, J. W. HEADLAM. Commerce and Finance, HARTLEY WITHERS. Industrial Legislation, C. SMITH. Social Reform, C. DELISLE BURNS. A World State, J. A. HOBSON. Religion, H. G. WOOD. The Growth of Humanity, F. S. MARVIN.

'The essays are edited with every care, and together make a book which cannot but prove interesting and suggestive to thoughtful readers.'—*Scotsman.*

'The essayists are all of them experts in their own spheres, and the collected essays form a storehouse of suggestion as well as of valuable information.'—*Glasgow Herald.*

'The object of the book will appeal to all people of goodwill. . . . The general impression left is that the unity of Western Civilization is still a matter of speculation and hope. But in mere faith there is something magnificent, and who shall say that it shall not prevail.'—*Times.*

PROGRESS AND HISTORY. Essays collected by F. S.

MARVIN. Third Impression, 1919. Crown 8vo (7¾×5¼), pp. 314. 4s. 6d. net.

The Idea of Progress, F. S. MARVIN. Progress in Prehistoric Times, R. R. MARETT. Progress and Hellenism, F. MELIAN STAWELL. Progress in the Middle Ages, Rev. A. J. CARLYLE. Progress in Religion, Baron von HUEGEL. Moral Progress, L. P. JACKS. Government; Industry, A. E. ZIMMERN. Art, A. CLUTTON-BROCK; Science, F. S. MARVIN. Philosophy; Progress as an Ideal Action, J. A. SMITH.

'An important book . . . provokes thought on every page and deserves careful reading.'—*Glasgow Herald.*

'Will be a stimulating tonic for those who are inclined to believe that our alleged progress has landed us in the worst outburst of barbarism that the world has ever witnessed. . . . The book is helpful and inspiring.'—*Economist.*

RECENT DEVELOPMENTS IN EUROPEAN

THOUGHT. Essays arranged and edited by F. S. MARVIN. Second impression, 1920. Crown 8vo (9×6), pp. 306. 6s. net.

General Survey, F. S. MARVIN. Philosophy, A. E. TAYLOR. Religion, F. B. JEVONS. Poetry, C. H. HERFORD. History, G. P. GOOCH. Political Theory, A. D. LINDSAY. Economic Development: 1. The Industrial Scene, 1842; 2. Mining Operations; 3. The Spirit of Association, C. R. FAY. Atomic Theories, W. H. BRAGG. Biology since Darwin, LEONARD DONCASTER. Art, A. CLUTTON-BROCK. A Generation of Music, ERNEST WALKER. The Modern Renascence, F. MELIAN STAWELL.

'Admirable both in style and substance.'—*New Statesman.*

'A remarkable presentation of recent developments in European thought .. all the essays are instructive and free from dullness.'—*Glasgow Herald.*